PARANORMAL REALITIES II

Keith Johnson

With

Sandra Johnson

To Emma :)

Keith E. Johnson

NEAR Publishing

WARWICK, RI

Paranormal Realities II

Copyright 2010 by Keith Johnson

All rights reserved. No part of this book may be reproduced or transmitted in any form or by any means without written permission of the author.

ISBN 978-0-615-45415-3

Cover design by Raymond Dowaliby

Foreword by Brian Harnois

My own first personal encounter with something which could be defined as "paranormal" took place when I was 11 years old, having been invited to a sleep-over at my best friend Josh Gavel's house in Woonsocket, Rhode Island. We were both fully awake, and talking with each other, when to our surprise we both witnessed a full-bodied apparition walk through the bedroom, and then disappear right through a bedroom wall. Needless to say, we spent the remainder of that night sleeping on the floor of my friend's parents' bedroom! After this experience I was hooked trying to find an explanation for what not only I, but also Josh had witnessed. Both Josh and I then decided to follow the "Sherlock Holmes" routine, by researching any available information on the house and its former occupants. We first visited the Woonsocket Public Library, and then the Woonsocket Town Hall. And it was while researching the records at the Town Hall that we discovered that there actually was a former resident of Josh's house, who was a Vietnam Vet, and who had committed suicide by hanging himself in this house! This was my very first experience in the field of paranormal investigation.

During my junior high and high school years, my interest in researching anything to do with the paranormal dramatically increased. Because this was an era before the Internet was available, I would often visit the local library, and would take out any book that I could find having to do with the subject of the paranormal. I would also make use of the copy machine, and

Brian Harnois guests on Ghosts R N.E.A.R.

copy page after page after page of these books to add to my personal reference collection. Unfortunately, this was also a time when the field of paranormal investigation was not nearly as publicly accepted as it is today. Certainly it was not socially acceptable within the general student population at school, and anyone who expressed a serious interest in the paranormal was opening themselves up to a great deal of ridicule. I was the kid in high school and junior high who repeatedly became the brunt of jokes for my interests. I found myself labeled a Satanist, a demon-lover, an idiot, and a fool. People would ask me, "Why are you doing this stuff, Harnois? What's wrong with you??" Of course, little did my contemporaries at the time have any idea just how popular the field I was studying would eventually become.

Almost immediately following my high school graduation I joined the military, becoming an Air Force M.P. During my four years of military service I did experience a couple of chance encounters with what might be considered things of an inexplicable nature. Unfortunately, since they occurred during military operations, the information is classified, and I am not at liberty to discuss the exact locations or to detail the phenomena. Let me just say that one involved a location in the South where a suicide had taken place within a dorm, and another had taken place at a Massachusetts location believed by some to be a "gateway to Hell!"

After leaving the military and returning to civilian life, I was naturally anxious to continue pursuing my interest of investigating the paranormal, which to me had become much more than a hobby. It was a personal quest to find the truth. However, instead of limiting myself to investigating local cemeteries and abandoned buildings, I wanted to begin doing some significant research. Not only that, but I was also looking for an opportunity to be able to help other people who were being frightened by the paranormal, including situations where inhuman, or demonic spirits might possibly be involved. This opportunity finally presented itself when I met Jason Hawes, and was invited by Jason to become a member of The Atlantic Paranormal Society, also known as TAPS. And it was through TAPS that I had the opportunity of meeting and getting to know my close friend and mentor in this field, Keith Johnson. Jason assigned Keith to personally train me, not only in paranormal investigation, but in the much more intense fields of angelology and demonology as well. Two things that Keith emphasized to me that were especially important, were about taking the proper safety precautions, and about having respect for the situations I'd be confronting.

Also, it was Keith who guided me through my first actual demonic case, which took place with TAPS at a 19th Century farmhouse up in Skowhegan, Main, in January of 2001. There was a great deal of activity taking place at this location, and it culminated with me assisting Keith in a religious cleansing of the entire house as well as the surrounding property. Many, many more cases would of course follow in my career. However, during these many investigations, I've always kept in mind the original training that I received from Keith, and the tremendous influence he's had on my career.

Throughout the year leading up to the Sy Fy TV series Ghost Hunters, Keith and his lovely wife Sandra (who was also a member of TAPS) and I were a close-knit team, and the three of us were out on investigations practically every weekend. In fact, at that time, Keith and Sandra and I were actually the nucleus of TAPS. On those rare occasions when we weren't investigating either a home case or some other site, we'd still usually get together, either at our favorite Chinese restaurant or at a local coffee shop, to discuss our current investigations. Quite often Sandra would arrange for TAPS members to meet as a group in a private room at the Warwick Public Library, where we'd hold evidence review sessions. (Sandra always had incredible organizational skills!)

In August of 2004, Keith and his wife Sandra branched off from TAPS and founded New England Anomalies Research, or NEAR. Because of my commitment to Ghost Hunters at the time, and later to Ghost Hunters International, I was unable to join Keith and Sandra on paranormal investigations for a period of about four years. However, because of family commitments, I eventually had to step back from the incredibly hectic demands of being involved in Ghost Hunters International, a TV show that meant I'd have to be oversees for months at a time. As much as I enjoyed investigating in some of these fascinating and exotic locations, I was simply unable to take that much time away from my family.

Now, in the present, with the responsibilities of a young family and a schedule that is far less hectic, I continue to regularly keep in touch with Keith Johnson and his wife Sandra. We occasionally still make time to work on paranormal cases together, as well as attending conventions together several times per year, as much as our schedules allow.

It is my sincere desire that the reader of 'Paranormal Realities II' which is Keith Johnson's second book detailing his true paranormal experiences, will obtain some insight into the realities of some of the often inexplicable and sometimes frightening phenomena which we ourselves and many others have experienced, and continue to experience. In reading this book, I invite you to join us in our ongoing quest for answers to these intriguing and very real paranormal phenomena!

Brian Joseph Harnois

Contents

Chapter 1: Shadow Man	1
Chapter 2: Hearth and Home	28
Chapter 3: The House on Atwood Avenue	41
Chapter 4: Paranormal Encounters in Chicopee, MA	50
Chapter 5: Long Island Haunting	57
Chapter 6: Shades of H. P. Lovecraft	65
Chapter 7: The Brooklyn Demon Case	70
Chapter 8: Walkin' Rosie	127
Chapter 9: Followed Home	129
Chapter 10: A Visit from Ted?	153
Chapter 11: Oakie Pokie	156
Chapter 12: The Maine Possession Case – Part 1	166
Chapter 13: The Maine Possession Case – Part 2	185
Chapter 14: The Dover Demon	231
Chapter 15: Spirit Well	239
Chapter 16: The Secrets of Precious Blood Cemetery	241
Chapter 17: The Hauntings of Old Slater Mill	257
Chapter 18: The Phantom Dogs of Hell's Gate	269
Chapter 19: Brian's Uninvited Guest	274
Chapter 20: A Skeptic's Encounter	281
Chapter 21: Paranormal Realities	283
From the Demonologist's Assistant	288

Chapter 1

Shadow Man

    Fairly exhausted from working the night shift, Ron – a slim, dark-haired 32-year-old husband and father of two young girls – slumped into a chair at his kitchen table. It wasn't just his regular evening work hours that were causing Ronald's present fatigue. It was also the series of unexplained events, which were now taking place within the lower section of this house where he and his wife and their two young daughters now lived. Sure, mysterious occurrences had always been known to happen now and then, on all three levels of this antiquated structure. But now, ever since he along with some other family members had tried communicating with whatever spirits might be here, by using the Ouija board, it seemed that the activity had suddenly and dramatically begun to increase. And he knew he wasn't losing his mind, because other people were experiencing it as well, including Ron's cousin (who resided on the next floor), Ron's wife, and recently even their two little girls.

    And yet, there seemed to be few people outside of his immediate family with whom he could discuss the peculiar events which were now taking place in his home fairly regularly. Friends and co-workers in whom he confided often either found it mildly interesting or amusing, without really taking the subject matter seriously…or worse yet, they would even sometimes ridicule him about it. And yet, Ron knew there were people out there who DID take these matters seriously… even organizations, which were willing to travel to haunted locations to investigate; including people's private homes. He'd seen this on various television programs, and he'd also recently begun searching out some local groups on the Internet. One local paranormal investigation group in particular had caught Ron's attention. This was The Atlantic Paranormal Society, or "TAPS," which was headed by some guy named Jason Hawes. For one thing, they were located in Warwick, Rhode Island, so maybe they wouldn't mind driving the distance to just over the Massachusetts border where Ron lived. Also, it said on their site that they did not charge people for their investigations, which certainly sounded appealing.

So now, the only thing preventing him from contacting TAPS and requesting an investigation, was his aunt, who resided on the third floor. At least several times now, Ron had suggested to his Aunt Louise that they invite a group of real, experienced paranormal investigators over to the house, to have the strange activity officially looked into… and each time she'd adamantly vetoed the idea. "But Auntie," he'd tried to reason with her, "these people would maybe be able to document what's been going on in this house for so many years. Especially since it's really been picking up, after we've used the Ouija board so many times. And maybe they'd even be able to help put a stop to it all somehow." But, no, she stubbornly refused to have complete strangers parading though this house, with their cameras and other equipment, invading their family privacy. Unfortunately, it was also Aunt Louise who actually owned the house, so of course she had the final say.

A slight tapping sound, barely perceptible and muffled, suddenly interrupted Ron's thoughts. It was coming from the direction of the basement. By the time his head had whipped around to face the closed basement door, the light tapping had stopped. Just as well, Ron figured. Even if it turned out to be his late Uncle Raymond just letting him know he was still here, there was still no way in hell he was going to open that basement door even a slight crack… let alone go down there by himself to investigate!

Then again, maybe he was just allowing this place get to him. What he needed more than anything else right now was a cigarette, before going in to join his slumbering wife in their bedroom, and crashing for the night. Because their youngest daughter had been born with breathing difficulties, they'd designated his and his wife's bedroom at the end of the hallway as the "smoking room". This was Ron's intended destination as he yawned, stretched, and then wearily pushed himself away from the kitchen table, rising up into a standing position.

Ron had taken only a few shuffling steps forward towards the outer hallway, when he abruptly froze in his tracks. There it was again, visibly silhouetted against the wall of the hallway, as if peering into the kitchen area... the semi-distorted, shadowy figure of a man, perhaps just over six feet in height. For what seemed like an eternity (but in reality was perhaps no more than a few seconds), Ron stood transfixed to the spot, observing this dark figure in silence. And then, just as suddenly as it had first appeared, the "shadow man" was gone.

This made three sightings in just over a month. Rather than continuing on to his designated smoking room, Ron instead turned and headed back towards the kitchen, and from there continued out the front door. Standing outside on his front steps a few seconds later, Ron hastily pulled a cigarette from his shirt pocket and placed it between his lips. With trembling fingers, he then took out his small butane lighter, lit his cigarette, and inhaled deeply of the smoke. This was it! Whether his aunt objected to it or not, Ron was now determined to contact these TAPS people, and ask them to at least investigate the first floor section of the house, where he and his immediate family resided. There had to be someone who would confirm that he and the rest of his family weren't losing their minds, or suffering from mass hallucinations!

Thus is was that on a Saturday afternoon, in September of the year 2000, a small group consisting of four members of The Atlantic Paranormal Society set out from Warwick, Rhode Island, to a three story residence located in Taunton, Massachusetts. Besides Jason Hawes and myself, also present on this case were TAPS members Valerie Southwick and Andrew Graham. Since the client had informed us beforehand that we'd have limited access to the house this afternoon, and that this would basically be little more than an initial interview, we brought along only a minimal amount of equipment with us.

Upon our arrival we were greeted and welcomed in by Ron, a casually dressed young man in his early thirties, with dark hair, about six feet in height and of wiry frame. "Thanks very much for coming, guys," he said. "I'm Ron. And this is my wife, Laura."

"Hi, guys," said Laura, a pleasant young woman with long dark hair.

"Hi Ron and Laura," said Jason, shaking hands with them. "I'm Jason Hawes, of The Atlantic Paranormal Society. These are three of my fellow investigators: Valerie... Keith... and Andrew."

"Very nice to meet you," said Ron, as he and his wife Laura shook hands with us. Ron then led us into the kitchen to begin our initial interview with him, while Laura went to tend to their two little daughters who were playing in the other rooms.

After we'd sat ourselves around the kitchen table, Ron served us each a glass of cola, and then joined us to begin the interview. When I'd switched on my tape recorder, Jason asked, "So Ron, how long have you and your family lived in this house?"

"Well, my grandparents originally lived in this house," said Ron. "So the house has been in my family for, I'd say, well over sixty years now."

"That's quite some time," observed Jason. He then asked Ron, "Now, would you give us a basic summary of what you and your family have been experiencing here, and the reason you decided to contact us?"

"Well, there's a lot of activity that takes place on all three floors of this house," said Ron. "My Aunt Louise lives on the third floor. She's the one who presently owns this house. My mom lives on the second floor, along with my cousin, and I live with my family down here on the first floor."

Valerie asked, "Which area of this house would you say is the most active for paranormal activity?"

Without hesitation Ron replied, "The basement, definitely the basement. I'm thirty-two years old, and I will not go down there by myself. Once a month I go down there to fill the hot water heater, but I refuse to go down there alone."

"Why is that?" asked Valerie.

"You just get that feeling of always being watched down there," Ron explained. With a nervous laugh, he added, "It's such an uncomfortable feeling that even in the daytime; I won't go down there unless my wife's down there with me. She often goes down there by herself, and she tells me, 'Come on, there's nothing wrong.' But if it's at night, then forget it; I won't go down into the basement even if someone's with me! Even if a fuse needs to be changed, it'll just have to wait until morning. My mother tells me that there also used to be a piano down there that used to play all by itself."

"Really?" I asked.

"Yeah, but that was quite a few years ago, long before I was born," Ron explained.

Jason asked, "Do you know approximately how old this house is?"

"From what I understand, it's at least two hundred years old," said Ron. "I've heard stories from my mom who grew up in this house that this whole block was originally part of an estate, although I'm not sure who owned it. Supposedly, this house was once divided up into two sections, and the side we're on now was used as some sort of a sewing factory. And one of the guys who worked there was having an affair with one of the girls, and his wife found out, and supposedly stabbed the girl with a pair of sewing shears. At least that's the story I've heard since I was a little kid in this house."

"Interesting," said Jason. "So, what else have you and your family been experiencing here in this house, besides the sensation of being watched in the basement?"

"Well, my mom's experienced things since she was a little kid in this house," said Ron. "She's woken up and seen people standing at the end of her bed. My aunt, too, who just went out, she seems to really be in touch with the other side, or whatever."

"Sensitive?" asked Jason.

"Yeah, she's real sensitive that way," said Ron. "My uncle died suddenly a couple of years ago, and one night soon afterwards, my aunt woke up to the strong scent of flowers filling her room. Then she looked toward the foot of her bed and saw my uncle standing there. He told her that he had died of a heart attack. Sure enough, the autopsy report came back a couple of days later, and confirmed that he'd died of a heart attack."

Glancing at Jason and the others, I commented, "Sounds like a transitional apparition. If so, then it probably wouldn't have remained here very long." They all nodded in agreement.

Ron added, "But my aunt doesn't really want to get involved with this sort of thing she just wants it to basically leave her alone."

Jason asked, "What other type of activity have you or any other family members been experiencing here?"

Ron replied, "Well, there's definitely two spirits here now that I know of. Now, the rooms on the other two floors are set up exactly like they are on this floor. And one night just recently, my cousin, who lives on the second floor, saw a little girl come into the kitchen where he was. As he watched, this little girl just looked at him, and then walked right through the back door, which leads into the hallway. And afterwards, he remembers feeling incredibly sad, which is really unusual for him."

Jason then asked Ron, "So, what have you and your family been experiencing here on the first floor?"

"We've seen the basement door suddenly slam shut on its own, after it's already just been opened from the other side," said Ron. "You'll go to reach for it, and it'll shut again. You don't see anything, but there's something there."

Valerie asked, "Have you experienced any noticeable fluctuations in temperature in any of the rooms?"

"Sometimes, it doesn't matter which room, but it'll suddenly get real cold for a moment, just before something happens," Ron explained.

Andrew said, "You mentioned that there are two spirits here now, that you know of."

"Yeah," said Ron. "There's the little girl spirit, and then there's also the 'shadow man'."

"The 'shadow man'?" asked Jason.

"That's what we refer to it as," said Ron. "I myself have seen the 'shadow man' down here on the first floor, moving along the walls and through the hallway. It's about six foot tall, around my height, at least the size of a full-grown man. I have the feeling that the shadow man may be my uncle still hanging around."

"How often do you see this shadow figure?" I asked. "And is it usually seen at any particular time of the day or night?"

"It can be anytime of the day or night," Ron replied. "Sometimes I won't see it for maybe a week or more. And then at other times, I'll see it maybe two or three times within a twenty-four hour period. Since I get out of work late I'm usually up until after two AM, so that's when I'll sometimes catch a glimpse of the shadow man, moving along out there in the hallway."

I asked, "Are there any sounds which accompany the appearances of the shadow man?"

"Not usually," Ron replied, "although once in awhile I'll hear footsteps in the house on the same day or night. And then there was the time recently when our family picture dropped off of the wall, right after I'd happened to mention my uncle."

Valerie asked, "Ron, how do you personally feel about the shadow man and the little girl being in this house?"

"These things don't really bother me," said Ron. "I mean, I know they're here. But whenever I see the shadow man, I'm like, 'Okay, how ya doin'?' I guess I'm just used to them being here."

"So, you don't feel threatened at all in this house?" asked Valerie.

"No, not really," said Ron.

Jason asked, "Is there anything else which you and your family have been experiencing?"

Ron replied, "Well, like I said, we sometimes hear footsteps walking around in certain rooms, when there's no one there. Sometimes we'll even hear the footsteps walking by us in the same room we're in."

Turning to me, Jason asked, "Keith, did you have some specific questions you wanted to ask Ron?"

"Yes," I said. "When was the last time you saw this shadow figure, Ron?"

"Maybe two days ago, just before I contacted you guys," said Ron. "Things have been kind of quiet the past couple of days, since then."

"Do you or your other family members have any specific religious beliefs?"

"Yes, we're Roman Catholics. Non-practicing."

"To your knowledge, Ron, have you or has anyone else in this house ever used any type of divination device, such as automatic writing or a Ouija board?"

"Yes, a long time ago me and my cousins used to play with a Ouija board all the time in this house," replied Ron.

"Oh, really?" asked Jason. "So, you have used a Ouija board in this house?"

"Oh, yeah," said Ron. "Not anymore because I've got my two little girls here. A long time ago me and my cousins and some friends of ours used to play with the Ouija board, a lot, and some really weird things used to happen."

Andrew asked, "What type of activity did you first begin to notice, right after using the Ouija board?"

Ron explained, "Well, there was one night that we were all using the Ouija board, and I remember that it was snowing outside that night. While we were playing, the name 'Frankie' was spelled out on the board for us. And when we asked who Frankie was, the spirit spelled out 'I'm five years old. I'm cold. Come see me.' So I asked 'Where are you?' And then it gave us directions, which led to the cemetery across the street, to a tombstone of a little boy whose name was 'Frank'. Sure enough, he'd died when he was five years old."

Andrew asked, "Have you played with the Ouija board recently?"

"No," said Ron. "After I got married and had kids, I told myself, I don't wanna mess with it no more. But my oldest, the seven-year-old talks to a little girl who she says plays with her, even though this little girl can't be seen. It could be just, like, an imaginary friend. Or it could be because kids are a little more open to these things."

"That's true, generally they are," I agreed. "Have either of your daughters or your wife ever seen the shadow man?"

"No. At least they haven't mentioned it," said Ron.

Valerie asked, "How does your wife feel about the activity in this house?"

" I've talked with my wife about it," said Ron, "but she doesn't believe that our daughter could be seeing a ghost. I mean, even though my wife has seen things herself in this house that she can't explain, she still refuses to admit that ghosts could exist."

"Why couldn't they exist?" asked Jason. "After all, you exist. We didn't make up the laws of the universe. I didn't believe that my daughter really had an imaginary friend named 'Bobby', until one day something unseen grabbed the vacuum cleaner right out from her grandmother's hands. It would be naive to think that we're the only things that exist."

"Exactly!" Ron agreed. "Who can explain why we exist?"

Jason asked, "Now, about these houses around here near the cemetery... do the families who live there have a lot of little kids as well?"

"No, no one in the immediate neighborhood has any young children my daughters' ages."

"Your kids are pretty much the only kids within the area?"

"Yes," said Ron. "But, I've known people who've lived in the area over the years, like within seven or eight houses, and some of them have also experienced things in their houses."

Jason explained, "I'm just trying to get a grasp as to why, if there is something in the area, it would be coming to this particular house."

"It could be at least partly because of my daughters being the age they are," said Ron. "And also because, like I said, my uncle died in this house. At least that's what I think the shadow man is."

Before we concluded our initial interview, Jason asked if anyone else had any more questions at this time. Turning to Ron, I asked,

"Have you ever tried to directly communicate with any of the entities in this house? I mean, outside of the Ouija board."

"Have I ever tried talking to them?" asked Ron. "No, not really, but I do believe that the shadow man could be my uncle, just passing by and letting me know that he's still here, maybe watching over us."

"Is there anything else you'd like to add?" I asked him.

Ron replied, "Just that, like I said before, my mother and my aunt grew up in this house too, and they've always seen things, like people standing over their bed at night."

"So pretty much all of the adults in this house have experienced something, even including your wife, correct?" I asked.

"Yes, pretty much all of the adults have," Ron agreed.

My final question for Ron was, "What would you like to see accomplished by our visit here today?"

"Well, if at all possible, I'd like for you to find some sort of proof of what I've been experiencing, if only to prove that I'm not crazy," said Ron.

Jason asked him, "And if we do find evidence of activity, would you then want us to perform a cleansing, to try and put a halt to what you and your family have been experiencing?"

"Yes. Definitely," said Ron. "Like I said before, aside from the basement, I'm pretty comfortable being anywhere in the rest of the house. Even the shadow man doesn't really bother me. So it would mainly be for my kids."

As the interview concluded, Jason suggested to Ron that we all begin a tour of the house. "Sure, that'd be great," said Ron, adding, "The only thing is, because of my aunt, we can only go through this floor and the basement. She doesn't want anyone going through the other two floors."

Jason asked, "Is your aunt aware that you've asked us to come over to investigate this house today?"

"Oh, yeah, she knows," said Ron. "Like I said, she's out for the afternoon, but she knew you were coming over. And that was fine with her, as long as you confine the investigation to down here. You know, if it were up to me, I'd certainly let you up to the other two floors as well." Ron also explained to us that he understood some of the methods of paranormal investigation, since both he and his brother had recently been visiting allegedly haunted locations. Some of these locations included a few nearby historical cemeteries and buildings, as well as Belcourt Castle in Newport, Rhode Island.

After sharing a quick glance with the rest of us, Jason said, "Well, I think that now, with your permission, Ron, we'll do a walk-through of the first floor, and then we'll set up some of our equipment here and in the basement as well."

"Yeah, sure, that'd be great," Ron said agreeably.

Jason then asked, "Ron, would you be willing to lead us downstairs to show us around the basement? Obviously you won't be alone down there. We'll be down there with you."

A bit hesitant, Ron replied, "Uh... yeah, sure, I guess I could do that. Let me ask my wife Laura if she wants to come downstairs with us."

Ron then excused himself, rose from the kitchen table, and went into another room past the hallway. We could overhear Ron and his wife speaking in muffled voices for a minute or so, after which Ron returned to the kitchen and informed us, "Laura says she's busy with the kids, but I suppose I could show you the basement, as long as we all go down together."

"Fair enough," said Jason.

With Ron reluctantly leading us, we made our way down a narrow set of stairs into the musty smelling basement. From the onset, Ron seemed uncomfortable being down there, and anxious to return upstairs, even though the four of us were with him. Observing Ron's level of discomfort, Jason asked him, "Are you going to be okay down here?"

"Yeah," he said with a nervous laugh. "I'll be okay as long as we don't stay down here too long."

"We'll just have a quick look around," Jason assured him. "The air is kind of hard to take down here anyway. You might even have a mold problem. I'd have that checked out if I were you."

Ron reminded us, "Well, like I said, this is the oldest part of the house."

Glancing around, I had to agree. "You're right, this is pretty old."

The structure of the basement itself appeared to be typical for just prior to the turn of the last century, having been somewhat converted for modern conveniences such as a washer and dryer. While we were down there, Ron mentioned, "We also have cubbyholes on each floor of the house, and in each of these cubbyholes, there's a small circle burnt right into them. They're all identical, and from the looks of them, they weren't done recently."

"Really?" I asked, becoming interested. "What's the story behind these circles?"

With a shrug, Ron replied, "I really have no idea who put them there, or what their purpose is. They've been there for at least as long as I've been living here, which is pretty much all of my life."

"Do you know if anyone who's lived here has been seriously involved in the occult, maybe from a past generation?" I asked.

"No, not that I know of," said Ron. "But like I said, this is an old house, so who knows?"

I asked. "Do you suppose either or your aunt or your mother would know anything about the origin of these circles?"

"No, neither of them does, because I've asked them both about it before."

"I see. So you have no idea at all what these circles may have been used for, or why they're here."

"No, I have no idea at all," said Ron, adding with a nervous laugh, "I sure hope it wasn't for occult practices. For all I know, it could've just been kids playing games."

"Anything's possible, I suppose," I told him.

We then decided to return upstairs, much to Ron's relief.

Once we were back upstairs, Jason announced that we would now be separating into two teams, to begin investigating what we could of the house. Turning to Ron, he said, "With your permission, Ron, we'll be spending a certain amount of time in each of the rooms here, as well as in the basement. I understand we're restricted to the first floor and the basement, and I hope we won't be disturbing your wife and your children down here."

Ron assured Jason, "No, not at all. In fact, Laura and the kids and I will all stay together in the TV room while you guys are doing your thing. So don't worry about us at all. And again, we really do appreciate you guys being here and helping us out."

"Not a problem," said Jason. "Since we've only got the first floor and the basement to deal with, this shouldn't take us very long at al. Certainly no more than a half-hour to forty-five minutes at most."

"Sure, go for it," said Ron. "Just give me a moment to let Laura and the kids know."

While Jason and Andrew investigated the parlor and the adult's bedroom, Valerie and I took recordings and photographs in the bedroom that the two daughters shared. Valerie and I found nothing at all unusual in the girls' bedroom, aside from the fact that they'd obviously been allowed to decorate the wooden headboards of their beds with crayons.

The four of us then grouped together and once again ventured down into the basement, to take photos and audio recordings. I especially took an interest in the small circle that was etched upon the floor. We'd been down there for several minutes, when Valerie suddenly announced that she herself felt a little uncomfortable being in the basement. Jason quickly asked her to describe exactly what she was feeling.

"I just have the impression that we're not alone down here, and that we're being watched," she explained. "I don't mean to sound like Ron, but I suddenly have kind of an uneasy feeling being down here."

"Would you feel better if we went back upstairs, Val?" Jason asked her.

"No, not yet" she replied. "If there is something down here, I want to be able to experience it for myself." Several seconds later, Valerie closed her eyes, slowly shook her head, and told us, "I'm not feeling it now. It's like whatever was down here a moment ago is gone."

"Interesting," said Andrew, glancing at our surroundings.

While we were still downstairs in the basement, Jason asked me, "Keith, I'd like to know your take on the situation in this house, and with this family."

"Well", I said, "especially after what Valerie's just experienced, I'd say there's a possibility of least some amount of paranormal activity down here. So I wouldn't say it's entirely in Ron's imagination. However, despite what Ron told us, I also get the impression that he's not as comfortable with the other activity in this house as he claims. And if the circles on each floor are any indication, there's a strong possibility that occult practices have taken place in this house. Plus, there's the story of a jealous wife having stabbed another woman with a pair of sewing shears many years ago. If that's true, then that's another reason negative energy could've been drawn into this house."

Andrew said, "I agree, that's my impression as well. I also think that for whatever reason, Ron and his family members are holding out on us. And there's some reason his mother and his aunt refuse to talk with us."

"You could be right about that," said Jason. "And it certainly doesn't help that we don't have access to the rest of the house." With a sigh he told us, "Well, we'll have to review whatever evidence we may have collected later on. But for now, I think it's time we grouped together back upstairs and had a conference with Ron and his family... or at least with Ron, since he's the only family member so far who seems willing to communicate with us."

Before we returned upstairs, I placed a small tape recorder on a bench in the basement, and left it recording.

Back upstairs we once again sat down at the kitchen table with Ron, who'd just returned from having a cigarette. Jason wasted no time in getting to the point. "Okay, Ron, here's the scoop," he said. "First of all, we do believe what you've told us, and we want very much to help. You're obviously in a situation that you have activity here, and you'd like the situation to be dealt with, be it through a cleansing or whatever. And if we're going to cleanse the house, then we'd pretty much have to go from room to room."

Sounding reticent, Ron said, "Well, like I said, I'm trying to work on my aunt. At this point she says that she doesn't want to get involved in this, but yet she thought that my having you here today was a good idea. You know, I told her that I contacted The Atlantic Paranormal Society, and she said, 'Oh, that's a good idea, Ron. Maybe we'll finally find something out.' And then later on, for some reason she wasn't quite as receptive to the idea." Ron punctuated his statement with a nervous little laugh.

Just then, Ron's 7-year-old daughter came rushing into the kitchen. Ron called her over. "Hey, Ann Marie!"

As the blonde-haired little girl attempted to climb onto her father's lap, she asked him, "What are you doin'?"

"Just talking to some nice people," he said. "Hey, Ann Marie, you remember what me and Mommy talked to you about?" As the little girl continued to squirm on her father's lap, Ron said, "Honestly, do you remember what we talked to you about?"

But Ann Marie's attention was not focused on the conversation. Sliding off of her father's lap and scampering away, she said, "I'm gonna go see Jodi. Bye."

"Okay. Bye," Ron called after her. He explained to us, "That's the one who talks to the little girl. She's always talking to people, so I don't know. She loves to play with her dolls, and she'll treat them as if they're real. She'll change their clothes, and you'll go into her room and if you're too loud, she'll say, 'Shh! Baby's sleeping.'"

"Who's Jodi?" I asked.

"Oh, Jodi's her older sister," said Ron. "But sometimes, it's hard to tell if she's talking to one of her dolls, or to her imaginary playmate. She has different names for all of them. Really hyper kid."

Valerie commented, "She sounds like a perfectly normal little girl for her age, just trying to imitate her mother. So why are you concerned, Ron?"

Ron shifted uncomfortably in his seat. "Well, you're right, maybe it's nothing to really be concerned about, but… it's just the way she sometimes talks to her invisible friend when she's alone in her room, and she describes her as wearing old fashioned clothes. And it's very similar to the description that my cousin gave, about the little girl he saw up on the second floor."

I asked, "In your opinion, Ron, do you feel there's any connection between the 'shadow man' and this little girl in the old fashioned clothes?"

"Well, yeah, I think there could be," said Ron. "After all, both my girls sometimes play with the invisible little girl, although maybe Jodi's just humoring Ann Marie. And I'll usually see the shadow man not too long afterwards."

Jason then said, "From what you're saying, Ron, you have activity here, and it sounds like human spirit activity."

"Yeah, it's definitely nothing more than human activity, I'd say," Ron agreed.

(For my own part, however, I was somewhat concerned about the shadow entity that Ron had described, especially after what Valerie had just experienced in the basement. Also, I was wondering how Ron expected us to further assist him and his family, either in the form of verification or deliverance.)

Jason then echoed my own thoughts, by explaining to Ron, "The thing is, you have activity on all three floors in the house, including the basement. Now, one way we could possibly bring these spirits out is by provoking them into revealing themselves. The thing is, Ron, if we provoke it down here, that doesn't necessarily mean it's only going to act up down here. It might start acting up on the third floor."

"Well, if my cousin was here, then I could at least take you up to the second floor. Because like I said, he and my mother have both seen things up there," said Ron

Jason emphasized, "Well, if you're looking to get rid of this activity, then it's going to have to be a family effort. The whole family's going to have to work together for a short period of time."

Sounding indecisive, Ron said, "See, I'm not sure if I really want to get rid of it, or kind of like, maybe find out for sure that there's definitely something in this house."

Jason asked, "But what do you intend on doing after finding out? Just keeping it around for fun?"

"No, I mean, it doesn't bother me. I mean, if I get rid of it, that's fine, but, it's like... do I want to get rid of it? No."

Jason again attempted to lay it on the line to Ron, by explaining, "You see, the thing is, these entities are doing certain things to make themselves known, especially to your daughters. Now, when your daughters grow up and get older and they don't see these things anymore, these things are going to become more of a hassle, to try to make people know that they're still there. They're going to feel forgotten or whatever, and that's when all hell can break loose. These spirits could start becoming malicious, even if they're human spirits."

Ron said, "Well, like I said before, I think that the shadow man I've been seeing could possibly be my uncle, and maybe he could be feeling that he's no longer needed to look over the two girls."

"But you've also played with a Ouija board in this house, too," Jason reminded him.

"Yeah, we used to play a lot."

"So you've also fooled around opening up doors and stuff, so how do you know? Your uncle could be here, or it could be other things coming in. This other little girl that your daughter's seeing, and that your cousin saw... that's definitely not your uncle."

"No, I don't think that's my uncle. It's definitely something else. And it's been maybe a couple of weeks since that happened with my cousin. No one's ever mentioned seeing the little girl before, until just recently. But the most active one is the shadow, the black shadow. Whatever it is, that's mainly the most active one. It's been seen in my room, and my aunt's front room. My cousin's seen it, and my mother's seen it. It's been seen on all three floors."

To reiterate, I asked Ron, "And how often did you say you've been seeing it lately?"

"The black shadow? At least once a week," said Ron. "Sometimes everyday, three or four times a day. But it's usually once a week, during the day or night. It doesn't matter, either way. But that's the most common one to see. And it's a big shadow. That's why I think it could be my Uncle Raymond; because he was a tall, husky guy."

"But you personally have never seen it on any of the other floors?" I asked.

"No, I hardly ever go up to the other floors," said Ron. "Like I said, my cousin and his girlfriend and his daughter live on the second, and my aunt lives by herself on the third. Sometimes the kids will go up to play with my cousin's daughter, and sometimes I'll go up with them. But I don't usually spend too much time up there."

Andrew interjected, "But your aunt has the ultimate say about everything that goes on in the entire house, correct?"

"Yes, she owns the house and has the final say about everything," Ron confirmed.

"Are you and your aunt close?" I asked him.

Ron replied, "Well, yeah, we're pretty close. But, like, we don't see each other all the time, because like I said, she lives alone up on the third floor."

"So it's not as though you all usually have Sunday dinner together, right?" I asked.

"No," said Ron. "In fact, we almost never all have dinner together, unless it's for a special occasion, like Thanksgiving or the kids' birthday parties."

After a few seconds of silence, Jason bluntly told Ron, "Well, without provoking or anything else, I can't give you a hundred percent verification that you do have activity here. Does it seem like you do? Yeah. Do you get weird senses in certain spots in the home? Yeah. So my own opinion is yeah, you do have some kind of activity. But I can't give you absolute verification with the limited setting we have to work with here. We're confined to a certain area."

"Yeah, that's true," Ron quietly agreed.

Jason continued, "First off, when we go to homes - and everybody here will tell you – when we go into a room, it's not like the activity is going to happen in that one room. The entity involved will play around with us. It'll often be upstairs while we're downstairs, and will tend to move downstairs while we're upstairs, to avoid us. That's why when you're cleaning a house, you have to clean every single room there is. These things hide, and whatever room you miss, they're hanging in."

"Even every crawl space," I added.

"That's right," said Jason. "Crawl spaces and attics, just for example. They'll tend to hide anyplace they can, to keep from being revealed and possibly expelled."

Ron asked, "But why are they doing these things in our house now? Are they scared, or just trying to make themselves known, or what?"

Jason replied, "There's all sorts of reasons as to why entities are here, if they're human spirits. It could be unfinished business, or it could be emotional attachments, or they could be just feeding off of the energy in this home. There could be somebody who's sensitive here drawing them in. Or it could be your children. They're seen by your children, so they're here. Finding the exact answer as to why they're here can sometimes be a little tough. But, as far as cleansing the house…"

"You'd need access to the entire house," Ron finished his sentence for him.

"Exactly," said Jason. "So it's kind of like opening a can of worms. You have to do it in sequence. You have to do it right, or we're going to be back here all the time. And if we provoke it or we try to clean the house down here, I'm not gonna to lie to you, all hell's gonna probably get raised on another floor of this house. Because they're gonna be pissed that we're trying to get 'em out."

"Hm-hm," Ron nodded in agreement. "So they'd be saying, 'My play area here is clean, so I'm just gonna move over to this new play area.'"

"Yeah, but if we can't do the whole house, then this area's only clean for a temporary amount of time." Jason explained. "And then they'll be back, and they won't be amused."

Ron then asked, "How often would you say, when you're cleaning a house, do you find spirits that are pissed off by what you're doing?"

"You mean how often do we get a reaction, once we start cleaning a house?" asked Jason.

"Yeah," said Ron.

"If it's done right, there's times when you get all sorts of phenomena going on from the spirits which have been provoked. And then there's times when you get no reaction at all," Jason explained.

"But do things usually go smooth during a cleansing?" Ron wanted to know.

"Sure, things often go smoothly. Also, sometimes they don't," Jason said candidly. "You just have to go the whole nine yards here, and you can't do it half way in this type of situation. It has to be a group effort, when you come down to it. We don't have all the answers in this world, as to why these things happen the way they do."

"I wish you really could cleanse this place," said Ron. "It's like everybody else is all for it, except for my aunt. You know what I mean?"

"I totally understand your predicament," Jason told him. "And I want to help you. But the only thing is, I'm limited to what I can do for you."

Ron reiterated, "Everyone else in the house agrees that it's okay to get help for our situation, except for that one obstacle. And that's the biggest obstacle that I'm still trying to work on. Everyone else says, 'Okay, let's do it.' And I also want to do it. But then she has final say."

"I totally understand that," said Jason. "Like you say, you get sensations in this house, especially in the cellar, and even one of our group members has confirmed that. But I'm not seeing things walk right in front of me, so I'm also limited to what I can tell you at this point. So that's pretty much where we stand."

Resignedly, Ron shrugged and said, "Yeah. I understand. And who knows? Maybe my aunt will see reason, after all."

Jason said, "So what we'll do now is review whatever evidence we may have collected here today, and we'll let you know our findings. Then, hopefully, you'll have us back for a follow-up visit."

"Thanks," said Ron. "And thanks especially for coming out all this way; I really do appreciate it."

"Not a problem," said Jason. "I just wish we could have helped you more today."

With a weak smile, Ron said, "Just knowing that you people don't think I'm crazy has helped a lot."

Valerie also smiled at Ron, and reached across the kitchen table to briefly squeeze his hand. "Everything will be all right, if we all just work together," she told him.

"Yeah. I know it will," said Ron, sounding unconvinced.

Sensing that Ron desperately wanted some sort of reassurance before we left, I told him, "In the meantime, Ron, keep in mind that we're only a phone call or an E-mail away, day or night. And if you want, I'd personally be willing to talk with your aunt, to let her know what we're about and that we're hear to help."

"Thanks. That's good to know," said Ron, brightening up just a little.

Andrew then accompanied me down to the basement to retrieve my tape recorder, while Jason and Valerie gave Ron some departing words of advice and encouragement. Through the open doorway we could overhear Jason telling him, "What Keith said was true, Ron, about us being available day or night if you need to contact us, even if you just feel the need to talk."

By the time we were on our way out, Ron's attitude appeared to be somewhat uplifted. As we stood on the front steps, Jason reminded him, "So, we'll be going over our evidence, and we'll definitely be in touch with you by the middle of next week to let you know our findings. In the meantime, if you experience anything else or if you have any questions at all, don't hesitate to give us a shout."

Standing in his doorway with a lit cigarette between his fingers, Ron said, "Yeah, if anything else happens, I'll definitely be in touch. Thanks again for coming over today, and for everything you've done."

"You're very welcome," I said, shaking his hand. "It was nice meeting you, and I look forward to seeing you again."

"Yeah, it was nice meeting you, too," said Ron. With determination in his voice, he added, "You know, I'm really going to try and convince my aunt to let you guys investigate the other two floors when you come back, and to do a cleansing of the entire house. When I explain to her in detail about the way I've seen you people handle things today, I'm sure she'll change her mind about letting you guys have access to the upstairs rooms."

Jason shook his hand firmly and said, "Great. It's been a pleasure meeting you, Ron, and we'll probably be in touch with you by the middle of next week, if not before."

"Nice meeting you, Ron," said Andrew.

Valerie also said, "Yes, nice meeting you, and please tell Laura for us that it was nice meeting her, too."

"Will do," said Ron. "Thanks again for coming, guys, and I'll talk to you again real soon."

During our late afternoon drive back to Warwick, Rhode Island, we discussed the various aspects of Ron's case. Although we'd all noticed some obvious inconsistencies while interviewing Ron, we also agreed that he desperately wanted help. Up front in the driver's seat, Jason commented, "It sure is a shame that his aunt takes that attitude, about not letting anybody go through the upper two floors of the house."

Seated beside him, Valerie said, "Well, who knows? Maybe Ron will be able to prevail upon his aunt to see his side of the situation, after all."

"Only time will tell," said Jason. Glancing at me in the rearview mirror, he said, "I'll tell ya, Keith… if we do come back for a cleansing of all three floors of that house, we've got one heck of a job ahead of us."

"That we will," I agreed. "And despite what Ron told us in the beginning, the poor guy's obviously very frightened of what's been going on in his house, including the 'shadow man' he's been seeing."

Jason said, "There's also the fact that Ron claims that he and his brother have been getting into paranormal investigation. But obviously, Ron should first be concentrating on resolving his own issues."

Seated beside me, Andrew commented, "And I still say that Ron's aunt probably knows something about that circle that's etched into the basement floor, plus the fact that there are supposedly identical circles on each of the upper floors. I mean, the family has lived there for generations, and the aunt's lived there all her life. You'd think she'd have at least some clue as to why the circles are there."

"Well," said Jason, "maybe we'll find out more of the whole story, if we wind up coming back in a week or so. Of course, that depends upon if Ron manages to convince his aunt. But in the meantime, we'll simply go over whatever data we may have collected there today, and then give Ron a review of what we've found so far."

"That sounds fair enough," said Andrew.

Back at home that evening I listened to the recording session that Valerie and I had conducted in the girls' bedroom. It revealed nothing unusual. I then listened to the audiotape that I'd left recording in the basement of Ron's house. About ten minutes or so into this recording, a faint tapping sound could be heard next to the microphone, which became progressively louder. The tapping then abruptly ceased. At first, I merely attributed the tapping sounds to a curious rodent. However, what sounded very much like a human sigh could then be heard from nearby, although there had definitely been no one down in the basement at that time. Although it was not much of an EVP, at least it was something.

At our weekly meeting of TAPS, we discussed our findings from the Taunton house with the other members. Since all of the combined data that we'd taken in the house on Saturday afternoon proved to be basically inconclusive, we unanimously agreed that the only course of action left to us in this situation, was a full investigation of the entire house. "At any rate", said Jason, "we've promised Ron a reveal of our findings so far. So if we don't hear from him by mid-week, I'll contact him, and then I'll let everyone know what the scoop is."

Unfortunately we never did hear from Ron again, either by E-mail or by phone. Attempts to contact him proved equally unsuccessful, as his wife would simply inform us that Ron was unavailable. Since there were other clients who seriously needed our assistance, Jason eventually told us to file the Taunton case as "inactive." Whether or not Ron and his family members continued to catch occasional sightings of the "shadow man" as well as the other illusive spirits in the three-story Taunton house, remained a mystery. Perhaps his illusive aunt who lived up on the third floor really did have something to hide, as Andrew had suggested. Or maybe she was simply averse to the idea of having strangers traipsing through her entire house, even if it was to verify the paranormal activity they'd allegedly been experiencing for years. At any rate, as the legal owner of the house, she obviously did have the ultimate say.

Be that as it may, it is a fact that the phenomenon known as "shadow people" seems to be reported with increasing frequency. These apparitional figures are often described in appearance as being blacker that black – in other words, seeming to stand out in a darkened room – and are usually in humanoid form, but with no visible facial features, and wearing what appears to be a cowled monk's robe. Their appearance is often similar to that of the classic Grim Reaper, minus the scythe. Occasionally they are also described as wearing a wide-brimmed hat. Although they can be of any size (sometimes even appearing as a "small alien" figure in shadow form) they are most often reported as being tall, usually around six feet in height.

Shadow People are usually associated with a haunting, either of a place or of a person. Rather than being spirits of deceased humans, they are generally believed to be inhuman entities, perhaps belonging to the demonic realm. During the beginning stages of a haunting in which shadow people are present, these shadowy figures will quite often be perceived from one's peripheral vision, as opposed to straight on. As the haunting progresses, however, they will seemingly become bolder, and tend to be observed full on within people's darkened bedrooms, or perhaps hovering at the tops or bottoms of staircases.

One theory concerning these shadow entities is that they are trans-dimensional, meaning that they may perhaps flit from their own dimensional plane of existence into ours, and back again. Some people theorize that they may originate from our past or even our future, or perhaps from an altogether separate world from our own. Similar to Poltergeist activity, the visitations of shadow beings can last anywhere from weeks, to months, to even years. Although they have been known to simply "go away" of their own accord, in some situations they will seem to be stubborn, and must be coerced into ceasing their appearances. This can usually be accomplished by a variety of means, ranging anywhere from a polite verbal request, to the burning of sage or blessed incense within a home, to a complete and thorough religious cleansing.

But whatever explanation one prefers for the existence of these mysterious otherworldly beings, the Shadow People are apparently a reality, one that a great many people will attest to. And more and more frequently, they appear to be intentionally making their presence known to us.

Recently, Sandra and I were in State College, Pennsylvania, having been invited to give a presentation on demonology at the annual Penn State Univ-Con paranormal conference. While in this college town, we were given accommodations in an extremely pleasant little cottage-type bed & breakfast. It was a house near to the university, which was known as the Yellow House. It was an enjoyable stay, and it was not until the very morning that we were getting ready to leave that Sandra happened to catch a glimpse of a small "shadow entity" flitting about on the back porch. (This back porch was contained within the house, with solid walls and a door leading to the back yard.) Sandra happened to be in the kitchen area when she saw it. At first she only glimpsed it for a moment out of the corner of her left eye. Sandra then turned and was able to get a good enough look at it to ascertain that it was definitely humanoid in form and that it was little more than perhaps two feet tall. A peculiar sensation came over Sandra immediately after witnessing it, which she described as a tingling sensation from her ankles to her thighs (the height of the entity). And although Sandra had been exposed to numerous paranormal situations before, she'd never experienced a sensation quite like this. As she watched, the shadow figure quickly darted from the porch and dashed across the back yard, finally disappearing behind a small, historic-looking building nest door.

Just before leaving that last morning, Sandra and I struck up a pleasant conversation with a local woman who was involved with the restoration of this building. She informed us that for well over a century, the building had served various functions, originally as a church, then as a one-room schoolhouse, and finally as a local grange hall. She also explained that a few years ago, a mini-tornado had hit the area, and that a fallen tree had destroyed the roof of the now abandoned building. Because the old building held so much local history, a community effort was now being made to restore it. The woman was kind enough to give us a tour of the building as well as the grounds surrounding it, during which we were shown a small historical cemetery located at the far side. This small overgrown cemetery, consisting of several headstones dating from the mid-to-late 19th Century, dated back to the time when this building functioned as a church.

Although Sandra and I had been unaware of this cemetery, since it had been hidden from our view in the B&B that we'd stayed at, the shadow entity Sandra had seen earlier had dashed from the porch directly to where the cemetery happened to be located! Sandra afterward speculated that the shadow entity she'd seen might have been drawn either from this small cemetery, or from the building itself. Either way, it had certainly seemed intent on making its presence known to Sandra, if only for an instant. As an additional piece of evidence, I'd been making an audio recording while the local woman had been giving us a tour inside of the grange building. When I played the recording back, and was listening to the woman telling Sandra about her husband's plans to renovate the windows, I clearly detected an EVP of a male voice quickly whispering, "No!" It seemed to be objecting, which would certainly indicate some degree of intelligent interaction. Perhaps the shadow entity that Sandra had witnessed was attempting to convey the message, that it did not appreciate intruders in its territory!

Chapter 2

Hearth and Home

(The actual names of the clients in this story have been changed, in the interest of their privacy.)

When moving into a new home – especially a historic home – people are almost always curious as to the general history of the place they are moving into, as well as the history of the previous inhabitants. However, even if one does happen to meet the current or previous owners during the transaction, this often does not familiarize the new occupants with the complete history of the home. It is not usually until they become acquainted with neighbors and others in their community, that they begin hearing about details pertaining to the house they now own. In some instances, the new occupants will sometimes be informed of a person of particular interest or an event that may have taken place in the home. And it is usually only at this point that most people will invest the time to make a personal visit to the local town hall or library and look up any records pertaining to the history of the house.

Of course, on the other hand, the complete history of a particular house or building is not always readily available. Sometimes the particular nuances of the people who lived in the home before are discovered in increments, such as a child's graffiti scribbled on a bedroom wall or someone's personal initials carved into a kitchen counter. There are also times when a somewhat more disturbing message is stumbled upon, the meaning of which is not always entirely clear at the outset.

The following story involves one such case, in which a family moving into a historic mansion soon found themselves faced with more than they'd originally bargained for.

Newport, Rhode Island, is of course well known for it many beautiful, historic houses and mansions, many of them dating back to the Victorian Era. It was to one of these mansions that several members of The Atlantic Paranormal Society were called to investigate.

According to the family who'd contacted us, they'd recently come into ownership of a Victorian Era mansion located in Newport. Although their new home had obviously once been quite elegant, it was now in need of many repairs to restore it to its former grandeur. However, almost as soon as the reconstruction had begun, some bizarre activity began to take place, in both the main house and in the adjoining carriage house as well. According to the workmen, tools they'd just been using would suddenly be missing, only to be found afterward in odd places. Lights would mysteriously turn off and on by themselves within the two buildings with no explanation, even when they were vacated and securely locked. One day while the workmen were all downstairs on the first floor of the carriage house, a child's ball had suddenly come bouncing down the stairs, even though there was supposedly no one on the upper floors. This was all the workmen could take, and they finally refused to return to the house to continue on the reconstruction. Naturally, the husband and wife who'd recently purchased the mansion were anxious to move into their new home. They wanted to know if we could provide some answers and hopefully offer a solution to their present dilemma.

The team chosen to attend this investigation consisted of Renee Laverdiere, Rich Einig, Jenn Rossi, Fran Ford and myself. Our founder Jason Hawes had some personal matters to attend to but said that he'd most likely meet us at the location an hour later. It was an overcast early evening in the autumn of 2002 that we arrived at the mansion. It was immediately apparent that the house had been quite magnificent in its heyday. The couple that now owned the property, Robert and Maria, were waiting for us outside of the front entrance of the main house when we arrived. Waiting along with them were also two members of the work crew – the foreman and his chief assistant - who were there to relate what they'd personally experienced. Robert and Maria gratefully welcomed us and invited us in.

The century-old Victorian house was large and quite spacious. Recently it had been gutted and was being restored from the first floor up. Our hosts apologized for the condition of the house and suggested that we move onto the carriage house to conduct our interview with them.

Robert, Maria and the two workmen led us through the first floor of the main building – making certain to securely lock all doors behind them - to the carriage house, which was at the back of the property. We then followed them as they led us up to the second floor of the much smaller carriage house. Robert invited us to make ourselves comfortable in the temporary seats they'd brought up for this occasion. "Please excuse these primitive conditions," he apologized. "I'm afraid we didn't have much time to prepare for this, what with all that's been going on."

Rich assured him, "That's quite alright. Trust me; this is a lot better than many of the conditions we're used to." The rest of us all agreed.

Robert and Maria turned out to be a very warm and intelligent young couple. Robert had actually met Maria while on a business trip to Columbia. Maria was quite lovely, with long dark hair, large dark eyes and a bright smile. They explained to us that they currently resided in New York, and were naturally quite anxious to move into their new home. Robert also explained that the foreman and his assistant were personal friends of Maria's, who did not really have a command of the English language. However, since Robert as well as Maria spoke fluent Spanish, they'd both be serving as translators. (We were informed that the other members of the restoration crew, who were also visiting from Columbia, were presently being put up at a local hotel.)

Before we began the interview, Rich told our hosts, "We're actually expecting one more person. Our founder, Jason, is supposed to be joining us here in about an hour or so."

"Well, I'll certainly look forward to meeting him," said Robert.

Rich asked, "Would you mind if I videotaped this interview? It will be kept strictly confidential, for our purposes only."

"Please, go right ahead," Robert told him.

As soon as Rich had mounted his video camera on a tripod, and the rest of us had switched on our tape recorders, we began the interview. The two workmen reiterated that they no longer felt comfortable staying in either of the two houses, especially the carriage house that we were presently in. This was where most of the activity seemed to be taking place. Cabinets were opening up by themselves downstairs in the kitchen area, and pots and pans could be heard banging, even though they were absolutely certain there was no one else in the house. Aside from tools seemingly vanishing and turning up in unusual places, small amounts of pocket change were also reportedly disappearing form their pockets and reappearing in odd places throughout the houses. Sometimes they'd even find small amounts of money that was totally unaccounted for, only to have it completely disappear soon afterwards. Finally, there was the incident of the ball bouncing down the staircase from out of nowhere, which had badly frightened the entire restoration crew. Since then, they'd been too spooked to spend much time in either of the houses any longer.

"Do you still have this ball that came bouncing down the stairs?" I asked.

Robert translated the question, and the foreman answered no, it had disappeared.

At one point during the interview, Fran asked the foreman, "Excuse me, but is there anyone over in the main house right now?"

When Robert translated the question, the foreman answered himself, "Oh, noooo, all gone to hotel."

Fran said, "It's just that I've been seeing lights going on and off inside the main house, through the windows. In fact, I'd say at least four people would have to be in there right now."

Everyone instantly rushed over to glance out the window but the light show seemed to have stopped. The foreman and his assistant began rapidly conversing with each other in Spanish before the foreman turned to Maria and said something. Maria translated, "They say this happens all the time when no one is in there, and they've seen it many times before."

Renee asked Robert and Maria if they themselves had experienced anything within either of two buildings. They replied that they'd experienced only minor activity. Both had experienced sudden temperature changes in the main building and felt the eerie sensation of being watched by unseen eyes. Maria felt especially uncomfortable about the basement of the main building and did not like venturing there.

Jenn asked Maria, "Is there anything in particular about the basement which makes you feel uncomfortable?"

Maria replied, "It's just so dark and scary down there it gives me the creeps. I don't like it at all down there."

Robert added, "Also, there's some strange graffiti on the chimney down there in the basement. I'll show it to you guys when we take the tour of the house."

"Have you done any research on the property or researched the previous owners?" I asked.

Robert explained, "This place was actually a wedding present for my wife Maria and me. I do know that the main house was used as a nursing home for a number of years and was then privately owned."

"Has anyone at all lived here since?" I asked.

"The owners supposedly rented the place to some young people," said Robert. "But from what little I was told about them, they weren't here all that long. I really don't know much about them except that they supposedly weren't very reasonable tenants."

Before our interview concluded, Rich asked Robert and Maria if they had anything they'd like to add. Robert took hold of his wife's hand and said, "Just that we'd very much like to feel comfortable here before moving in and making this our permanent residence."

Fran and I reminded them, as they'd been informed earlier, that our team also offered a possible solution in the form of a spiritual cleansing. I explained, "At the very least, it might introduce some positive vibes into the surroundings to help dispel the negative vibes."

Robert said, "If you could possibly do anything to get rid of whatever's here so we can finally get the work done and move in, we'd sure appreciate it." His wife Maria thoroughly agreed that if we could help, she would be forever grateful.

Before we began tour of the two buildings, Jenn tried contacting Jason and left a message on his cell phone. It was now beginning to seem doubtful that he'd be joining us. I in particular was feeling sorely disappointed about Jason not being there. However, we'd be certain to give Jason a full report of the investigation at our next TAPS meeting.

The tour of the carriage house did not take very long at all since it was the smaller of the two buildings. As our hosts led us through the carriage house, it was plain that the two workmen were becoming increasingly uncomfortable. They spoke rapidly in hushed voices to each other while darting nervous glances about at their surroundings.

We were then escorted though the backyard and back over to the side entrance of the large main house. We could see through the windows that the large interior of the house was now completely darkened. Robert took out his keys and began unlocking the door. I half expected to hear the footsteps of scurrying intruders because of the lights shutting on and off that Fran had witnessed. Robert pushed open the door, switched on an overhead light and invited us to enter. To all of our mutual relief there did not seem to be anyone hiding out in there, at least not anyone we could immediately detect.

As we entered, we soon became aware that the first floor of the main house was much warmer than it had been when we'd passed through it less than an hour earlier. In fact, although it was an overcast autumn evening and rather cool outside, here inside on the first floor the temperature was almost sweltering. A quick check of one of the thermostats read that the temperature had been turned up to 85 degrees. We asked if anyone had turned the thermostats up. Robert replied, "It is rather warm in here, isn't it? But I wasn't aware that anyone had turned the thermostats up in here. That could certainly cost me a pretty penny in heating expenses." He and the two workmen then began setting the thermostats back to normal room temperature, as we continued on.

All three floors of the house were empty and spacious, having been completely gutted. The rooms were devoid of any furniture or trimmings. Only on the first floor was there any sign that the building was just starting to be restored at all to its former elegance. We of course complimented Robert and Maria on their new house and commented on just how wonderful it would look once the restorations were completed. Robert thanked us for the compliments and again voiced his frustrations over the renovations being halted.

The last section of the house we were led to was the basement. The two workmen friends of Robert and Maria refused to even accompany us down there. Maria herself was extremely uneasy about venturing down there and would only do so with a great deal of reassurance from her husband. As expected, the basement was expansive and musty smelling. Several overhead light bulbs served as the only illumination dispelling some of the gloom. The walls throughout the basement were painted white, although the paint was now quite grimy and peeling. There were also a few archways built into the walls, which resembled those that might be seen within a chapel. Somehow, they seemed oddly out of place within the structure of the basement. I asked Robert if these arches were a part of the original structure. He replied that they might well have been a more recent addition to the basement, although he had no idea exactly when or why they would have been added.

Among the few rooms that comprised the basement, Robert indicated one that was what he referred to as the "cold storage room." As Robert led us in, we could easily see why he called it that. The atmosphere in this room was noticeably more dank and chill than the rest of the basement. Renee, Fran and Jenn were filled with an overwhelming sense of heaviness as they stepped into this small room and felt uncomfortable remaining in it for more than a minute or so. Maria refused to step inside this small room at all. Sweeping his video camera around the enclosure, Rich commented to Robert, "I can see why you call this place the 'cold storage room.' It feels just like a morgue in here."

"You've got that right," said Robert. "And I have to wonder if this room was actually designed for some sort of cold storage." The three of us then also stepped back out.

Rich continued videotaping our tour of the basement while the rest of us were snapping photos and taking audio recordings. Maria was now clinging to her husband and obviously becoming increasingly uncomfortable down here in the basement. As we continued on, one of the archways in particular caught our attention. Strangely, this one was built directly into the house's center chimney. We also noticed an unusual illustration that had apparently been spray-painted onto the center of the chimney. It was a crude black and red spray-painted "symbol of Baphomet" goat head set within an inverted pentagram, apparently denoting satanic worship. Fran gasped audibly upon seeing it.

The emblem seemed to have been recently spray-painted there, sometime within the last several years. Renee commented, "No wonder the workmen are reluctant to come down here."

Calling Rich over, I asked, "Rich, could you possibly get a close-up shot of this?"

"Absolutely," he said, stepping forward with his video camera.

However, no sooner had Rich begun to take some footage, then his camera shut down "That's funny," he said. "The camera batteries were just freshly charged and should have lasted at least another forty-five

Keith just prior to performing a house blessing.

minutes. I'll have to feed some wires down here from upstairs, if that's okay."

Robert told him, "Sure, go ahead. In fact, the guys upstairs have some extra extension cords." While Rich was busily attaching the extension cords to his video camera and leading them down into the basement, Jenn informed us that the fresh batteries in her tape recorder had also suddenly died. "They were working fine just a moment ago," she said.

I then asked Robert and Maria, "Do you folks have any idea who could have painted this illustration on the chimney?"

Robert replied, "As far as we can tell, it must have been one of the more recent tenants, who were temporarily renting this house."

"Do you know any specific details about them?" I asked.

"Not really," said Robert. "I was simply told that there was a wild group of young people who were thought of around the neighborhood as being 'weird' and people thought they might be practicing witchcraft. But if you people are familiar with this sort of symbol, I want you be totally honest with me as to what it means."

Fran, being Pagan, was particularly unnerved to hear the pentagram being associated with witches although she mentioned that this information was also very revealing. She explained, "Seeing the goat headed Baphomet spray-painted right on the chimney, which is the 'heart' of a house, makes me wonder just what kind of rituals were performed here and what offerings were made."

I asked Fran if she could elaborate a little. Robert was also anxious for her to share what she knew about the location of the symbol. "Well," said Fran, "I'm sure you know all about the history of fireplaces and how important it was keeping one's hearth fire going as long as a house was standing. Fireplaces were called the hearth of a home, meaning the heart of the home, where meals were shared and families basically lived in their kitchens next to the hearth fire. During the olden days, especially during the winter, they'd spend a lot of time gathered there to keep warm. And to see a ritualistic symbol that is associated with the dark arts painted on the chimney in that basement… which I believed was used to carry any ritual offerings up and out to do their work... now THAT disturbs me! It may even have been used to call stuff into the house in a reverse ritual."

Listening to all this, Maria was plainly becoming increasingly uncomfortable being down there in the basement. She was clinging even more closely to her husband Robert and urging him in Spanish to escort her back upstairs. But after all, Robert had asked us to be honest with our findings and he seemed anxious to know the whole truth. He was also eager for our advice as to how he might best deal with the situation. Fran suggested to him that the symbol should be removed by sandblasting or using a belt sander with salt water and bay leaves sprayed on the plaster and brick, before and during the removal. And then the area should be covered over with a fresh coat of clean, white paint, preferably with a small amount of blessed holy water and sea salt added to the can.

I also reminded them that I was prepared to perform a full religious cleansing of both the main house and the carriage house. Both Robert and Maria once again agreed that they would very much appreciate that, especially if it would help bring closure to the situation and allow them to finally move in.

Rich returned downstairs with the extension cords connected to his video camera. While Robert escorted his wife Maria back upstairs, Rich successfully proceeded to take video footage of the entire basement, including the hearth with the satanic symbol spray-painted on it. As requested by the clients, I then proceeded with the house blessing, beginning right where we were in the basement. Naturally I paid special attention to the center chimney, anointing it with blessed oil and dousing it with holy water, all the while reciting prayers to hopefully nullify any negative spiritual attachment.

We then returned back upstairs, and went as a group from floor to floor and room-to-room as I read Bible passages aloud and anointed each room with holy water. As we continued throughout the rooms in each of the three floors, Rich followed us with his video camera, while Renee and Jenn took temperature readings and audio recordings. Fran also held onto a brazier of incense to spread the fragrant, purifying fumes of Frankincense and Myrrh. I made certain to be very thorough, blessing every door, every window and every possible egress.

Eventually we reached the top floor, and were standing as a group at the top of the wide staircase. While blessing this area in particular, I had begun to sense the tension building in the atmosphere surrounding us. As always, I had my own tape recorder with me, recording audio throughout. Since Robert and Maria were not with us at the moment, having decided to leave us to our work for a bit, I suggested to the others, "How about if we take a short break, and listen to some of our recordings?"

Everyone was agreeable to this. After rewinding my audiotape for a minute or so, I played back the portion of the tape of my blessing of the very area that we were in. There was the sound of my voice on the tape saying, "Be gone any unclean spirits, I command you to leave now in the name of Jesus Christ!"

We then heard a whispered yet very clear EVP of a male voice saying "Oh fuck!"

Fran, Renee and Jenn gasped in astonishment at this clear vulgarity. I played it again and it was unmistakably clear. Rich commented, "Whatever's here, Keith, it obviously doesn't want you to be doing the blessing up here." Everyone else wholeheartedly agreed.

The EVP had a peculiar inflection to it. It seemed to be a sigh of exasperation, or perhaps resignation, with what may have been a slight British accent.

Fortunately, we were able to complete the investigation and the blessing of the main house without further incident. The carriage house, being much smaller, took even less time. It was then time to wrap things up and present our conclusions to the clients. We shared the recording of the EVP with Robert and Maria. Not surprisingly they were taken aback by what they heard. But we also informed them that the blessing of the entire premises was now completed. They were both extremely grateful for our intervention and announced to us that the atmosphere within the two buildings did feel noticeably lighter. Even the foreman and his assistant agreed that the entire place now felt better to them. Robert asked, "So, does this mean that whatever negative spirits that were in here are now completely gone?" Maria looked at us with an expression of hopefulness.

We explained to them that only time would tell if the activity would remain dormant. However, we also advised them on ways of protecting themselves, as well as keeping the blessing effectual. Fran again emphasized the importance of completely removing the symbol of Baphomet from the basement hearth or at the very least painting over it. Robert assured her that he'd personally sandblast the image away himself, before painting over it. Before we left, he told us, "Again, I absolutely can't thank you people enough for all you've done for us tonight." Maria also sincerely thanked us, her eyes filling with tears. Robert even offered us cash compensation, but we told him this was not necessary.

"Well, hopefully we'll have you all over for dinner here, once the restorations are completed," said Robert. "And be sure to thank Jason personally, from me, for sending you people out to help us."

We assured him that we would. He and Maria wished us all a safe ride home.

A few weeks later Fran received a call from New York- it was Robert. He told her that all was quiet and he'd like to again thank TAPS very much. We were all relieved when Fran relayed the message to the rest of us at our next meeting. Those of us who had been there recalled how very upset Robert's wife Maria had been about what could possibly be plaguing their new home and how she was refusing to live in it at all unless the negativity was gone and the atmosphere peaceful. Since none of the disturbing activity had reoccurred, the construction crew now felt comfortable enough to continue the renovations in both the main house and the carriage house.

Because of our caseload, we eventually lost touch with these clients. At least they still had our contact information and had been encouraged to get in touch with us if they were experiencing further problems. Rich, Fran, Renee, Jenn and I always wondered about them and if they eventually moved in and stayed. We never did receive a dinner invitation. Hopefully they were simply occupied with moving into their beautifully restored Newport home and getting on with the business of enjoying life, perhaps even starting a new family.

Thinking back on the obscene EVP that as captured on my tape recorder that night, Fran Ford recently commented, "That is one moment in the investigating archives of my brain that I will never forget. I think we were all a bit taken aback by this. And if I remember correctly, you played the recording back for us because you had sensed something and the clients weren't there at the time; they had gone out for a bit."

Of course, this was not the only historic Newport home that we'd eventually wind up being called in to investigate because the owners were experiencing unusual activity soon after they'd begun renovations. Perhaps owing to its rich history as a historic coastal port, Newport in general seems to be rather a hotbed of paranormal activity. Simply ask anyone who has taken one of the Newport ghost tours or spent any length of time touring one of the famous historic Newport Mansions located along Bellevue Avenue.

Chapter 3

The House on Atwood Avenue

Most of us in the field of paranormal research and exploration, very early on in our careers, develop an attachment to certain haunted locations and they soon become our favorite places to investigate. For me personally, upon first starting out as a young teenager, it was the abandoned Darby Road Inn located in North Scituate, Rhode Island. For John Zaffis, it was the haunted Phelps Mansion in Connecticut. (Both of these structures have long since been demolished.) And for my friend Brian Harnois, it was a nondescript, abandoned two-story house located along Atwood Avenue in the town of Johnston, Rhode Island. The house was set on a slight elevation, painted a faded colonial brown color and appeared to be perhaps fifty or sixty years old- although it was difficult to precisely estimate the age of the property. For some reason, those who had periodically lived in this unassuming house had stayed on average only a year or less and then the house would be up for sale again. In fact, the last family living there had stayed only a few months before moving out, finally leaving the house abandoned for at least two years. Back in the mid-1980's, my close friend Peggy lived with her mother directly across from this house. Neither Peggy nor her mom had a clue as to why no one had lived there in so long since there was nothing particularly odd or unattractive about the structure. In fact, the only thing they definitely knew about the history of the house was that a husband and wife had recently lived there and that the wife had suffered from some sort of debilitating illness.

The reason that Peggy would sometimes mention the house to both my brother and I was that, according to those in the local neighborhood, the house had a reputation as being "haunted." And it was generally assumed that this was the reason it had stood unoccupied for so long. Since Peggy was also an enthusiast of the paranormal, Carl and I asked her if she herself had ever experienced or witnessed anything unusual about the house in the several years they'd lived in such close proximity to it. The only things both Peggy and her mom had witnessed were lights turning on and off in certain rooms of the house in the late evening hours, even though the house was supposedly no longer receiving electric power. And there would never be any cars parked in the driveway or in front of the house at these times. If there were any intruders in the house, they certainly didn't seem to be using flashlights since entire rooms would be illuminated. Peggy, being psychically sensitive herself, always experienced what she described as "negative vibes" emanating from the house. She would usually avoid walking past it, especially after dark. Peggy's mom also felt uncomfortable about the house and preferred to stay clear of it.

Deserted house.

It was not until the late 1990's that Brian Harnois first heard about the allegedly haunted house on Atwood Avenue. At the time, Brian was the lead investigator of the Rhode Island Paranormal Society, an organization he had founded. It was two of his group members – Theresa and her boyfriend Eric – who first brought the house to Brian's attention. They described it to him as bearing a resemblance to the "Freddie Krueger" house in "The Nightmare on Elm Street" and asked him if he'd like to check it out with them. Brian's interest was instantly peaked and it was not long before an after-hours investigation was planned for the house.

Shortly after 8:00 PM on a Friday evening Brian met up with Eric and Theresa. They met at Theresa's house, since she herself happened to live on Atwood Avenue and, in fact, her own residence was well within walking distance from the house they were about to investigate.

They soon arrived at the house itself, which was naturally in complete darkness, and managed to gain access through a two-by-four foot basement window near the back. Once inside, they switched on their flashlights and began inspecting the lower levels of the house. Almost instantly, all three investigators simultaneously experienced a sense of foreboding within the interior of the sparsely furnished first floor. They also found it strange that there was still any furniture at all within the house, as if the previous occupants had perhaps been reluctant to take everything with them. When Brian began leading the way upstairs to the second floor, he suddenly began feeling himself being pushed back by some sort of invisible force. The pressure moving against him became increasingly more forceful until he thought he would stumble backwards into Theresa and Eric behind him. It was only by tightly holding onto the railing of the old wooden banister that Brian was able to maintain his balance. Theresa cried out, "Brian, are you alright??"

Brian replied, "Yeah. It's just that I felt something pushing me back for a moment. Something obviously doesn't want us going up there to the second floor." Somehow the three of them eventually managed to make it up to the second floor. When they did, they discovered a strange glowing ring of light on one of the walls, about the size of a man's hand. What was strange about this light was that it had no apparent source. A thorough check proved that it could not be any sort of reflection from an outside window. Even when Brian placed his hand over it, the light mysteriously continued to glow.

They had returned to the first floor when Brian and Eric suddenly witnessed what appeared to be some sort of a shadowy, human-like figure moving up behind Theresa. "Hey!! Theresa, watch out!" Brian exclaimed.

Theresa let out a shriek. Eric instantly rushed forward and protectively caught his girlfriend around her waist.

Both Brian and Eric quickly shined their flashlights around the room but there was no sign of anything unusual. They then described to the frightened girl exactly what they'd just witnessed.

With a sigh Brian told his team members, "Okay, guys, I think all three of us have had enough excitement for one night. I'm beginning to see why nobody would stay here for very long. There's definitely some kind of unnatural presence in this place." Eric and Theresa readily agreed to call it a night.

However, the three of them also mutually agreed to come back for a follow-up investigation in a week or so and pick up exactly where they'd left off.

The return investigation of the Atwood Avenue house was scheduled for early Friday evening of the following week. Unfortunately, for various reasons, it turned out that none of his team members would be able to make it that night. A strange feeling of illness and foreboding had come over Theresa, as Friday evening approached, and Eric was reluctant to leave her alone. They apologized to Brian saying that this would probably not be a good night for them to return to the house. Brian told them he understood. However, he was determined to return to the house for a follow-up investigation that evening, even if it meant going in there and exploring by himself. Upon returning to Atwood Avenue that night, Brian once again parked his car in Theresa's driveway and walked over to the abandoned house. Just as he'd done the week before, he gained entrance by squeezing through the small basement window near the back. The oppressive feeling was there again and, if anything, it was even more palpable than it had been on his previous visit here. Except, of course, this time he was in there facing it alone.

Brian reached the first floor and his flashlight again revealed the familiar dusty, cobweb-enshrouded furniture. It was then that he seemed to hear a low, masculine-sounding voice speaking… though not exactly out loud. It was more of an impression somehow being conveyed to him. It seemed to be derisively telling him: "You arrogant punk!" Brian felt the hair on the back of his neck rise up. Even more than the last time, he was getting the distinct impression that something did not want him here. And yet he'd made it this far and was determined to stay for at least a short while longer.

Concentrating, Brian silently projected his thoughts right back to whatever seemed to have spoken to him: "If you really want me to leave so bad then show yourself to me... or at least give me some sign of your presence and then I'll leave." He stood there for a moment, scarcely daring to breathe as he waited for a reaction in the form of a knock or perhaps another message from the harsh, deeply masculine voice. But no immediate response was forthcoming. Carefully shining the beam from his flashlight on the dusty steps, Brian slowly began making his way up the staircase to the second floor. He examined the wall in the hallway where he, Eric and Theresa had seen the mysterious ring of light the week before. It was no longer there.

Brian then went back downstairs. In fact, he was just about to leave when, from the corner of his eye, he caught a sudden flash of movement. He glanced over to his right- just in time to catch a quick glimpse of the same shadow form that he and Eric had seen near Theresa. Brian instantly shined his flashlight in the direction of the shadow figure but it had vanished.

After this second visit Brian was completely intrigued with the house on Atwood Avenue, as well as with whatever malevolent entity or entities it contained. He soon decided to make it his personal home base of paranormal investigation.

Brian eventually disbanded the Rhode Island Paranormal Society. When he joined TAPS, one of the first things he excitedly shared with us was about what he and his teammates had experienced in the Atwood Avenue House. He was naturally anxious for some of us to accompany him on his next investigation there. Since Theresa and her boyfriend Eric had also joined TAPS, they certainly wished to be included in a return investigation to the abandoned house on Atwood Avenue.

It was some months, however, before an actual TAPS investigation of the house was arranged. When a date and a time were eventually scheduled, several members of TAPS agreed to participate. The assembled team consisted of Brian, Jason, Andrew, Rich, Heather, Valerie, Eric and Theresa. Brian would of course be leading the investigation. (I was unfortunately unable to join them on this investigation, due to family obligations.)

After Jason and Rich had parked their cars in Theresa's driveway, everyone made the brief walk together along Atwood Avenue to the abandoned house. Upon their arrival Jason said, "So, this is the place. You guys were right, it does look like something from a horror flick."

Rich asked, "So, Brian, how do we get in?"

Brian replied, "Oh, there's only one way inside. We have to climb in through a small basement window in the back, one by one."

However, Jason came up with an easier means of access for himself and the team. After finding out where the back door was, he then proceeded to kick it open with a loud crash! "I guess we can all go in now," he announced to the others.

During their investigation in the house that night, the TAPS team experienced only a minor amount of activity. There were some odd light anomalies captured on film, including some orb activity. However, most of this could be attributed to the dust that had been stirred up by the investigators moving around. Theresa felt the sensation of being touched on the middle of her back, at one point, and both Heather and Theresa were becoming increasing uncomfortable in the house. Rich, Brian and Eric did catch a fleeting glimpse of the shadow figure downstairs on the first floor but were unfortunately unable to capture it on film. At the end of the night, everyone agreed that the trip to the abandoned house had been at least an interesting excursion.

Long after the official TAPS investigation of the abandoned house on Atwood Avenue was concluded, Brian maintained an avid fascination with the house. He would often visit the place on a Friday or Saturday night, providing a TAPS investigation had not already been scheduled. Sometimes Eric and Theresa would still accompany him there, but if they were not available, Brian would also just as much enjoy going there by himself. The house eventually became almost like an old familiar friend to him and certainly his ongoing investigations there had become a treasured hobby. According to Brian, he would sometime briefly see the by now familiar "shadow figure" passing by while he was in the house. However, the figure no longer seemed to pay him any mind. It would silently pass by, as if it was either unaware of his presence or no longer even cared that he was there. Perhaps, by now, the shadow entity had even come to tolerate his visits to the house. In fact, Brian certainly no longer had the feeling that he was unwelcome there.

There was an occasion when Brian had approached me and asked me if I'd consider performing a religious cleansing within the house. He was concerned about the possibility of someone eventually buying the home and moving into a potentially negative haunting. But because TAPS soon became very busy with other cases that required our immediate attention, the religious cleansing never took place. In fact, as the TAPS caseload continued to steadily increase, Brian was given the added responsibilities of Case Manager. Now even he had to take an extended amount of time away from his favorite location.

Nearly a year would elapse before Brian would again visit the abandoned house on Atwood Avenue. He had naturally always wanted to take my wife Sandra and I inside this house that we'd heard so much about. Finally, our opportunity came. Brian, Chris Finch, my brother Carl, Sandra and I were returning home from an evening investigation of the Ram Tail mill site in Foster. During the drive, our conversation turned to some of the past investigations we'd done all done together. The Atwood Avenue house naturally came up. Carl and I began mentioning how our friend Peggy, who lived across from it, would avoid walking past it because of the uncomfortable vibes she'd experienced. Brian suddenly suggested, "Hey, I've always wanted to take you guys there. How about if we stop over there right now and just quickly check it out?"

"Sure," I said, "if everyone else is in agreement. After all, we already have our equipment with us."

The others said that they were also game for it. Sandra and Chris especially wanted to visit Brian's legendary Atwood Avenue house. "Alright, then!" Brian said with excitement. "Let's do this!" Brian soon made a quick detour off the main highway, and pulled onto Atwood Avenue.

As we neared our destination, I asked Brian, "Do you suppose the place is still accessible?"

He replied, "Well, to be honest, I haven't been by there for months. But the last time I drove by, it wasn't up for sale or anything. So it should still be accessible."

However, when we arrived at the site minutes later, Brian was in for quite a shock. The abandoned house on Atwood Avenue no longer stood there! "What the-??" he exclaimed, unbelieving. He then quickly swerved into a small parking lot across the street, put his Malibu into park and jumped out. In an instant, he had bolted across the street to where the house had stood for so many years. Sure enough, it had now been reduced to rubble, and from what we could see of it, the demolition had occurred fairly recently. In the illumination shone by the headlights, we could see Brian darting about the ruins with his arms waving frantically. I could not help but feel terrible for him.

When Brian finally returned and got back into the driver's seat, he cursed and pounded the steering wheel... then gave a deep sigh and lowered his head in exasperation. Clearly this was like losing an old friend to him. The rest of us sympathized with him and told him just how shocked and sorry we were, as well.

During the remainder of the drive back home that night, Brian did manage to cheer up a bit. He reminisced with us about his many investigations at the Atwood Avenue house, both with group members and privately. We agreed that it was curious that the place had never been put up for sale since, according to Brian, both the interior and the exterior of the house were in relatively good condition. We also speculated with him about what might eventually be put up on the now vacant lot... and what would become of the shadow figure that Brian had seen there on at least several occasions.

Now in a much more optimistic frame of mind as he drove along Rt. 295, Brian smiled and said, "Hey, who knows? Whoever moves into whatever house or business winds up being built on that spot, might just wind up giving us a call someday. I can just imagine someone contacting us and complaining, 'I'm seeing a shadow person walking around inside this building!'"

"You're probably right, Brian," I agreed with him "And in the meantime, there'll still be many other places for us to investigate and many more adventures. Tomorrow's another day."

Chapter 4

Paranormal Encounters in Chicopee, MA

Sandra and I first met Mike Dion when he attended a Paranormal Investigation class held at the Adult Education Center in Boston, given by New England Paranormal. Steve Gonsalves, founder of New England Paranormal, was leading the class while Sandra, my brother Carl and I were assisting him by speaking on the topic of demonology. Brian Harnois was also with us, to speak on some of the technical equipment used in paranormal investigation. Mike Dion sat in one of the front seats and was extremely attentive throughout the class. He readily asked questions whenever there was something he wished to know more about or to have clarified. It soon became apparent that Mike had more than a passing interest in paranormal investigation. In fact, Mike had even announced himself to us, before the class had begun, by drawing an illustration of a "welcoming ghost" on the chalkboard.

Not surprisingly, Mike had his own true-life experiences that had initially sparked his interest in the realm of the paranormal. He shared these with all of us near the end of the class that evening. Afterward, Mike joined us for an evening out at the Hard Rock Café in Boston and we soon became friends with him. It was not long afterward that Mike was invited by Steve to become a member of New England Paranormal, starting out as a trainee. He soon became a full member and, before long, proved himself to be quite capable.

Throughout the past several years both Sandra and I have had the opportunity to frequently team up with Mike and other members of New England Paranormal- usually when our assistance is required on cases where inhuman spirits may be involved. Mike Dion is the previous co-director and case manager for New England Paranormal and has been an avid senior investigator for both New England Paranormal and The Atlantic Paranormal Society. Sandra and I have also worked closely with Mike during paranormal investigations.

The following two accounts, given to us by Mike Dion, are what originally peaked Mike's interested in the paranormal. Both of these true events occurred in the city of Chicopee, Massachusetts- within one street of each other- and were separately experienced by Mike Dion and his eldest son Thomas. The street names have been changed to protect the privacy of Michael and his family. Both of these instances happened about two weeks apart.

Burton Street Encounter

On Friday afternoon, March the 1st, 2002, 16-year old Thomas Dion was taking his dog, Princess, on her daily walk around the block. The time was approximately 4:50 PM as he turned off of the street where he lived and onto the next, which was Burton Street. Thomas had made it about halfway down the street, all the while listening to his portable CD player, when he suddenly heard the screeching of tires directly behind him. It sounded as though someone had just slammed on their car brakes. Instantly turning around, Thomas spotted two blonde haired children – a girl of perhaps age eight and a boy of perhaps ten – standing in the middle of the road. They were apparently oblivious to the fact that a dark bluish green car was rapidly bearing down on them from behind. It was also curious that they seemed to have appeared out of nowhere. Thomas had just passed by the spot where they were now standing only seconds ago. Before Thomas could react, the oncoming car impacted the two young children with a loud thud and the vehicle then continued on. It was an obvious hit-and-run.

For a moment Thomas merely stood there in shock, gazing at the two seriously injured children lying there in the street. Realizing that it was now up to him to respond to this emergency situation, Thomas issued a quick command to Princess to stay put, threw off his headphones and rushed over to the two children to offer whatever assistance he could. Although he'd never seen either of them before, as he approached, the two children pathetically began calling out to him by name: "Tooommm...Tooommm..."

Kneeling down beside them, Thomas was about to assure the two hurt and bleeding children that help would soon be on the way. Looking up at him with pain and fear in their eyes, the young boy and girl both pleadingly called out his named once more. "Tooommm… Tooommm…"

Then, as Thomas reached out to touch them to offer some comfort, both of the two young children suddenly vanished from his sight, leaving him staring at the empty pavement beneath.

In shocked disbelief at what he'd just witnessed, Thomas shook his head and blinked. But there was no denying it… the two children, who he'd been looking down at only seconds before, had now completely vanished from his sight. In fact, it seemed as though they'd both simply "evaporated" before his eyes.

Utterly dumbfounded by what he'd just experienced, Thomas struggled for a logical explanation but could come up with none. Could he somehow have hallucinated the car, the whole hit-and-run incident and even the two young children themselves? Certainly, in all his sixteen years, he'd never experienced anything remotely similar to this.

Dazed and confused, Thomas glanced up and down the street in both directions. There were no cars coming. Nor was there anyone outside in the immediate area who might serve as a witness to substantiate what he'd just experienced… or at least to confirm to him that he'd imagined the whole thing. After regaining his full senses, Thomas concluded that the only thing to do now was simply to return home and discuss this bizarre experience with his parents. He turned to his patiently waiting dog. She did not appear to be particularly excited. "C'mon, Princess, let's go," he said, picking up the leash once again. He then continued on his way, this time not bothering to switch his portable CD player back on.

About 5-10 steps later, Thomas again heard the screech of tires. Turning around, he watched with unbelieving eyes as he saw the same two mysterious children standing there, glaring intently at him. The same dark bluish green car was bearing down upon them. Once again, before Thomas had the chance to react, an identical gruesome scenario was played out before his eyes. The car impacted the two children with a dull, sickening thud and then screeched away, leaving the young boy and the young girl injured and bleeding on the pavement. "Tooommm," they both pathetically wailed again, somehow knowing his name. Just as before, Thomas rushed over to them to offer what assistance he could.

This time, however, with the initial shock of the first experience having worn off, he decided to analyze the situation from a more objective standpoint. Taking in his surroundings, Thomas observed that something about the immediate area appeared noticeably different. The surrounding neighborhood in general now possessed a different look to it, and although Thomas had been down this street dozens of times before, he'd definitely never seen it this way. It actually seemed as though he was now viewing Burton Street as it would have appeared perhaps a decade or more ago. There were now fewer houses and some of the houses that were there seemed to have somehow changed in detail. For example, one of the existing houses was now without an additional garage, while another one now lacked vinyl siding... while still others were painted a different color altogether and sported different trim.

"Tooommm...Tooommm," the two children again called out to him. Thomas instantly sprinted over to them and knelt down beside the injured boy and girl, exactly as he'd done before. Not unexpectedly, they once again vanished before his eyes. Glancing up, Thomas also noticed that his surroundings had now reverted back to normal.

Feeling completely baffled by this phenomenon, Thomas walked back over to Princess, and absentmindedly asked, "Well, Princess... am I losing my mind, or what?" He then picked up the dog leash and again began continuing along Burton Street.

Once again, after ten or so steps, the same scenario played out, with the children crying his name after being hit by the car. He watched the scene, along with the altered surroundings, hoping to find some clue as to what reason there was for these weird sightings to be happening to him. As anticipated, the phantom boy and girl again vanished before he could offer them any type of comfort or assistance. Was some unknown force simply playing some kind of cosmic game with him?

Thomas finally reached the end of the street... and when he turned the corner the phenomena stopped happening. He continued home without further incident with Princess trotting briskly in front of him as though nothing at all out of the ordinary had happened. Upon his arrival home, Thomas relayed the story to his mother and later that day to his father, as well.

Redwood Street Encounter

Only a couple of weeks after hearing of his son's ghostly encounter on Burton St., Mike Dion had his own strange experience while leaving his home on Redwood Street, which runs parallel to Burton. It was around 6:00PM in Mid-March of 2002 and Mike had just received a phone call from his mother. She needed assistance with his uncle whom just days before had suffered a mild stroke. His uncle was a rather large man and now required assistance getting to and from the bathroom. Mike assured her he would be right over and proceeded out of his house to the car.

Pulling away from the driveway, Mike looked back at the living room window to wave goodbye to the family, which was one of those little traditions that he and his family always did whenever someone was driving away. He noticed that there was no one in the window and had started to glance away to look back at the road when he caught a glimpse of his youngest son waving to him from his bedroom window. Mike looked back at his son, waved for a second and then turned his attention back to the road in front of him. Suddenly he beheld something that seemed to defy any rational explanation.

About fifteen feet in front of the car, he saw a swirling mass of smoke approximately six feet high and four to five feet wide. The only thing Mike could initially liken the twisting, rope-like mass to, would be an image from a scene in the movie "Poltergeist", in which a white smoky substance is descending the staircase. In fact, the undulating mass in front of him appeared so thick and prominent, he instinctively reacted by slamming on the brakes to avoid hitting it.

After his car had nearly come to a complete stop, Mike let up on the brake pedal and simply began coasting through the smoky substance, with his mouth wide open in amazement. His car was completely engulfed by whatever this was. Mike saw that the smoke in some areas was thick enough to totally prevent him from seeing through it, even though the sunlight should have allowed at least some visibility. Also, as he was driving through the substance, Mike observed that the smoke was slowly twisting around in different directions as though blown by a slight breeze. What was most unusual, however, was that on the left side, about three to four feet above the street, there was a separate, glittering area in the smoke that was perhaps about the size of softball. It appeared to have either many tiny lights in it or contained some type of material that would cause this unique sparkling effect.

Dumbfounded by the whole experience after passing through the rope-like cloud of smoke, and still in awe of what he had just witnessed, Mike drove on to his mother's- reminding himself that he was desperately needed.

The entire way there, approximately a five-minute drive, he could scarcely get his jaw back up, as he kept repeating to himself, "What in the world was that? What in the world was that?" In fact, in his haste to get to his mother's, Mike suddenly realized that he'd been far too startled to even look in his rearview mirror to see if the smoky substance was still hovering there. He then thought to himself, "When I get to my mother's... I'll check the front bumper to see if there is any trace of residue to explain whatever the heck it was I've just driven through." When he arrived at his destination he examined the front bumper. Any visible trace of evidence that might have been present previously, had since evaporated.

On the way back home from his mother's, Mike speculated, "Maybe there is a manhole cover there and I just never noticed it before." As it turned out, there was no manhole cover. However, there was now a visible wet section on the pavement, directly underneath the exact spot where this phenomenon had occurred, even though it had not been raining in the area.

Both of these peculiar instances involved specific phenomena which Thomas and Mike have never experienced before or since and for which they have no logical explanation. Did Thomas happen to experience some sort of "time displacement" in which he repeatedly found himself transported back to Burton Street, as it may have appeared some years before? Since the two mysterious children both interacted with him, this experience cannot be defined as merely "residual" or playback. Also, these two phantom children were calling out to Thomas by name, even though they were both completely unfamiliar to him. Whatever the explanation, this experience seems to have been intended for him, and him only, at that very time and location. This phenomenon, therefore, falls into the category of "intelligent." What remains a complete enigma is the source, or identity, of the "intelligence" which may have been engineering this phenomenon.

And what of Mike's experience, which took place later in the same month, only one street over on Redwood Street? While on the surface it does not easily fit into the categories of either "residual" or "intelligent," one has to wonder if this anomaly also had somehow been intended for Mike Dion alone to experience, at that very time and location. Perhaps it even falls into some completely separate, unique category that has yet to be satisfactorily defined. Based upon Mike's personal description, the "twisting, rope-like, smoky thing" he drove straight through even bears some similarity (albeit on a much smaller scale) to certain phenomena that has been reportedly witnessed in such places as the Bermuda Triangle. As Mike himself humorously added when relating this experience: "I don't take drugs, so we can rule that out."

Any definitive explanation for the phenomena, which Thomas and Michael Dion separately encountered, remains elusive. Like the majority of people going about their daily business, neither Thomas nor Mike happened to have a camera or any other recording device with them at the time, although they now make certain to carry such equipment on their persons wherever they go... just in case!

Chapter 5

Long Island Haunting

It was on a mild early autumn evening in the year 1968 that young Ronnie Burns drove in the direction of the old cemetery located along Town Line Road in Commack, Long Island. His teenage girlfriend Yvonne sat in the passenger's seat beside him. Originally they'd planned to stop by the local burger joint for a snack. But first, Ronnie felt compelled to visit the historical cemetery in which the body of local ghost legend Lewis Wicks reposed. Perhaps it was partially because of the Ouija board sessions that Yvonne's best friend Marion had been conducting. Supposedly, she'd recently had some success in contacting the spirit of Lewis Wicks, who had informed her through the Ouija board that he was in a state of unrest as the result of having died an untimely death.

Ronnie himself had also recently experienced a rather vivid dream in which he'd seen Lewis Wicks leaning up against a cow barn, with one spurred boot propped up next to the partly opened door for support. He was wearing old-fashioned clothes from the 1800's including a long coat and a wide-brimmed hat. There may have been a wagon wheel propped against the barn as well. But for some reason, Ronnie just couldn't shake this image from his mind and he knew he simply had to visit Lewis' grave this evening before taking his girlfriend out for a bite to eat.

Although it was dark by the time they arrived at Town Line Road, a large yellow full moon had just risen over the nearby treetops. Ronnie soon spotted the cemetery just up ahead and began pulling his old 1961 Impala over onto the right shoulder of the road. He finally parked his car nearby to the cemetery entrance and shut off the engine. Turning to Yvonne, Ronnie asked, "You coming with me?"

"No," Yvonne refused. "I'll stay right here. And please don't be too long. This place gives me the creeps, especially at night."

"Don't worry, I can see Lewis' gravestone right from here. I'll be right back," Ronnie promised her. He then got out of his car and began approaching the cemetery while Yvonne watched him from her open window. Glancing over his shoulder, Ronnie added, "Just give me a shout if you see any cops coming, okay?"

Although the cemetery gate was closed, Ronnie was easily able to hoist his tall, wiry frame over the low metal fence that surrounded the cemetery. Because the nearest streetlight was burned out, Yvonne was indeed thankful for the moonlight, which allowed her to keep Ronnie in plain view.

It did not take long for Ronnie to find the exact headstone, which was only about 125 feet away from where he'd parked his car. Bending forward and squinting, he was just barely able to read the name of Lewis Wicks inscribed on the stone. He began wishing that he'd thought to bring along a flashlight, but this visit to the cemetery had been a last minute decision. A breeze soon began to pick up and the clouds that were moving in were now partially obscuring the moonlight. Ronnie soon found it necessary to get down on his hands and knees to try and read the rest of the inscription. Squinting, he read, "Sacred to the Memory of Lewis Wicks, who was killed on Thursday the 4th of Oct. at 2 o'clock P.M. by a wagon loaded with hay running over his breast. AD 1821, age 56 years." He also thought he could just barely make out words saying, "…who has left an affectionate consort and numerous friends to lament his loss," although in the dim lighting he couldn't be certain. Ronnie then said aloud, "Spirit of Lewis Wicks, if you can hear me, please give me a sign that you are here." To his surprise, less than a minute later, Ronnie began experiencing a cold, clammy sensation throughout his body. In fact, it reminded him of the way he felt that night when Yvonne's friend Marion had been conducting a Ouija board session in her bedroom and they'd suddenly heard scratching and knockings emanating from within the bedroom walls. Marion had even claimed that a spirit had sat down on the bed right beside her.

While positioned there in front of the gravestone, Ronnie could see the grass surrounding him begin to become matted out in spots, perhaps from the breeze which had now picked up considerably. He suddenly began experiencing the uncanny sensation of being watched by unseen eyes. Glancing up, he was astonished to behold a thick mist of vapor, which had somehow appeared directly over the gravestone. The thick vapor quickly began to congeal, seemingly taking on a human-like shape. Ronnie instantly jumped back and continued to watch with unbelieving eyes as first a head, and then shoulders and an upper torso began to form. Within less than a minute, he found himself staring at the nearly complete, hazy outline of a man who he estimated to be about 5' 11' in stature. Ronnie could even make out some dim facial features. The ghostly figure also appeared to be wearing a wide-brimmed hat and a long coat; very similar to the one Lewis Wicks had been wearing in his dream. Completely unnerved, Ronnie lowered his gaze; unable to look into the phantom's ghostly features any longer.

And then, just as suddenly as it had first appeared, the phantom image quickly evaporated from view. Ronnie shook his head and blinked several times, wondering to himself if he'd just imagined the whole thing. He then turned and dashed out of the cemetery, nearing injuring himself as he vaulted his tall, lanky body back over the low metal fence.

As soon as Ronnie returned to his car and jumped back into the diver's seat, he found Yvonne nearly in a state of panic. "Ronnie," she said in a trembling voice, "let's get out of here, now!"

"Why, what's wrong?" he asked her.

"Don't asked questions, just drive," Yvonne insisted. "We've gotta get the hell outta here!"

Without having a chance to tell Yvonne about what he himself had just experienced at the grave of Lewis Wicks, Ronnie started the engine, switched on the headlights and peeled out onto the road, causing the back tires to spray up a thick cloud of dirt and gravel. It wasn't until the cemetery was completely out of site, as Ronnie continued speeding down Town Line Road, that Yvonne regained her composure enough to explain what had frightened her so. Ronnie's hair literally stood on end as Yvonne described to him what she'd seen. From her open window in the passenger's seat, she'd also witnessed the mist hovering like a ball over the gravestone he'd been crouching in front of, and had watched as the mist had quickly formed into the hazy image of a man.

The fact that Yvonne had seen the exact same image, including the way it had formed out of a mist hovering over the gravestone of Lewis Wicks, convinced Ronnie that neither of them had been imagining the experience.

This was not to be the last encounter Ronnie Burns was to have with what he believed to be the ghost of Lewis Wicks. Yvonne's best friend Marion supposedly continued to keep in communication with Lewis' restless spirit through Ouija board sessions held in her basement and in her bedroom, during which she'd illuminate the room by lighting black candles. In fact, according to Marion herself, she was in regular contact with three separate spirit entities. One was supposedly the spirit of Lewis Wicks, another was a kindly, guardian spirit and the third was a malevolent spirit, perhaps even a demon. (In fact, according to Marion, the malevolent spirit had even attempted to engage in sexual relations with her.)

One evening, not long after their mutual cemetery experience, both Ronnie and Yvonne had another odd sighting. Ronnie was driving with Yvonne, nearing Town Line Road, when Yvonne told him that she absolutely refused to go past the old historical cemetery at night again. Feeling a bit uncomfortable about going past the cemetery himself at night, Ronnie pulled onto another rural road known as Commack Road. Since they had over an hour before Yvonne had to be back home, Ronnie decided to pull into a nearby field on the right to spend some time alone with his girlfriend.

About hour or so later, when it was time to leave, Ronnie started his car and turned on the headlights. As he did so, the headlights suddenly shone on something moving just up ahead of them. "Ronnie, there's someone out there," Yvonne alerted him.

As Ronnie peered through his windshield, the headlights fully illuminated what appeared to be the white-clad figure of a man, dressed in old-fashioned clothing, sprinting across the mist enshrouded field just up ahead. Whoever he was, he also appeared to be wearing a long, whitish cape that trailed behind him, which Ronnie described as looking like a "Liberace-style cape." Then, as Ronnie and Yvonne watched, the peculiar figure completely vanished into the darkness.

Whoever the strangely dressed individual might have been, they never found out...although the style of clothing did appear similar to that of the image they'd recently seen in the cemetery on Commack Road.

    Not very long afterward, Ronnie happened to have a job that was in the next town over, about eighteen miles away, working the graveyard shift in a machine shop. Instead of returning home after dropping his girlfriend off at home, Ronnie would sometimes pull alongside one of the rural roads in Commack and catch a few hours of sleep before setting out on the long drive into work. It was on was on one of these nights, as Ronnie was dozing in his newly acquired 1953 Ford with an alarm clock set on the dashboard and his head leaning against the driver's side door, that he was abruptly awakened by someone pulling on the door handle. Startled, he instantly snapped to full alertness and glanced out the window but could see no one. At first he thought he might simply have been dreaming. However, the door handle soon began rattling again to the point where he could distinctly hear it being tugged and could even feel the vibration of the door against his left arm.

    Thinking it might be a police officer, Ronnie again looked out the window. Still, no one was in sight. "Who is it? Who's there?" he asked. The jerking on the door handle then instantly stopped. Ronnie got out of his car and looked around for a moment, even stooping and checking underneath his car, but there was no sign of anyone. He then got back in and tried to relax. But seconds later, he could hear heavy footsteps, or boot steps, circling around the outside of his car. He reached over and opened his window as much as he dared, and sure enough, the heavy treading sounds continued loud and clear. There was even the sound of gravel loudly crunching underfoot, as whatever it was passed directly by his partly opened driver's side window. Desperately, he looked around for any trace of a living person, but there was no one in sight. At one point Ronnie stepped out of his car and apprehensively walked around a bit, even going so far as to get down on his hands and knees and glance underneath the car. However, there was no explanation for the noise he'd heard or for the violent pulling on the door handle.

He got back into his car. For a moment, Ronnie considered calling out, "Lewis Wicks, is that you out there?" Instead, he did the next best, sensible thing. He quickly rolled up his window the rest of the way, locked the car doors and scrunched down upon the front seat with his eyes tightly shut- until the sound of the heavy footsteps eventually ceased.

About this same time, a mysterious disturbance broke out in a home that was located almost directly across from the old historical cemetery on Commack Road. At least two members of the family involved were personal friends of Ronnie Burns. One of the sons in this family, 17-year-old John, actually broke down in tears while he was explaining the situation to Ronnie. Apparently the disturbance was of a spiritual nature, involving poltergeist-like activity. This activity included household items such as dishes and furniture being moved within the house by an unseen force as well as family members being physically attacked. A priest was finally called in an effort to deal with the situation. According to Ronnie's friend John, the priest was eventually successful in ridding the family and their house of the disturbance. However, throughout this ordeal, the priest was also physically attacked while assisting the family. At one point he was even violently thrown down by this unseen force. Rather than being deterred, the priest continued with the deliverance session until it was concluded.

Ronnie could not help but wonder if this spiritual disturbance had somehow been connected to the house's close proximity to the historical cemetery across the street on Commack Road (where he himself had experienced his ghostly encounter not long before). He also wondered if there might have been some connection to the Ouija board sessions that Yvonne's friend Marion had been conducting in her home, which was also located nearby in Commack.

It was not until thirteen years later, when Ronnie had returned for an extended visit to his original home city of Warwick, Rhode Island, that he began doing some actual research into the historical personage of Lewis Wicks. On an afternoon in 1983 Ronnie, accompanied by his mother, paid a visit to the Warwick Public Library. With the assistance of a kind librarian, they began researching the history of Commack, Long Island. What they discovered was that Lewis Wicks had owned a substantial amount of property in Commack, making him a very prominent citizen. As his gravestone had stated, he had died on October 4th, 1821 (at 2:00 in the afternoon) at the age of 56 and had indeed had the misfortune of being run over by a hay wagon. Ronnie always had the feeling that the spirit of Lewis Wicks had deliberately chosen him to communicate with back in 1970. Perhaps his restless spirit simply wished for Ronnie to tell his story so he would not be forgotten.

Ronnie Burns himself, who recently happened to be in Warwick, Rhode Island visiting his neighborhood buddy from years ago, Alfred Law, related the details of this account to me. Al happens to be married to my wife Sandra's sister, Donna. Ronnie had seen me on the TV series "Ghost Hunters," and when he found out that his old friend Al was actually my brother-in-law, he was naturally anxious to meet Sandra and myself, and to tell us all about his personal brushes with the supernatural. Al obligingly introduced us to Ronnie and we subsequently heard the details of his experiences, as best as he could recall them.

Ron Burns visits the grave of Lewis Wicks.

Ronnie Burns, who is now in his early 60's and who still resides in Commack, Long Island, hopes to one day obtain documented proof of the Long Island Haunting, which he and other close acquaintances of his had personally experienced back in the early 1970's. The grave of Lewis Wicks is still there in the old Commack

Cemetery for all to see, located just off of the Jericho Turnpike, and the story of the "banishment" which took place in the house nearby is still remembered by some long-time residents of Commack to this day. According to Ronnie, this incident was even mentioned in a story that once appeared in Reader's Digest.

Perhaps some evening the ghostly apparition of Lewis Wicks will actually reappear, this time in the presence of multiple witnesses, and Ronnie Burns' story will finally be vindicated. Members of the Long Island Paranormal Investigators are currently looking into strange sightings and other incidents surrounding the old Commack Cemetery, which continue to be reported to this day. Ronnie has even issued a word of caution to his old friend Al Law, who he's also invited to visit Commack Cemetery with him: "You better bring some shoe polish for your hair, Albert, 'cause it's gonna turn white!"

Chapter 6

Shades of H. P. Lovecraft

"Mock not the crows of Swan Point, for they are the guardians of those souls which here linger."

- Carl L. Johnson (excerpted from the annual graveside tribute to H.P. Lovecraft)

In March of 1987, my brother Carl, being an avid fan of Rhode Island Gothic horror writer H.P. Lovecraft, decided to organize a literary service of tribute to this master of the macabre, and asked me to assist. The date of this service would be scheduled for Sunday, March 15th; the 50th anniversary of Lovecraft's passing. As to where the tribute service was to be held, Carl could think of no better location than at the author's burial site, located in Providence's expansive Swan Point Cemetery. He then contacted the cemetery's caretaker and made arrangements to hold the tribute there. A week prior to the event, he also placed an announcement pertaining to the tribute in a local publication. In the announcement, Carl invited anyone who wished to do so to bring readings from Lovecraft's works, or literature of a related theme, to be read aloud at the gravesite. Initially, Carl was hoping that perhaps a dozen or so local Lovecraft enthusiasts might decide to attend, although he had little idea as to what the response might be.

Carl and I both arrived at the Phillips plot in Swan Point Cemetery suitably attired in black. As we began setting up for the service, it was not long before people began arriving in cars, on bicycles and on foot. Eventually, to our surprise, a crowd of well over a hundred spectators had gathered to join us in paying tribute to the life and works of H.P. Lovecraft! Not only that, but the event was covered by Channel 10 television as well. Word had apparently traveled fast among devoted Lovecraft fans. No less a personage than S.T. Joshi, president of Arkham House Publishers arrived with an entourage from New York.

Also among the attendees was Brett Rutherford, a renowned poet, author and playwright who was so impressed with the tribute that he was afterward inspired to write his famous poem "At Lovecraft's Grave."

Carl and Brett Rutherford also became fast friends as a result of this service of tribute. Later in 1987, Brett authored an original biographical stage play about H.P. Lovecraft entitled "Night Gaunts" with Carl in mind to portray the lead role of Lovecraft. This production was twice performed at the Providence Athenaeum on Benefit Street in Providence to standing room only, the first time in 1988 and the second time in 1991. In a review of the play which appeared in the Providence Journal, Carl's "eerie resemblance" to Lovecraft was commented upon. (This is not all that surprising, since while subsequently researching our family history, Carl and I discovered that we are blood related to H.P. Lovecraft on our mother's side.) Around this time, Carl also organized the H.P. Lovecraft Commemorative Activities Committee, of which he is founder and president.

Since the first of these graveside tributes was held in 1987, they have become an annual Rhode Island Tradition. Carl at one time decided to take a couple of years off, but popular demand soon compelled him to resume them. Far from being a dry dissertation on a deceased author, they are extremely entertaining and intriguing, with participants from all over the East Coast (and sometimes far beyond) sharing selected readings of their choosing. The H.P. Lovecraft Commemorative Activities Committee also occasionally conducts walking tours of Providence's East Side, where Lovecraft resided for most of his life, and from which he drew inspiration for many of his chilling tales.

For this chapter, my brother Carl has graciously agreed to be interviewed about H.P. Lovecraft and the annual services of tribute that he, himself organizes.

"Fantasy-horror fiction writer Howard Phillips Lovecraft, born in Providence, Rhode Island on August 20th, 1890, was a true American original," says Carl. "His macabre tales spanned the gap between those of Edgar Allan Poe and Stephen King. Typical 'Lovecraftian' themes –

evident in 'The Call of C'thulhu' and 'The Doom That Came To Samath' – deal with the powerlessness of the human race in a malevolent, godless universe; a fear of madness; and the downfall of civilization. His demon-gods were cosmic entities that could, with the wave of their tentacles, enslave mankind or drive to insanity the hapless populace of our planet. Yet, while his writing could be categorized, Lovecraft the man remained a mystery. Some viewed him as an obscure, pulp magazine writer and neurotic misanthrope, while others encountered a gifted author, witty conversationalist, and a generous friend and mentor.

"On March 15th, 1937, a horror story of courage and dignity maintained while enduring unremitting physical pain came to a close, as an author who had come to regard himself as a literary failure succumbed to intestinal cancer and nephritis, five months short of his forty-seventh birthday. In the years following his abbreviated life, the very name of Lovecraft has become synonymous with gripping supernatural suspense and he is widely regarded as the peer of Edgar Allan Poe, who he revered. Although he was known to have had many shortcomings, such as fervent prejudices in his younger days and an inability to take the sensible advice he offered to younger writers, his consideration and valiant spirit emerged to outweigh those flaws. It is through these annual services of tribute that we briefly endeavor to honor that spirit which shines forth in the legacy of H.P. Lovecraft."

Mist forming at Swan Point Cemetery.

Interestingly, it has also been noted that something quite out of the ordinary nearly always seems to occur at these graveside tributes honoring the memory of H.P. Lovecraft, often involving a sudden and unanticipated change in weather conditions. To cite an example from the service presented on March 16th, 1998, a snow flurry fell upon the scene for the precise duration of a dirge being sung by an attractive "Goth-type" young woman clad in a black velvet cloak and hood. Then, bright sunshine just as suddenly reappeared. Vaporous distortions have inexplicably occluded photographs of the gravesite and surrounding area, taken during the services. Also, flocks of crows sometimes congregate to interrupt readers, their cacophonous scolding seemingly cued to enhance portions of Locvecraft's horror tales as they are read.

When I asked Carl to comment on the possible paranormal implications, he replied with a wry smile, "Maybe Mr. Lovecraft has been, in his own way, letting us know of his bemusement at all the commotion surrounding him by augmenting the proceedings. Yet, that is mere speculation and of a decidedly 'unscientific' nature. After all, Lovecraft personally referred to himself as a 'scientific materialist' and professed to have no belief in the supernatural whatsoever."

There are a few other locations in the East Side section of Providence where H.P. Lovecraft's spirit or "shade" has reportedly been perceived. One such location is 598 Angell Street, where Lovecraft resided for a brief time prior to his death at age forty-six. Another place is the Ladd Observatory, located at 210 Doyle Avenue. An avid fan of astronomy from a very young age, Lovecraft was a frequent visitor to this antiquated observatory in his youth. He even possessed a key to the Ladd Observatory given to him by a family friend who worked as a caretaker there. It is perhaps for this reason that Lovecraft's ghost is said to haunt the dark recesses of this building. Still another location where Lovecraft's spirit has allegedly been sighted is 187 Benefit Street, where his body resided at the time of his funeral.

And then there was the occasion when the final resting-place of H.P. Lovecraft was disturbed by some wannabe grave robbers. Sometime during the night of October 13th, 1997, under the cover of darkness, a group of unknown perpetrators stole into Swan Point Cemetery and made their way to the Phillips plot, apparently intent on unearthing H.P.L.'s mortal remains. Fortunately, they only managed to dig down about three feet before relinquishing their task. The following morning, Swan Point security officers discovered a gaping hole three feet deep, directly over Lovecraft's grave, along with a single footprint in the surrounding soil. Those responsible were never traced. The hole they'd left was promptly filled in, the ground re-seeded and nighttime security at Swan Point was increased. By all accounts, this act of vandalism was not sufficient to rouse the spirit of H.P. Lovecraft since there have never been any reported sightings of his restless shade wandering the cemetery grounds.

Due to the fact that officials at Swan Point Cemetery no longer allow photography or news media on the cemetery grounds – this being an issue of privacy – the annual H.P. Lovecraft tributes have recently been relocated to take place on the front lawn of the Ladd Observatory at 210 Doyle Avenue. Our long-time friend Christian Henry Tobler, who is a noted author of several books on German Medieval longsword and field combat, traditionally emcees them.

Immediately following proceedings at the observatory, however, attendees are always invited to drive to Swan Point Cemetery, 585 Blackstone Boulevard. There, those who wish may briefly pay their respects at the Phillips family plot where H.P. Lovecraft is interred. And if you are planning on attending one of these tributes, who knows? You yourself may just be "lucky" enough to catch a glimpse of the shade of H.P. Lovecraft himself!

If you would like any information on upcoming events organized by the H.P. Lovecraft Commemorative Activities Committee, please get in touch with us at http://www.nearparanormal.com, or contact Carl at ConstableCJ@Hotmail.com. Also, feel free to contact the folks at "http://www.quahog.org", who are always a wealth of Rhode Island info.

Chapter 7

The Brooklyn Demon Case

(The names of the clients in this story have been changed to protect their identities.)

It was in April of 2003 that TAPS received an urgent sounding email from a young woman asking for our assistance. Her name was Cheryl, a single mother who lived alone with her eleven-year-old daughter in Brooklyn, New York. Brian Harnois, in his position as TAPS Case Manager, responded to the email and before long he was on the phone with Cheryl. According to Cheryl, she and her daughter were sharing their house with at least two spirit entities, possibly more, and one of them was frightening her daughter. When Brian asked Cheryl how long she'd been experiencing unusual phenomena in her house, she replied that it had been going on for several years but recently it had dramatically increased. Brian asked her if there were any other witnesses to the activity in her house, other than herself and her daughter. Yes, she replied. Her cousin Barbara was a frequent visitor to the home and had also experienced some of the activity. Because of what her daughter was also being put through, Cheryl was rather desperate to know if we could possibly offer any help, or at the very least, investigate her situation. Brian assured her that he would contact the two TAPS founders, Jason and Grant, and request that they call together a meeting to discuss an issue of imperative importance. In the meantime, Brian promised to remain in touch with her and asked Cheryl to contact him, day or night, if anything else should happen. Cheryl thanked him, expressing how grateful she was to him for not thinking she was just another nut case.

True to his word, Brian wasted no time in contacting Jason and Grant, as well as the senior members of TAPS. A meeting was arranged, during which we discussed what few particulars we actually knew of the case. By the conclusion of our meeting, it was unanimously agreed that Cheryl and her daughter's situation warranted an investigation. Cheryl was elated when Brian telephoned her, shortly after our meeting ended, and informed her that we'd decided to take on her case. She gave us specific directions to her home and arrangements were made for us to make the trip to Brooklyn on the 17th of May 2003. Several TAPS investigators were selected to go. Unfortunately, Sandra and I would be unable to attend since this was the weekend of Sandra's birthday and we had made plans with our son weeks in advance. However, both Heather and my brother Carl would be attending as well as Renee, so there would be three investigators present who were experienced with the study of inhuman entities. At Carl's request, I let him borrow my 35MM camera as well as my small Panasonic tape recorder, along with some fresh audio cassette tapes.

Following a drive of about three-and-a-half hours, the TAPS crew arrived at the three-story brownstone house in Brooklyn, which was their destination. Cheryl Pezzullo, a petite dark-haired woman in her early thirties, welcomed them in. (She had arranged for her 11-year-old daughter Druscilla to spend the night with her father so that she would not be in the way of the investigation.)

Cheryl's cousin, Barbara Dolan, who was only slightly older than Cheryl, was also there to assist with the interview. As Barbara explained, "Cheryl and I were more like sisters than cousins when we were growing up, since Cheryl was an only child." Grant commented, "You certainly look as if you could be sisters. There's quite a family resemblance."

After each member of the TAPS investigation team had been introduced to Cheryl and Barbara, Jason assured them, "Just so you'll know, we're not going to be prying into your private stuff tonight. I just want you to be able to relax and take it easy."

Cheryl said, "Thank you. I want you to know how much we appreciate all of you coming all this way tonight. Really, this means so much to me. My daughter and I have been in quite a desperate situation, lately, and we really had nowhere else to turn."

"Not a problem," said Jason. "I want you to feel as comfortable as possible with us being here. So, if you'd like, we can begin the initial interview."

Everyone was soon gathered together in the kitchen. Carl asked, "Do you have any objections to us tape recording the interview or to our taking photographs this evening? Everything will be kept completely confidential."

"We have no objections at all," said Cheryl. "Take as many recordings and pictures as you'd like. I'm really hoping you'll find something to prove that what's been happening isn't all our imaginations."

Carl switched on the cassette recorder. Investigators Fran, Heather and Jenn began taking down notes as Jason and Grant commenced the interview. "Well," said Grant, "let's go through exactly what has been happening. You say that the activity which you've been experiencing has picked up lately and that it's been frightening your daughter."

"Oh yes, it's been upsetting Druscilla quite a bit, to the point where she's having a great deal of trouble sleeping in her own bedroom," said Cheryl. "At first Druscilla was hearing voices whispering, both in her bedroom and out in the hallway, although she could never make out exactly what the voices were saying. But lately, she's also been seeing things."

"Seeing things?" asked Grant. "What sort of things has she been seeing?"

Cheryl replied, "She says she's been seeing an old woman dressed in black with long gray hair, peering into her room and smiling at her. And Druscilla describes the woman as having no eyes, just black holes where the eyes should be."

Carl and Heather shared a brief glance with each other. Although they were both aware of the fact that the manifestation having no eyes could be significant, they refrained from commenting, so as not to alarm the family.

Jason asked, "Has anyone else seen this woman who has no eyes?"

Cheryl and Barbara both shook their heads no.

Carl asked, "What activity have the two of you been experiencing?"

Cheryl explained that while in the house, both she and her cousin Barbara had experienced sudden rapping sounds in the walls accompanied by the pervasive feeling of being watched. They'd also heard heavy footsteps emanating from the second and third floor rooms when they knew for a fact that those rooms were empty at the time. "And there's stuff that's been happening to us, like, when I'm on the phone…I'll be talking with Barbara about you guys coming and there will suddenly be interference. And then there was the message we received on the answering machine, even though no call had come through."

Renee asked, "What did the message say?"

"It was just some sort of garbled message in a male voice," said Cheryl. "But the thing is, there's really no way it could have recorded because no call was indicated. Because I have Caller ID, even if no number came up, it should at least have been listed as unidentified."

"Also," said Barbara, "back when we were children, both Cheryl and I used to see some kind of ghostly figure in different rooms of this house. I know that was a long time ago but I still remember it quite clearly."

Heather said, "I notice you have two cats here. Do they ever seem to react to something unseen?"

"Oh yes," said Cheryl. "Every so often they'll suddenly get very skittish at a certain corner of whatever room they're in. One time, I even saw one of them hissing at the third floor closet, even though the door was closed."

Jason asked, "Is there a particular spot in this house where you personally feel the most uncomfortable?"

"The basement…definitely the basement," said Cheryl. "I just go down there to do whatever it is I have to do and then I rush back upstairs as quickly as possible."

Barbara said, "I hate being down there, period. Even if someone's with me I can't stay down in the basement for any length of time."

Heather asked, "Why does the basement in particular make you both feel so uncomfortable?"

"It just gives us a really creepy feeling to be down there," said Cheryl. "We feel like we're being watched all the time we're down there, even more so than the other rooms. Barbara feels terrified of the basement and Druscilla doesn't really like being down there for any length of time."

Barbara added, "It probably has a lot to do with the history of the basement. As you can tell, this house is pretty old. During the days of Prohibition, back in the 1930's, the basement was used as a 'speakeasy.'"

"Oh, really?" asked Carl. "So, in other words, in order to be admitted, customers back then would have to identify themselves by whispering a certain password at the door, hence the term "speakeasy.'"

"Exactly," said Barbara. "And from what I've heard, a great deal of gambling and prostitution also went on in those rooms down there. I'm sure the place has seen its share of bloodshed as well."

"Sounds delightful," said Brian, shaking his head.

Grant asked, "To your knowledge, has this house ever been blessed by a member of the clergy, or otherwise?"

Cheryl replied, "A Catholic priest did come in to bless this entire house shortly after my daughter Druscilla was born."

"How thorough was he during the blessing?" asked Grant. "Are you sure he went into every single room?"

"Well, I'm not quite certain if he got every room because I didn't go with him," said Cheryl. "I figured he knew what he was doing so I just gave him access to the house and let him to his thing. I know he went to all three floors and into the basement."

Jason then suggested, "Well, maybe we should do a walk-through of the house now, to get better acquainted with the entire structure."

Both Cheryl and Barbara offered to give them a tour of the thirteen-room house. Barbara apologized, "You'll have to excuse the clutter;

most of this is just garbage. I've been in the process of Fen Shui-ing and I ran out of industrial size trash bags."

"Fen Shui-ing?" Brian asked.

Carl explained, "It's basically aligning yourself to your surroundings and creating an empathetic atmosphere; one that's spiritually conducive."

"Thank you, Carl," said Barbara. "That's exactly what I've been trying to do here, to try and make the place more livable for both Cheryl and Druscilla."

Fran noticed a picture of a young girl on the wall. "Is this your daughter?" she asked Cheryl.

"Yes, that's a recent school picture of Druscilla," said Cheryl.

"She's very pretty. She looks like you," said Fran.

"Thank you, very much," said Cheryl. "Hopefully, with your help, we can make the situation here a little less frightening for her."

Grant then asked Cheryl, "Now, what are you experiencing on the first two floors?"

Cheryl replied, "Well, that was when Barbara and I were children. I was haunted- and so was Barbara- but we didn't tell each other until we were adults."

"That's what she mentioned," said Grant.

"Right," said Cheryl. "It looked like... I don't want to sound, you know, crazy, but..."

"Just say it," Grant encouraged her.

Cheryl explained, "From what I remember from when I was younger, it looked like a little, weird, sneaky guy. He had an evil grin and wore a little black hat. Barbara has also been haunted by the same guy with a black top hat."

Grant suggested, "Like a 'Snidely Whiplash' kind of character?"

Cheryl said, "From what I understand, what Barbara saw was taller. I don't know if he was kneeling at the bed when I saw him or if he was standing. But as a young child of about four or five, I recall him being short."

Following a complete tour of the first floor, Cheryl and Barbara led the TAPS members upstairs to the second floor. Grant asked, "Now, how old is this house?"

Cheryl replied, "It was built around 1910. So it's seen a lot of changes over the years."

"Are you familiar with the history of the house?" asked Grant.

"Not at all," said Cheryl. "At least not before my grandfather lived here. It's been privately owned by my family ever since." Cheryl also mentioned that her grandfather was known to have had ties to organized crime many years ago, and that her father had been emotionally abusive to both her and her mother. "I believe that you can bring things in, which may have something to do with the activity here," she said.

"Absolutely," Grant agreed. "Absolutely. It makes the path easier."

Carl added, "Perhaps these manifestations you've been experiencing are symptoms rather than causes in and of themselves. They are a problem but they stem from actual events."

Cheryl explained that not a great deal of activity seemed to happen on the second floor, aside from occasional footsteps that were unaccounted for. She'd had tenants renting out the second floor area for several months, though they'd recently moved out. "I guess they didn't like the disembodied footsteps at night either," Cheryl said with a light smile.

They then proceeded up to the third floor. Barbara and Cheryl first led them into the bedroom that had belonged to Cheryl's father. Although the double bed in one corner of the room was neatly made, the covers were extremely worn. The entire bed was covered with a noticeable layer of dust, signifying a long period of neglect. Cheryl explained to the TAPS crew, "We almost never go into this room because we get a very uncomfortable feeling in here, almost as bad as in the basement. As I said, my father was very emotionally abusive to both my mother and myself."

Grant asked, "Where are your parents now? Are they still living?"

"My father is," said Cheryl. "He's been declared mentally unstable and he lives elsewhere, on state aid. We very rarely see him. As for my mom, she died when she was 34-years-old, which happens to be the same age as I am now."

Jason asked, "Could you tell us a little more about your mom and how she died?"

Cheryl replied, "Her name was Ann-Marie, although she went by the nick-name of 'Buffy.' Both Barbara and I were told that she died of a drug overdose. At least, that's supposedly what the autopsy report said. However, Barbara and I were never completely satisfied with that."

"Was your father ever physically abusive to either you or your mom?" asked Jason.

"He was more inclined to threaten than to actually abuse," said Cheryl, "although we did sometimes have to do things like hide the scissors from him."

Grant asked, "Is there anything else you'd like to tell us about your family history?"

Cheryl replied, "Yes, I think I should mention that my father's father had mob ties. Talk about having skeletons in your family closet, so to speak."

"That's quite alright," said Grant. "That's a past generation and you certainly had nothing to do with it."

"I'm glad you feel that way," Cheryl told him. "There's also an old journal in our possession that my grandfather kept. I'll have to scout around for it when I have some time. I'm not sure how many details of his life in this house are documented in it but it just may contain some interesting info."

Cheryl and Barbara then led everyone over to a closet. A visiting psychic had claimed some sort of unholy entity inhabited the closet. Grant asked, "Did you pay for a psychic to come here and investigate?"

"No, we didn't even ask for the psychic to come here," said Cheryl. "The people who called her in were actually some tenants who I had living up here on the third floor. I guess they were experiencing activity up here such as disembodied footsteps and the feeling of being watched. So they had her here when I wasn't even home. But when the psychic came to this closet she suddenly became terrified and told them, 'The devil's here in this closet!' And then she fled the house and refused to come back."

"Interesting," said Grant. "Of course, there are all sorts of psychics. There are those who are legit and then there are those who are versed in parlor games. Obviously, having been exposed to the paranormal a lot, we're a little bit more sensitive. Are we psychic? Maybe… maybe not. We don't claim to be. But that is a tool in our bag."

Fran added, "Like anything else, if you use it and you exercise it then you'll become more attuned."

Grant agreed saying, "You do… you become more focused."

With a sudden wave of relief Barbara said, "Oh my gosh, you know what? I have to say this; thank God I'm not crazy!"

Everyone laughed. Grant commented, "I wish I had a dollar for every time someone says that."

All that remained now of the house tour was the basement. Back downstairs, Grant turned to Barbara and said, "Now, you don't have to go downstairs if you don't want to. I understand that it's a sensitive issue."

Barbara told Grant that she'd prefer to remain upstairs with the others, explaining that whenever she went down into the basement she felt as if she were being chased out of there.

Cheryl agreed to accompany Grant, Brian, Carl and Renee into the basement. She switched on the basement light and carefully led the way down the narrow stairs. Once they were down in the dark, musty basement Brian commented, "Now, I know why Barbara especially hates this part of the house. The atmosphere does feel extremely oppressive."

"I'm sorry it's so dark down here," Cheryl apologized. "Let me turn on another overhead light so you won't trip over anything."

As they cautiously moved about the basement, Carl noticed a smaller set of stairs at the far end. "It looks like it could be an escape route," he commented to Cheryl.

Cheryl said, "That actually leads out to my backyard. I imagine it may have been used for smuggling in liquor years ago."

"That would make sense," Carl agreed.

Cheryl then stepped over to an area in the center of the basement and indicated a section of the floor. "You see where there's a spot here that's been cemented over?" she asked.

Everyone moved forward for a closer look. "You're right," said Grant. "In fact, it looks as if it was some sort of hole in the floor, that's been cemented over."

Cheryl explained, "This was actually once a well that was cemented over some decades ago; I'm not sure exactly when. But there was once a rumor in the family that at least two people were killed and their bodies were thrown down there."

"R-Really?" Brian asked in astonishment. "Do you have any idea who they were?"

"No, not at all," said Cheryl. "Like I said, it was just a family rumor and it probably isn't even true."

Brian said, "Then again, maybe it did happen, considering the history of this basement. Maybe a couple of people were actually killed down here, back in the days when it was a speak-easy."

"Yes, I suppose anything's possible," said Cheryl.

Examining it a bit more closely, Grant said, "The only thing is, that was during the days of Prohibition, back in the 1930's. This looks as though it's been sealed much more recently."

Barbara said, "Yes, you're right. It wasn't cemented over until sometime in the 1970's when Cheryl and I were children. I think my family had it sealed for safety purposes, for us kids."

"Hmm," said Grant. "I'll have Jason take a look at this too, later on."

Back upstairs, it was time to begin the investigation. Jason and Grant assigned team members to various spots throughout the 13-room house. Carl and Brian ventured up to the third floor. Brian set up his infrared video camera facing the "haunted" closet with the door open. Carl placed the small cassette recorder he carried inside the closet and left it there. He and Brian began a walk-through of some of the other rooms on the third floor.

Renee and Jenn were assigned to the second floor area while Fran and Heather were asked to remain on the first floor with Cheryl and Barbara.

Jason also accompanied Grant down into the basement where Grant pointed out the well, which had been cemented over, and explained to Jason about the rumor of one or more bodies having been deposited down into it. After examining it for himself, Jason told Grant, "You're right about this having been sealed fairly recently. I'd say it was cemented over no more than thirty years ago, tops." He then looked squarely at Grant and said, "I'll tell ya, if there are human remains down there, there's certainly one way of finding out for sure."

"Yeah, but I don't know how agreeable Cheryl would be to having part of her basement floor torn up," said Grant.

"Well, that's totally her decision," said Jason. "Maybe later on we can discuss that with her. Anyway, let's set up some surveillance equipment down here and then head back upstairs."

Fran and Heather were in the kitchen interviewing Barbara about some of the other activity that had taken place in the house. Heather asked, "To your knowledge, Barbara, has anyone ever used a Ouija board in this house?"

Barbara replied, "Yes, when we were kids Cheryl and I used to play with a Ouija board quite frequently in this house. We knew that the place was haunted so we wanted to find out who the ghosts were."

"Did you ever get any results?" asked Fran.

"Yes, we certainly did," said Cheryl. "At first, it just seemed like we were having conversations with friendly spirits but after awhile we started getting a lot of foul language and vulgarities. So that's when we got scared and stopped."

Heather asked, "Do you still have the Ouija board now?"

"No, we destroyed it when we were teenagers," said Barbara. "I know it was just supposed to be a game, but after what came across, we were just too terrified."

Just then, Carl and Brian returned from upstairs. Carl asked, "Did I walk in on a conversation about a Ouija board?"

"Yes," said Barbara, "I was just explaining how Cheryl and I would play with the typical store bought variety, here in the house, back when we were teenagers."

Carl said, "Ah yes, the 'Mystifying Oracle' by Parker Brothers."

"Right, that's exactly what it was," said Cheryl.

"It's always been especially popular with teenagers," said Carl. "The thing is, it's like playing a game of Russian roulette. Most of the time, nothing overtly negative will happen. Some people play Russian roulette and never have an incident."

Heather added, "But it only takes that one time, by opening psychic doors to something unknown. It could be a negative presence, masquerading as something that's benign. But then, it's sometimes much more difficult to get rid of."

"It also could be tapping into a collective consciousness," said Fran. "By the way, where are the Ouija boards you used now? Are they still here?"

Cheryl replied, "No, we disposed of them quite a few years ago."

Carl asked, "You destroyed them, you got rid of them?"

"We destroyed them and got them out of the house when we were teenagers," said Cheryl.

"Just as well," said Heather.

The investigation continued, with the TAPS members splitting up into different teams and taking shifts in various rooms of the 13-room house. Aside from some feelings of oppression and being watched by an unseen presence in certain rooms, no one was experiencing any significant amount of activity. Fran and Renee conducted an EVP session in Druscilla's room while the other team members continued to take shifts in various other sections of the house.

Shortly after 1:00 AM Jason and Grant called everyone together, including Cheryl and Barbara. Grant said, "Whatever's in here is very, very coy. Although some of us seem to have felt a presence in this house, it's definitely lying low."

Cheryl told everyone, "I'm sorry that nothing's been happening in the house. It's just so unpredictable as to exactly when something will take place."

"No need to apologize," Jason assured her. "That's the nature of the game, so to speak. We have to review whatever data we've collected tonight, anyway."

"I don't know if this means anything," said Cheryl, "but for some reason I always seem to wake up at four o'clock in the morning. Either that or something wakes me up. And it's never at four-fifteen or four-thirty, it's always precisely at four AM."

"It could be significant," said Jason. "And I guess some of us will be staying here most of the night, as you requested, Cheryl."

"As long as any of you can possible stay, you're certainly welcome to," said Cheryl.

Jason told the other investigators, "Well it's getting pretty late so, if anyone wants to call it a night, that's okay with me. I know it's a long drive back to Rhode Island and Fran has to make it back to Massachusetts. Me and Grant will probably stay the remainder of the night."

Both Carl and Renee, who had driven together, decided to begin making the lengthy trip back to Rhode Island shortly after 2:00 AM.

After saying goodnight to everyone downstairs, Renee excused herself to go upstairs to say goodnight to Grant and Jenn. As she entered the third floor bedroom Renee saw Grant and Jenn sitting in darkness, taking some recordings. "Oh, I'm sorry," she whispered. "I was just coming to say goodnight since Carl and I are leaving now."

"That's quite all right, come on in," Grant whispered back, motioning to her. "Just join us for a few minutes in here, will you? We seem to be experiencing something, and I want to see if you can witness it too.

Quietly, Renee took a seat next to Grant and Jenn on the small sofa that was in the bedroom. "Why, what's going on?" asked Renee.

"Shhh," Grant hushed her. "Just look around the room for a moment and observe."

It was not long before Renee also witnessed what Grant and Jenn had been seeing – a black, somewhat hazy figure, with no distinct shape, which appeared to be moving along the bedroom walls as they watched.

"Oh my God," Renee gasped.

The room was in complete darkness… and yet, somehow this shadowy figure clearly stood out. Grant, Jenn and Renee visually followed the figure, as it seemed to be circling the parameter of the room. There was no real shape to this form; it was just a very black shadow in motion. At one point, it suddenly cut through the center of the room and then briefly returned to its circling motion before disappearing from view.

"Unbelievable," Jenn whispered. "And there's no denying we all saw it, too."

Renee gave a nervous laugh, and commented, "Wow! I'm so glad I got to see something before leaving tonight."

Rising from the sofa, Grant said, "That's why I plan to have at least two people in this room all night until we leave, just in case it happens again. I'm also going to make sure that Brian has his night shot camera running in here the remainder of the night."

By 4:00 AM, with most of the other investigators having left, Jason was downstairs with Cheryl and Barbara. Grant, Brian and Jenn were keeping vigil upstairs in the third floor bedroom, which obviously seemed the most active spot. Brian had his video camera positioned on a tripod, set to night shot. By this time, the three of them were having considerable difficulty keeping awake in the darkened bedroom, which necessitated them having to remain awake in shifts. It was presently Brian's turn to keep awake and he himself was nearly dozing off. Suddenly he became aware of a light flickering against the wall in front of him. At first he thought that it might be a trick of his eyes until he saw that the light appeared to be moving around the room in a pattern. He quickly alerted the others saying, "Hey, guys... I think we're getting activity in here."

Both Grant and Jenn snapped to full alertness. Since their eyes were well adjusted to the darkness, they could also clearly see the rectangular flash of light, about four feet in length and width. It was moving rapidly along the bedroom walls in a left-to-right direction. Grant and Brian quickly ascertained that no light source was causing a reflection from outside, such as passing headlights. The light show continued for several more seconds before it abruptly ceased.

Then something else began to take place in the room. Over near the bed a dim, cylindrical shaft of light suddenly appeared and slowly began elongating. "What the hell is that?" asked Brian.

"I have no idea," Grant whispered back.

As the three of them watched in awestruck silence, the oblong light widened and actually appeared to be taking on a vague humanoid shape. Within seconds, they could make out what resembled the semi-translucent figure of a person sitting upon the bed. Though it seemed human in shape, it possessed no discernible facial features. It then seemed to slowly rise from the bed into a standing position.

Both Grant and Jenn watched in silence as Brian rose from his seat and slowly began approaching the dim figure. When he stood directly in front of it, Brian paused and cautiously extended his left hand to touch it. The figure then dissipated from sight. "It's gone," Brian whispered.

Finding her voice, Jenn asked, "What did it feel like, Brian? I mean, was there any sensation when you put your hand in it?"

"Yes... it was like a cold, tingling sensation," Brian replied. "It wasn't shockingly cold or anything. It was more like just a cold static."

Grant said, "Well we certainly have something to report to Jason and the others. And hopefully we'll have some concrete evidence to show for it, too."

Since the dawn of a new day had now arrived, the TAPS crew members decided it was time to pack up their equipment and begin the trip back to Rhode Island. Before doing so, however, they once again convened with Cheryl and Barbara. Grant, Jenn and Brian explained to them what they'd witnessed upstairs, which certainly lent validation to what the family had been experiencing. Jason informed them that the next step would be for them to review whatever data they'd collected. "This can sometimes be a tedious process and it can take some time," he explained. "But we should be able to go over most of it before the end of the week. Then we'll be in touch with you about our findings."

Grant added, "In the meantime, if anything else happens at all, or even if you just want to talk, please don't hesitate to call."

Cheryl told them, "I understand. And again, thank you all so much for coming all this way and for spending the entire night."

"Yes, thank you," said Barbara. "Do you think you'll be coming back here again?"

Brian assured her, "Believe me, after what I've just experienced upstairs, we'll definitely be coming back to this house again!"

At our weekly meeting of The Atlantic Paranormal Society, held at a local coffee shop, we discussed the data that had been compiled from the Brooklyn investigation. Brian was understandably excited about the spectral figure that he'd actually been able to put his hand into upstairs in the third floor bedroom, witnessed by both Grant and Jenn. "I sure wish you'd been there to see it, Keith," he told me. "It was the most awesome thing I've ever experienced on an investigation! When

I came over and tried to touch it, it was like a momentary cold, tingly sensation. And then the spirit, or whatever it was, just faded away."

Renee said, "I only wish that Carl and I had stayed there just a couple more hours. Then we might've seen it, too. But at least I did get to experience the flashing lights up on the third floor."

Grant told us, "Unfortunately, we weren't able to catch anything significant on video. Brian's camera had stopped running at the time the spirit form actually appeared to us. All we were able to capture earlier in the room was some minor orb activity against the wall."

"Yeah, going home empty-handed was a bummer," said Brian. "I hope we can capture some evidence on our next trip there."

Jason said, "I wouldn't say we came away empty handed. From what I understand, Carl managed to catch a few impressive EVPs during the investigation."

"Yes," said Carl, "I gave the tape recorder I borrowed from Keith back to him the day after the investigation and asked him if he'd be so kind as to listen to it for any possible EVP. As Jason said, he managed to find at least a few interesting examples."

Everyone looked at me with anticipation as I took out my small gray tape recorder, placed it on the table in front of me and switched it on. The first example of EVP I played for them was during the initial interview. In the mist of the conversation, three taps could suddenly be heard. They were immediately followed by a low voice – presumably male - clearly saying: "Beatrice… right."

The other members gasped and moved forward. After I'd rewound the tape and played it again for them, Brian remarked, "That's so incredibly clear; it's definitely a 'class A' EVP!"

Carl said, "The question is, who is Beatrice? I don't recall either Cheryl or Barbara mentioning that name during the interview."

Heather suggested, "Maybe Beatrice was a family member who died in the house, and for some reason, a spirit in the house is trying to bring our attention to her."

Anxiously, Brian asked, "What other EVPs you got for us there, Keith?"

"There's one right after you and Carl had gone upstairs to the third floor and are about to place the tape recorder in the third floor closet," I said. "It sounds like the exact same voice which mentioned the name 'Beatrice' downstairs and it seems to have taken exception to you and Carl walking around the house." After fast-forwarding the audiotape to the correct spot, I pressed play and said, "Listen carefully to this."

There was the sound of Carl and Brian noisily treading up the stairs. This was followed by Carl announcing that he was about to place the tape recorder inside of the third floor closet. He then asked Brian if he needed a flashlight. Just as they were about to walk away, a low voice could be heard whispering: "Jesus, this is my house. Just walk slooow."

"Oh, man!" said Brian. "That voice sends chills right through me."

Grant agreed, saying, "It does have an extremely eerie quality to it, especially the way it elongates the vowel. And that was at the closet that's supposedly demonically infested, right?"

"That's correct," said Carl. "That's the closet which caused the psychic who was brought in to go fleeing from the house, claiming that the devil was inside it."

Brian asked, "Did you find any EVPs while the tape recorder was left inside the closet?"

"Just one very distinct sigh, after about a minute or so. You'll have to listen carefully."

After I'd played the sound of the breathy sigh for them a few times, Carl commented, "It sounds exasperated, as if it really doesn't want us there."

Brian said, "That's right. It felt we were intruding on its territory."

I'd finished playing the EVP examples for everyone. Based on the interaction of the entity, we all agreed we were undeniably dealing with an intelligent haunt. Grant asked Fran if she'd captured any EVP inside of Druscilla's bedroom. "No, unfortunately not," she said. "But I did throw some Reiki symbols in there, hopefully to offer her some psychic protection."

"Every little bit helps," said Grant.

We then began discussing what our next step would be regarding the Brooklyn case. Jason told us, "It's obviously a very precarious situation there. On the one hand, they definitely do have activity taking place in the house. On the other hand, the psychic who was brought in went running out of the house in a panic, claiming that Satan himself was in the third floor closet."

Grant said, "I'm sure that didn't help the family's peace of mind any."

"No, I'm sure it didn't," Jason agreed. "Anyway, I certainly think a follow-up investigation is in order before we draw any definite conclusions."

"Alright!" said Brian, perking up. He was obviously very much looking forward to returning to the Brooklyn house, especially after what he'd experienced there the first time.

Jason then asked Brian, "You've been in touch with Cheryl over the past week, haven't you?"

"Yes, I have," said Brian. "Cheryl's been experiencing some minor activity since our last visit. She's hearing footsteps coming from the empty second and third floor rooms at night and now the door to the third floor closet has been opening and closing by itself. Plus, she's still waking up at four o'clock in the morning."

Heather asked, "How's her daughter, Druscilla, doing?"

Brian said, "She's still pretty frightened about sleeping alone in her room at night. From what Cheryl told me, I guess Druscilla's been having a lot of night terrors."

"Poor kid," said Heather, shaking her head.

Jason asked her, "Heather, what's your take on the situation so far?"

Heather replied, "Well, based upon the history of the house, I'd say a great deal of negativity has obviously been introduced to the house over the years. There's definitely the potential for both human and inhuman spirits to be present there."

"Carl?" Jason asked.

"I have to agree with Heather on that," said Carl. "There's also the fact that both Cheryl and Barbara have previously used a Ouija board in the house. That may have drawn something of an inhuman nature into the house… or at least exacerbated the situation."

"Jenn, would you like to add anything?" Jason asked her.

Jenn replied, "After what I personally experienced, I'd have to agree that there is definitely paranormal activity going on in that house. And the people living there are understandably very frightened by it."

Jason then asked my opinion. "Well, of course I wasn't present for the investigation," I said. "However, Carl mentioned that 11-year-old Druscilla reported seeing a ghost woman outside of her bedroom, which had no eyes. That could possibly be an indication of a demonic spirit."

Jason nodded and said, "Then I guess our next step is to arrange for our return visit there, possibly for sometime within the next few weeks. Hopefully we'll be able to capture some more concrete evidence there. Then, if Cheryl is agreeable, we'll eventually arrange to have a spiritual cleansing done in her house."

Carl said, "And as I mentioned, either Brian or myself will be contacting Cheryl this week. We'll ask her if there's any significance to the name 'Beatrice.'"

"Good enough," said Jason. "I'll be very interested as to what you find out about that."

Later that week, Carl contacted Cheryl by phone as promised. He asked her if there's been any change at all in the activity within her house since they'd last spoken. "Nothing really significant," said Cheryl, "except that I had a somewhat disturbing dream the other night."

"Can you describe your dream?" asked Carl.

Cheryl said, "It was very vivid and it was just before I woke up at my usual four AM. I dreamt that Druscilla was sleeping on the couch in the parlor and I was sitting there in the parlor watching over her.

Then suddenly I turned around and there was a shadow figure standing there in back of me. I don't know if that means anything."

"It's hard to tell," said Carl. "With all that you and Druscilla have been going through lately, I suppose it could have simply been your subconscious mind reflecting your maternal instincts."

Cheryl agreed. "Yeah, you're right; I certainly do feel very protective towards her."

"How's she holding up, by the way?" asked Carl.

"Oh, she's doing okay," said Cheryl. "I give that kid a lot of credit for her emotional fortitude. It's mostly at night that she feels really uncomfortable. As you know, she's been seeing a professional counselor because of the night terrors she's been having. Although it's hard to explain to a counselor about everything else that's been going on here."

"I understand," said Carl. "Oh by the way, Cheryl, I wanted to ask you something. Are you're familiar with anyone named Beatrice in connection with your family or, if not your family, perhaps to the history of your house?"

"Hmmm... Beatrice," said Cheryl. She thought for a moment before replying, "No, not at all. I'm afraid that name doesn't ring a bell. Why do you ask?"

Carl explained, "While my brother Keith was reviewing the audio tape I used during the investigation, he came across an EVP of a voice saying the name 'Beatrice.' I listened to it, too. It's extremely clear."

"Really?" asked Cheryl, her interest picking up. "Well like I said, I've never known of anyone in my family or in this house named Beatrice. I'll give Barbara a call later on and ask if that name sounds at all familiar to her."

"Thanks, Cheryl, I'd appreciate you getting back to me on that if you find out anything," said Carl.

Cheryl said, "And again, Carl, I'd just like to say how much I appreciate you and the rest of your team for all your help with this."

Less than two hours later, Carl received another telephone call from Cheryl. This time she sounded rather frantic. "Carl?"

"Cheryl?" he asked. "What's wrong? Has something just happened over there?"

"No, nothing's happened." she said. "But I just got off the phone with my cousin, Barbara. I asked her if she'd ever heard of anyone named Beatrice either in the family or this house, just like you told me to. Well, she'd never heard of anyone named Beatrice either. But she said she'd call her mother, who now lives in Texas, and ask her. Well, she did… and when she mentioned the name Beatrice, her mother nearly passed out. She asked Barbara, 'My God, who's been talking to you? How do you know about Beatrice?'" Cheryl paused for a moment to compose herself.

"Cheryl, calm down," Carl told her. "What else did Barbara's mother say? Who was Beatrice?"

Cheryl replied, "Carl… do you remember Barbara and me telling you guys about my grandfather who used to live in this house and had mob connections?"

"Yes, I remember," said Carl.

"Well, apparently my grandfather had a mistress who was staying here for awhile, who supposedly became pregnant with his child. And then, suddenly she was missing. The last place she was seen was in this house but she was never seen again. And the name of his mistress was Beatrice!"

"What?? Then that's the person that the EVP could have been referring to," said Carl.

Cheryl explained, "It's been kept secret from our generation for all these years because, at the time, they suspected foul play. That's why my aunt was so taken aback when Barbara mentioned the name of Beatrice. And my aunt even said that there was a rumor that after Beatrice was murdered to hide the pregnancy, her body was dumped into the well downstairs."

"You mean the cemented over well in the basement?" asked Carl.

"Yes," said Cheryl, "and that's supposedly why she vanished without a trace. Like I said, it's just a family rumor. But it's kind of unnerving, just the same, knowing that there might be a dead body in a sealed well hole in my own basement!"

And so, here we had an example of an EVP, bringing to our attention a possible homicide victim from a past generation. Neither Cheryl nor Barbara had ever heard the name of Beatrice in reference to the Brooklyn house prior to this. When Carl brought this to the attention of our fellow TAPS members, Jason came up with the idea of returning to Cheryl's house with some of his heavy duty plumbing equipment and drilling into the basement well. He then intended to utilize fiber optics, in an attempt to uncover any possible human remains that may lie within. However, he was unable to obtain Cheryl's permission to do so. Not only was she reluctant to have a small section of her basement dug up, but it would also be difficult to hide the reason they were doing it from her daughter Druscilla, especially if they did find human remains. Also, I was of the opinion that this was a project better left to a professional forensics team, rather than risk contaminating any evidence that might be revealed.

On the other hand, my wife Sandra strongly felt that perhaps it might not be a bad idea if the TAPS team was allowed to safely drill into the well and try some dredging. Calling in the authorities would certainly entail a long and involved process, with an incredible amount of legal red tape to even initiate an investigation of this type. But suppose, we as paranormal investigators, had taken the initiative and somehow managed to dredge up anything resembling human remains. Then a full-scale investigation would be launched and perhaps a missing person's case from a past generation would be reopened. And what if the remains were ultimately identified as belonging to an unfortunate young woman, named Beatrice, who'd been disposed of decades before because of an inconvenient pregnancy? It would be an example of a homicide victim from a previous generation actually being "identified" by an EVP and would certainly serve as a landmark event in the history of paranormal research.

Perhaps the intelligence behind the EVP was even attempting to guide us in this direction. But regardless of our individual opinions Cheryl, as the homeowner, remained adamant in her decision not to grant permission for Jason to tear up a small portion of her basement floor to search for human remains and we were bound to abide by her decision.

Our second TAPS investigation in Brooklyn was scheduled for some weeks later. Cheryl had reported to Carl and Brian that the activity within her house was suddenly on the up-sweep again. Unfortunately, because of our local caseload at the time, not all could make this one, including myself. The TAPS crew this time was comprised of Brian Harnois, my brother Carl and Christopher Finch.

This time when they arrived at the three-story brown house in Brooklyn, Cheryl's daughter Druscilla was there to greet them, as well. Cheryl's cousin Barbara was also present. Despite what 11-year-old Druscilla had been going through, she was a very pleasant, sociable pre-adolescent, who was obviously delighted to greet the company. In fact, Druscilla was having such a good time chatting with her guests; she seemed reluctant to leave when her father arrived to pick her up that evening. "This is unusual for Druscilla," Cheryl explained after her daughter had left. "Usually she's anxious to leave this house for a night. I can tell that she really liked the three of you."

Carl said, "Hopefully, we'll eventually help to make this place more comfortable for her to live in."

Cheryl told them, "Believe me; I'd be eternally grateful if you could do that. As you know, the activity here has been picking up again lately and it's been upsetting Druscilla pretty badly."

Because this was Chris's initial visit, Cheryl, Barbara, Carl and Brian led him on a walk-through of all three floors to familiarize him with the layout of the house. Barbara chose to remain upstairs in the kitchen as the others brought Chris into the basement and showed him the cemented-over well.

Later, as Cheryl and Barbara were serving refreshments in the kitchen, Chris said, "Although this is my first time here, I've been thoroughly filled in about what's been taking place here and how it's been affecting your daughter. I'm sorry to hear that things have gotten worse lately."

"Thank you for your concern, Chris," said Cheryl, handing him a cup of freshly brewed coffee. "It has been especially hard on Druscilla. On the one hand, she enjoys having the privacy of her own bedroom. But on the other hand she's becoming increasingly terrified of being in there alone at night."

Brian asked, "Has Druscilla had anymore sightings of the woman with no eyes?"

"Yes, once, but she didn't see it full view," said Cheryl. "She glimpsed it more out of her side vision, just outside of her bedroom door."

"That's unnerving enough," said Brian.

They then began discussing the EVPs that were captured on analog audio tape during the previous investigation. Barbara commented, "I swear, my mother nearly dropped when I asked her if she had any idea who Beatrice was. All she could say at first was 'How do you know about Beatrice? Who told you??'"

Cheryl said, "By the way, I've been thumbing through that old journal that my grandfather kept. There's a lot of weird stuff in there but I couldn't find any mention at all of anyone named Beatrice. I guess it's not all that surprising, though, that he'd avoid writing about his mistress."

Chris asked her, "Do you really believe that Beatrice was murdered and that her body was hidden in the well that's in the basement?"

Barbara replied, "It's entirely possible. I know some pretty unsettling things have happened in the history of this house and that could've been one true incident."

Carl said, "It would certainly account for the male voice which brought her name to our attention. Another mystery is who that voice could have belonged to."

Chris suggested, "Maybe it was someone who knew about the crime. Perhaps it's an accomplice who's in a state of unrest and wants to come clean."

Barbara asked, "Do you think the voice could possibly be something else? I mean, like a demon or something?"

Brian said, "Well, that's what we're gonna try to find out tonight. But just out of curiosity, why do you ask?"

"Well, there's that evil looking little gnome-like creature that Cheryl and I both saw years ago," said Barbara. "But I also had some much more recent experiences at my own apartment in Manhattan, which I'll tell you about later."

Cheryl said, "I also found that EVP you got up on the third floor to be fascinating. It gave me the creeps, especially knowing it was right outside of the 'haunted' closet up there that the psychic went running from."

"Oh yes," said Carl. "That was the one that said, 'Jesus, this is my house, just walk slooow.' The entity certainty seems to be territorial."

Brian said, "It sure as hell didn't like us walking around up there on the third floor. That's why later tonight I want to try provoking it into revealing itself."

Addressing Cheryl, Carl said, "By the way, you also mentioned that this same closet door on the third floor has been opening and closing on its own, correct?"

Cheryl said, "Yes, it has. Sometimes when I've been up there I'll hear it slamming. One time I even saw it open and close all by itself."

Carl then said to Cheryl and Barbara, "My brother Keith performs religious blessings of houses which have negative spirit activity in them. In fact, he and his wife Sandra very much wanted to be here with us tonight but unfortunately Jason had to send him and some of the other members on a local case. However, I brought along some holy water with me tonight, courtesy of Keith. Later on, with your permission, we'll go throughout the house and sprinkle some in each room. This should help to lessen some of the negativity you've been experiencing."

"Thank you," said Cheryl. "I appreciate anything that can help, especially with what Druscilla's been going through."

Carl then said, "By the way, Barbara, you mentioned that you recently had some experiences at your own apartment. Did you want to talk about that now?"

"Yes, it's been both at my Manhattan apartment and here," said Barbara. "I remember that it was in the afternoon and I was feeling exhausted so I decided to lie down on the sofa for a few minutes. But the moment I closed my eyes this loud male voice came booming into my mind saying, 'You bitches! You bitches!' And I know that it had something to do with this house, I just know it did. And then another time, I was in my apartment when a cross necklace, that I was wearing around my neck, was suddenly wrenched off and it went flying. Both my son and his girlfriend were witness to it when it happened."

"Interesting," said Carl. "So, do you think that it followed you to your apartment?"

Barbara said, "I certainly believe that it may have, at least temporarily. And I think it was meant as a warning because it happened shortly after the first TAPS investigation took place here."

Carl asked, "What was the incident that took place here?"

Barbara replied, "Well, one afternoon I was in the parlor with Cheryl and Druscilla and they were both admiring another necklace I was wearing. It wasn't the cross but they were telling me how much they liked it when suddenly that went flying off of my neck, too. It was like it happened just because they were admiring it."

"That's right," Cheryl confirmed. "Druscilla was pretty shaken up when she saw it happen and she asked us if 'the ghost lady with no eyes' did it. I didn't really know what to tell her."

When the interview was concluded Brian, Carl and Chris unpacked their equipment, including a vial of blessed water that was stopped with a cork. Before they began Cheryl informed everyone, "I've also tried burning a sprig of dried sage throughout the house. On your last visit here Fran recommended that I try doing that."

Chris said, "It does seem to have a positive effect, at least temporarily. It depends on the strength of whatever negative entities may be involved and the faith of the person using it."

Carl added, "Some investigators prefer to use it for protection during a paranormal investigation. It does tend to lessen negative activity. Of course, not only is a smoldering object inside an older house like this a safety hazard, it could also contaminate evidence."

Barbara said, "I have to tell you something. I believe that, if there is a demonic spirit here, it must've gotten into Cheryl's father's mind. Trust me, the man was on the brink of madness. He was always very paranoid about females, too. In fact, when he found out that Cheryl's mom had just given birth to a baby girl, he started telling her, 'Kill it! Kill it! It's the Devil's child!'"

"Nice guy," Chris commented.

Barbara said, "Oh, you don't know the half of it, Chris. Some of the stories I could tell!"

"Well," said Brian, "if this is a demonic entity we're dealing with then I think it's a very low-class demon." He then reached for the bottle of holy water which they'd set on a nearby table. Strangely the bottle was uncorked, the cork lying on the table beside the bottle. "Hey... did anybody just open this bottle of holy water?" he asked.

Carl said, "No, I haven't touched it since I unpacked it and set it there," said Carl. Chris, Barbara and Cheryl hadn't touched it either.

Brian commented, "Well then, it looks as though something's already trying to give us a message."

Carl, Brian and Chris then walked through the house with Brian liberally sprinkling blessed water. They began in the basement and then throughout the first floor rooms, taking EFM readings and audio recordings as they did so. When the first floor had been spiritually cleansed they approached the landing of the stairway which led to the second and third floors. No sooner had they reached the bottom of the stairs on the first floor landing when Brian's EMF meter suddenly began spiking. "Check this out," he said, while doing a sweep of the immediate area. "I'm getting some high readings right over here. Three-point-two, three-point-three... there's no electrical currents here that would cause this type of fluctuation." Brian then pointed the EMF toward the hallway and instantly received a lower reading. "One-point-one...one-point-two."

Standing nearby, Barbara also noticed a definite change in the atmosphere. "The air right here is suddenly so thick you could cut it with a knife," she commented.

Chris quickly began gauging the ambient temperature around the immediate area. "I'm picking up a temperature reading of eighty-two degrees although it didn't seem that warm just a moment ago," he said. He then took a few steps into the parlor and checked his digital thermometer again. "It's only a degree lower right in here although it feels cooler."

"It seems isolated," said Carl. Speaking into the tape recorder he held, he added, "Entering the hallway, main staircase."

Brian even held the EMF close to an electrical outlet just outside of the hallway, which caused the indicator to waver only slightly. He then stepped back into the hallway near the staircase that caused the indicator to begin spiking once again. "Three-point-two...three-point-seven. This is so cool!" he excitedly told Carl. "Now watch when I come in here. Point one. Point one! We're getting proof tonight, dude. This is great!"

"Taking other factors into account," said Carl.

Barbara brought Cheryl into the hallway so she to could also experience the change in the atmosphere. "You're right," Cheryl agreed. "It feels noticeably thick and oppressive right here in the hallway, especially as you get closer to the stairs."

Gradually the oppressive feeling began to wane in the hallway. However, Chris was now beginning to feel a bit unsettled. He suddenly began wincing and placed a hand on his abdomen. Concerned, Carl asked, "Chris, what's wrong?"

"Oh... just feeling a bit queasy all of a sudden," he replied. "It's probably just a mild case of indigestion."

Over the next few minutes Chris began feeling worse, until he eventually doubled over and had to take a seat in the parlor. Carl asked him pointedly, "Chris, do you suppose the oppressiveness in this house could have something to do with the way you're feeling right now?"

"Possibly," he said. "I started feeling this way earlier while we were downstairs in the basement, performing the cleansing."

Carl suggested, "Perhaps it's affecting you in particular, because of your particular empathy." He then explained to Barbara and Cheryl, "Chris possesses a certain sensitivity, meaning that he's sometimes able to pick up on the emotions which are lingering in haunted places. These emotions he picks up on can either be active or residual."

"I've felt the same exact thing in this house so I can sympathize," said Cheryl.

"Me too," said Barbara. "That's why I refuse to step foot in the basement."

Moving over to Chris and gently placing a hand on his shoulder, Cheryl told him, "I'm so sorry this had to happen to you in my house, especially after you've come all this way just to help us."

Chris looked up at her and managed a smile. "I'm sure it'll pass," he said. "Maybe if I just rest up for awhile and stay close to a bathroom."

Carl told Cheryl and Barbara, "We'll continue with the cleansing of the upstairs rooms while Chris is resting up. It shouldn't take us very long." Brian then led the way as he and Carl ascended the stairs.

The cleansing of the second floor rooms took about a quarter of an hour. It was not until Brian was spraying blessed water in the last remaining second floor room that they overheard a "thumping" sound coming from upstairs on the third floor. Brian said, "That sounded like footsteps up there. Let's go!"

Together, they rushed up to the third floor and searched each room. Although there was no sign of anyone there, they noticed that the "haunted" closet door was halfway ajar. Brian asked, "Did anyone leave this door open when we were up here earlier?"

Carl replied, "No, I definitely remember it being closed."

They entered the main bedroom where Brian had encountered the spirit manifestation during the previous investigation. Brian did a sweep of the room with his EMF detector which registered only minor readings. They then decided to attempt some communication with the entity. Brian told Carl, "Maybe we should start recording this. I'm gonna try some provocation to see if maybe the spirit remembers me from last time."

"Go for it," said Carl. "I'll monitor the video and take audio recordings as well."

After they'd set up Brian's video camera on a tripod in a far corner of the bedroom, they lowered the overhead light and switched the camera to night shot. Brian then stood in the center of the darkened room and said, "If you are here then give us a sign of your presence. You showed yourself to us last time. Now we're asking you to appear to us again."

Carl added, "We've heard your voice, we've felt your presence. What connection is there to the name Beatrice?"

They paused and waited in silence for a reaction. Brian switched on his pen flashlight and glanced at his EMF meter, but the indicator remained still. After a wait of about twenty seconds, Brian again attempted to coerce the entity into revealing itself. "Why not show yourself to us? Are you afraid?" Again there was nothing but silence. "We wish to know what it is that you want and why you are bothering the family that lives here. Are you a coward? C'mon, give us a sign of your presence."

They again waited as Brian glanced around the darkened room. Carl then broke the silence by saying, "I'm suddenly starting to feel the energy in here is beginning to pick up."

Brian again glanced at his EMF. "Looks like were getting a slight fluctuation," he said. Anxious to get more of a reaction, Brian began throwing out a few cuss words.

Carl glanced into the viewfinder of the video camera. All he could see was Brian's darkened form standing there, his eyes eerily illuminated by the night shot and the visor of his baseball cap swaying back and forth like a duck's bill as he glanced around. After the provocation session they waited in silence, but nothing happened. "The EMF's registering nil again," said Brian.

Carl suggested, "Then maybe this would be a good time to complete the cleansing up here."

Brian agreed. As they moved into the adjoining room and began spraying the blessed water, Brian said, "Oh, I just remembered. I should check the video camera, in the room where we just were, to see if it's still running. Excuse me a second, I'll be right back." He then stepped out of the room.

"Take your time," Carl told him.

Less than a minute later, Brian quickly re-entered the room where Carl was. From the expression on his face, Carl could immediately tell that something had happened. "Brian? What's wrong?" asked Carl.

"Dude... I just caught a glimpse of something in the main bedroom," he replied. "There was some kind of partial manifestation in the doorway of the room."

Both of them immediately rushed back into the main bedroom but it was completely empty. Carl asked, "Is there any chance it was picked up on video?"

"No, I'm afraid not," said Brian. "The camera had already stopped running. And even if it hadn't, it wasn't pointed in the direction of the doorway so it wouldn't have picked it up."

"Can you describe to me exactly what you saw?" asked Carl.

"Well," said Brian, "I only saw it for an instant but I did manage to get a clear view of it. It wasn't exactly a full-bodied apparition...more like the outline of a pair of legs just walking by the doorway. And then they just stopped, before vanishing."

The two of them waited in the darkened bedroom for awhile longer but there was no further trace of any spirit manifestation. Finally Carl said, "I really don't think it's in here anymore."

Brian did a final sweep with his EMF meter and said, "I think you're right, Carl. I guess we should continue with the cleansing and then call it a night."

"Good idea," said Carl. "I think we're all pretty well exhausted by now and, with Chris not feeling well, we probably shouldn't stay too much longer."

After the cleansing of the third floor rooms was completed, Brian and Carl returned downstairs and informed Barbara and Cheryl of all that had transpired upstairs. Carl said, "Now that the entire house has been cleansed, things should quiet down here for the most part. What Brian's done through the sprinkling of blessed water in each room is to introduce positive energy throughout the entire house, which will hopefully help to dispel the negativity."

Teasingly, Barbara said, "The great archangel Brian!"

Cheryl told them, "Thank you, so much. It does feel somewhat more comfortable in here right now. Of course my main concern is whether or not Druscilla will start to feel comfortable in this house, once again."

Chris said, "Unfortunately, there are no guarantees. We'd be lying to you if we said otherwise. But I did get the distinct impression that the dominant spirit here has retreated."

"And like we mentioned earlier," said Brian, "if the activity does start to pick up again we'll make sure that Carl's brother, Keith, gets here to perform a complete blessing in this house."

Carl said, "In the meantime, you know that we're always only a phone call away."

"I know," Cheryl told them with a smile. Turning to Chris, she said, "And I'm so sorry that you were a little knocked back during the investigation, Chris. I hope you're feeling alright now."

Chris said, "Not to worry, I'm fine now. And who knows, it could've been just a mild case of indigestion."

Barbara also thanked the TAPS team for coming to help once again. With a small laugh, she added, "Just maybe I'll wind up asking you to come to my apartment, in Manhattan, if unexplained things keep happening there."

"We'd be glad to," said Carl. "But hopefully, once things settle down here, the activity in your apartment will also cease."

Throughout the first week following the second TAPS visit, there was a lull in the haunting activity in the Brooklyn house. Aside from the occasional random creak here and there, which is not uncommon in older houses, things were basically quiet. Druscilla even felt comfortable enough to begin sleeping in her own bed once again. Apparently the blessed water that Brian had liberally sprinkled throughout the house had taken a positive effect.

Just as the last time, Carl gave me the audio tape he'd recorded during the investigation and asked me to check for any possible EVPs. As it turned out, there were some... spoken in the same low, husky voice as in the previous recording. The first one I discovered was when Brian, Carl and Chris were speaking with Cheryl, and her cousin Barbara, about Cheryl having burned sage throughout her house to try to counteract the negativity. Surprisingly, the low male voice could suddenly be heard saying: "Smokers! Hot!" This was accompanied by the distinct sound of blowing into the microphone, as if the EVP voice was mocking the sound of trying to blow away the smoke.

The second EVP on the audio recording was when Carl and Brian were in front of the main staircase on the first floor. Brian was taking EMF readings and excitedly saying to Carl, "We're getting proof tonight, Dude. This is great!"

Carl responded by saying, "Taking other factors into account."

This was followed by the same voice, this time whispering so quietly as to be barely perceptible: "My house... back."

A third EVP heard right after Carl had commented about a picture in a poster that was hung on Druscilla's bedroom wall, saying, "It looks like Keith when he had long hair." For whatever reason, the voice whispered, "No."

There was also a fourth EVP, again whispering quietly, yet obviously somewhat perturbed by Brian's verbal provocation in the third floor bedroom. In response, it whispered to Brian: "Yeah... yeah. Fuck you, man!"

My fellow TAPS members were naturally intrigued when I shared the EVPs with everyone at the next meeting. Of special interest was the "Smokers! Hot!", complete with the blowing sound, and the vulgarity that had been directed at Brian. Excitedly, Brian commented, "Wow, it looks like I really DID manage to piss it off, after all!"

"Looks like you did, Bro'," Carl agreed.

Leaning closer to Brian, I quietly reminded him, "You know, that's not always the safest thing to do for all involved."

"Yeah, I know," Brian admitted.

Chris said, "And the 'Smokers! Hot!' EVP also seems to indicate that the smoke from the sage was actually bothering the entity."

"Good point," said Carl. "The thing is, this entity seems to have such an individual persona which comes through in the EVPs. It's unfortunate that we can't place a name to it. In fact, I opt for dubbing it 'Wise Guy' just for reference purposes."

Grant said, "Yeah, that sounds like a catchy name, Carl. 'Wise Guy' it is. What we need to discuss now is, what's our next step? We need to draw up a definite game plan."

Jason told us, "Well, because the activity in Cheryl's house has pretty much tapered off since the last visit, I'd say that our best call would be to simply keep in touch with her and lend our support, just as we have been doing."

The question then came up once again on whether we might be dealing with something more than merely a human spirit in this case. Based on what evidence we had so far, and from those who'd actually been there and experienced it, the general opinion among us was that there was a distinct possibility that an inhuman spirit might be involved. The manner in which a presumed spirit entity had been manifesting itself to 11-year-old Druscilla – as a leering woman lacking eyes – combined with the tiny, troll-like creature which Cheryl and her cousin Barbara had both seen in the house, seemed to indicate a demonic presence.

Grant commented, "It's obviously an intelligent haunt. We can pretty much gauge that from the way it's targeting Druscilla and from the interaction that's evident in the EVPs. And the activity does seem to have settled down for now, as a result of using holy water throughout the house."

"Also," said Carl, "the 'Wise Guy' entity has definitely been attempting to convey some sort of message. Perhaps it simply wants some degree of closure over the Beatrice incident."

Jason said, "Unfortunately, because Cheryl refuses to allow us to drill into that well in the basement, we may never have the complete answer." He then turned to me with a serious expression on his face. "Keith... if the activity does eventually begin to start up again, I definitely want you to go there with the team and do a complete, thorough blessing of the Brooklyn house."

"Just say the word, Jason," I told him.

Things remained relatively calm in Cheryl's house for another two days. Then, unfortunately, the activity restarted, picking up exactly where it had left off. Footsteps could once again be heard at odd hours of the night, mainly coming from upstairs in the third floor bedroom. Druscilla was again feeling extremely uncomfortable being in her own bedroom at night for any length of time and had even caught a shadowy glimpse of the female specter gliding past her bedroom doorway. Cheryl's two house cats were behaving even more strangely, acting as if they almost constantly sensed the presence of an intruder in the house. Nor was the activity confined to Cheryl's house in Brooklyn. Her cousin Barbara was also once again starting to experience things in her Manhattan apartment and felt extremely threatened. Cheryl telephoned both Carl and Brian, who were her main lifelines with TAPS, and informed them about all that was taking place. "Please, can some of you come back to help?" she pleaded to them through her tears. "It's not so much for me, but my daughter's so terrified. She doesn't have a father figure here all during the week so I'm the only one she can come to for protection." Cheryl added that Barbara usually visited at least once or twice during the week to help out. Lately, however, they'd been quarreling with each other, often over trivial circumstances, which was very uncharacteristic of them. "I know that it has something to do with being in this house," said Cheryl. "There's a certain pervasive gloom in here now that's even much worse than it used to be. But I'm a single parent and I can't afford to move. Besides, this house has been in our family for three generations now."

Both Brian and Carl comforted her as best as they could and reassured her that assistance from TAPS would be on the way as soon as possible. After getting off the phone with Cheryl, my brother Carl called me at work and related the latest developments in the Brooklyn case to me. "At this point," he said, "both Brian and I are agreeing that it may be demonic. So we'd especially appreciate your assistance with this when you and Sandra are available. Cheryl and Barbara are also very much looking forward to having you come to the house. This situation is now being considered a priority."

"Well, as I told Jason at the meeting, I'll be there as soon as it's arranged," I said.

The next day, while my wife Sandra and I were enjoying lunch together, I explained to her about the recent developments in the Brooklyn case. Since Sandra had also recently become a member of TAPS, she would also be welcome to attend the next visit to Cheryl's house, during which I'd be expected to perform a blessing of the entire house. Without any hesitancy whatsoever, Sandra agreed to be part of the investigation team and to personally assist me during the blessing.

The investigation/deliverance at Cheryl Pezzullo's house was arranged for a Saturday evening. Sandra and I would be would be making the trip with Brian, while my brother Carl would be meeting us there. This time the TAPS team would consist of only the four of us.

Traveling along the Brooklyn Bridge overlooking the sunset, Brian and Sandra and I shared some final discussion about the situation we would soon be facing at Cheryl's house. Brian told us, "Trust me, you'll be able to feel the oppressive atmosphere as soon as we walk in."

Sandra asked him, "Do you really think this could be an inhuman spirit that's causing all the activity in the house, even though Carl refers to it as 'Wise Guy'?"

Brian replied, "Based on what we've all experienced so far, I'd say there's at least one inhuman entity there. But like I told Cheryl and Barbara the last time we were there, I think it's a very low-class entity. As you both know, I really managed to tick it off."

"Yes," said Sandra with a wry smile, "that was quite apparent from one of the EVPs I heard."

"I do seem to have a knack for doing that," Brian said with a laugh.

"Let's just say you're not too popular in certain unseen circles," I told him. "But you know, you also have to be careful not to turn it into a personal vendetta, especially when you're possibly dealing with a demonic entity."

"Oh, no, I certainly know better than to risk that," Brian assured me.

When Sandra, Brian and I arrived at the three-story brownstone house in Brooklyn, New York, Cheryl Pezzullo and my brother Carl were outside on the front steps waiting to greet us. "Glad you made it," Carl welcomed the three of us. "Cheryl, you of course know Brian. And this is my brother Keith and his wife Sandra."

Cheryl was indeed a small, slim, attractive dark-haired young woman, although the stress she'd been going through was evident on her features. "Brian, it's nice to see you again," said Cheryl. "And I'm so glad to finally get to meet Keith and his lovely wife Sandra. I've heard so much about you both."

"So nice to finally meet you as well, Cheryl," I said, shaking her hand.

Also shaking her hand, Sandra said, "We've heard so much about you too, Cheryl. In fact, you're all Carl talks about lately."

Cheryl smiled and said, "I wish it was under better circumstances. I'm afraid the situation here hasn't been all that pleasant lately, as I'm sure you know."

"Well, we're going to do our best to remedy that tonight," said Sandra.

Brian said, "You bet we will, Cheryl. We'll be pullin' all the stops out, especially now that we have Keith with us tonight."

"And I very much appreciate you and Sandra being here tonight," Cheryl told me. "But you must be in need of refreshment after your long trip. Come on inside and I'll introduce you to my daughter Druscilla."

Sandra asked, "Oh, Druscilla's here tonight?"

"Yes, but just for an hour or so, until her father arrives to pick her up," said Cheryl. "In fact, if you wouldn't mind, I'd like you both to talk with her for a little while, to try to ease her fears a little. Carl's been telling me what a calming effect you both have on people. Also, if it's not too much trouble, I'd also like for Keith to maybe perform a small blessing over her."

Sandra and I assured Cheryl that we'd be glad to help in whatever way we could.

We were then invited inside the front kitchen area where Cheryl introduced us to her cousin Barbara Dolan, who was visiting, and to eleven-year-old Druscilla. "So good to meet you, Keith and Sandra," said Barbara. "And now I can certainly see the resemblance between Carl and Keith!"

"Yes, and I can also see quite a family resemblance between you and Cheryl." I commented.

Sandra agreed, saying, "Yes, in fact you look more like sisters than cousins."

"We've always been more like sisters than cousins, especially since Cheryl was an only child growing up in this house," said Barbara.

Cheryl's daughter Druscilla was a bright, pretty young girl who was obviously delighted to meet us and to have us there. She seemed to think of us as being "her" company as she sat at the kitchen table and excitedly chatted with us. "I could tell right away that you and Carl are twins," she said. "It must be nice. I've always wondered what it would be like to be a twin, or even to have a brother or sister."

"Yes, it is interesting to be a twin," I said.

"Are you both the same blood type?" asked Druscilla.

"Yes, we are, I said. "We're both A-positive.

"In fact," said Carl, "we could even have tissue transplants."

Sandra said, "However, Druscilla, just because they're twins, doesn't necessarily mean that they have the same personality."

Before long, it became apparent that Druscilla had taken quite a liking to Sandra and perhaps regarded her as a big sister figure. "I really like your hair," Druscilla told her. "You look like you're about twenty-two and you look like you could be an actress."

Sandra's eyebrows raised and she laughed, "Oh, thank you, Druscilla, we'll be friends forever."

Druscilla said, "I hope you don't mind me saying this, but you remind me of The Little Mermaid, Arielle. I mean, the lady who does her voice."

"Why, thank you, I don't mind at all," said Sandra.

"I'm trying to be polite," said Druscilla.

Sandra smiled, "Well, when you told me that I'm twenty-two and that I look like an actress, I think that was being very polite."

Druscilla then brought out her cats to show to Sandra. Later, she began entertaining us all by singing and acting out TV commercials for us.

Cheryl eventually told her daughter, "Druscilla, honey, I know you're really enjoying the company here but your father's going to be here soon to pick you up. Before you leave I'd like you to talk to them a little bit about what's been frightening you. Do you remember how we discussed this?"

"Oh yeah sure, I remember," Druscilla said brightly. "And you want them to do a blessing over me too, right?"

"Yes, honey, that's right," said Cheryl.

Led by Cheryl, we then all went into the parlor where Sandra and I noticed a collection of small angel statues and figurines of various designs adorning the shelves. Druscilla pointed to a beautiful Native

American style angel statue and said, "She's my favorite because she reminds me of Pocahontas."

"She's very beautiful," said Sandra.

Druscilla then sat on a small parlor sofa as Cheryl, Sandra and I sat close by. With all of the adults seated around her, Druscilla seemed relatively comfortable talking about the phenomena which she'd been experiencing in her home. She told us about the frightening woman with long white hair and no eyes that she'd seen grinning at her from the hallway outside of her bedroom doorway and how, even with her bedroom door closed, she'd sometimes hear footsteps and rapping sounds throughout the house. She herself was afraid to go either downstairs into the basement or upstairs to the third floor, even when her mother was with her. "Lately, even my cats don't like to be inside the house for very long," she told us. "And that's not like them at all."

Cheryl asked, "And how have you been feeling, Druscilla?"

"Frightened a lot of the time," said Druscilla. "I get afraid of the things that are going on in the house, especially outside of my bedroom at night."

I asked her, "But you believe in God and in Jesus, don't you, Druscilla?"

"Yes, of course I believe in God and in Jesus," she answered.

"And you know that you can always call upon Jesus and His angels for protection whenever you feel frightened," I said. "In fact, that's what I always used to do when I was very young, and it always worked. And you know that you have God's angels to protect you, too, and they're much stronger than any of the things that are frightening you."

"Yes, I believe in angels, too," said Druscilla.

"Good," I said. "You know, you can always call on God's angels to take away whatever's making you feel uncomfortable and send it right to Jesus."

"You're right," Druscilla said with a smile.

"And now," I said, "just like your mom was telling you a little while ago, Sandra and I would like to pray a blessing over you. Would that be okay?"

Druscilla happily told us, "Oh yeah, I've been looking forward to this!"

Turning to Sandra, I asked, "Sandra would you please read from the Gospel of Mark, Chapter Ten, verses thirteen through sixteen?"

"Of course," said Sandra. She opened the Bible we'd brought with us and read: "'People were bringing little children to Jesus to have Him touch them, but the disciples rebuked them. When Jesus saw this, He was indignant. He said to them, 'Let the little children come to me, and do not hinder them, for the kingdom of God belongs to such as these. I tell you the truth; anyone who will not receive the kingdom of God like a little child will never enter it.' And He took the children in His arms, put His hands on them and blessed them.'"

When Sandra had finished reading, I anointed Druscilla's forehead with blessed oil in the shape of a cross, saying, "As Jesus loved and blessed the little children, so we bless you in His name, Druscilla."

"Thank you," she said, smiling radiantly. "I feel a lot safer now."

"Do you have any questions for us before you leave tonight?" I asked her.

"Yeah," she said. "I keep hearing about someone named Luke in the Bible, and I'm wondering who Luke was."

"Luke was a physician," I explained. "And he was a friend of St. Paul. He was also one of the authors of the New Testament."

"Okay," said Druscilla. "I've been wondering who he was."

"Well, now you know, dear," I said.

Druscilla said, "And it's been so nice meeting both you and Sandra, I really mean it. I hope you'll both come here to visit again, really soon!"

After Druscilla had been picked up to spend the remainder of the evening with her father, Cheryl told us, "I'm so glad the way she opened up to you two like that. I could tell that she really, really liked you both."

Sandra said, "Well, we really liked her, too. And I certainly appreciated all the compliments she was giving me."

"Also, thank you so much for the wonderful blessing you did over her," said Cheryl. "I think Druscilla feels a lot safer now."

"It was certainly our pleasure, Cheryl," I said. "And now, before Sandra and I begin the blessing of your house, have there been any recent developments in the activity?"

Cheryl said, "Well, for one thing, Barbara and I have been arguing a lot, seemingly over nothing."

"And that's not like us at all," said Barbara. "As I explained, we've always been extremely close, more like sisters than cousins. But lately we've been at each others throats, on and off. And I know that it has something to do with this house, the way it affects people. Also, I've been getting these excruciating headaches while in my own apartment in Manhattan."

Brian informed us, "Cheryl's also recently had another sighting in this house, similar to the one I caught a glimpse of the last time I was here with Carl and Chris."

"Really?" asked Sandra. "Can you describe exactly what it was that you saw?"

"It basically just looked like an indistinct human form, from the waist down," said Cheryl.

Barbara said, "Both of us have also recently woken up with small bruises on our bodies, mostly on our backs and arms."

"They're relatively small bruises," said Cheryl. "I woke up with one on the back of my neck, as if someone had grabbed me from behind. And it hurt. In fact, I was at a doctor's appointment just the other day, and the doctor asked me, 'What is this fingerprint on the back of your neck?' Fortunately, due to the position of the fingerprint, he speculated that it may have been caused by 'rough sex.'"

Barbara said, "I'm also continuing to have some disturbing experiences in my Manhattan apartment. Aside from dealing with excruciating headaches whenever I talk about the activity here, I've also been waking up with bruises on my arms, just as Cheryl mentioned. It's as if someone came up from behind me and grabbed me."

"How does this make you feel?" I asked her.

"Sometimes I get scared but then I just get tough about it," said Barbara. "I figure, it can either get me or I can get it. But the scariest thing happened just recently. I woke up one morning and I couldn't move. It was as if something was sitting on top of my chest and I just couldn't breath for a while."

I then turned back to Cheryl and asked, "In your opinion, Cheryl, what would you say is haunting this house?"

Cheryl replied, "I think it could be more than one spirit. After all, a lot of evil's happened here. And I also think that there's one main spirit, which is demonic."

"I agree," said Barbara. "I believe that the restless spirit of Beatrice could be here as well as the spirit of Cheryl's mother, Buffy. But there's also another more malicious spirit, which seems to have affected the males in this house, especially Cheryl's father."

"Cheryl, where is your father now?" I asked.

She replied, "Right now I imagine he's living out of his car. He was an inmate at the Brooklyn Center for Psychiatric Care, for some time, but he's very good at playing the system. Last time I heard he was out."

Carl said, "He's degenerated to the point that he can't be around Cheryl or any of her family."

"Fortunately, we have a restraining order on him so he's not allowed to come anywhere near us or this house," said Cheryl.

"I'm sure that's for the best," I said. "But when your father was living here, Cheryl, did your father ever feel that there was a spirit presence in the house?"

Cheryl replied, "Yes, Keith, he did. In fact, he sometimes felt as if it was invading his mind and his body. And he always referred to it as 'The Intruder.'"

Before Sandra and I commenced with the blessing of the house, Brian and Carl led us down into the basement. They pointed out the well hole that had been cemented over, as Carl said, "Quite possibly, the body of Beatrice was deposited down this well."

"I don't think we'll ever find out for sure," Brian commented.

Carl said, "As I've mentioned, the 'Wise Guy' entity certainly seemed to be attempting to draw attention to Beatrice, as if it – or he – wanted closure. But you're right, Brian, we'll probably never know for certain."

"Hopefully," I said, "when Sandra and I perform the blessing, we'll at least bring some closure to the haunting activity in this house."

Sandra then switched on the camcorder she held to begin recording. Glancing through the lens, Sandra immediately saw a white, round object, appearing to be the size and shape of a golf ball, coming straight towards her. "Whoa!" she exclaimed.

"What is it?" I asked.

"I already got an orb," Sandra said with a startled laugh. "It looked really solid and it was coming right at me."

Brian said, "Oh yeah, it's down here. Can't you feel how hot it is? After all, this basement used to be a 'speak-easy,' back in the '30's."

None of the rest of us had seen it, even though we were standing right there. We momentarily wondered if this glowing ball of light which Sandra saw through the lens, seemingly solid and coming straight towards her, was meant as some sort of "warning" for us to proceed no further. Nonetheless, we continued with our investigation of the basement area for another twenty minutes.

Back upstairs, we reported our findings to Cheryl and Barbara. Sandra explained to them about the solid-looking globule, which had seemingly been shot straight at her. "I'm just glad I didn't drop the camera," she said. "I mean, I've seen anomalies through the video lens before, but this one appeared to be so solid and it just came right at me so fast."

We then further discussed the history of the house. Carl said, "Okay, so Beatrice is officially a missing person. A couple of people have corroborated that she was last seen in this house. By who, I don't know. But she was almost certainly a murder victim."

Barbara said, "And I told you that my mother filled in the blanks, about Cheryl's mother's situation."

"Yes," said Carl. "And I told Keith about it and went into a lot of detail with him. And that was how many years ago now? I know Cheryl was nine at the time."

Cheryl said, "That was twenty-three years ago now. So of course, Druscilla never got to know her maternal grandmother."

Carl said, "Also, back when you and Barbara were children, there were the Saturday night sessions with the Ouija board. That potentially increased the activity here."

Sandra asked, "Has anything else happened recently that you can think of?"

Suddenly remembering, Cheryl said, "Oh, now that I think of it, there is something. Just a couple of weeks ago I had a friend over here, named Michael. He's one of our best friends. Now he's not a psychic or anything like that, he just happens to be really sensitive. But he had a really bad reaction while he was here. Barbara was here too, so she also witnessed it."

"What sort of reaction?" asked Sandra.

Barbara said, "Well, at first I thought he was joking because he suddenly appeared to be out of breath and hyperventilating. But then I got a closer look at him and his face was blood red. He was actually sweating like he was being strangled. It was like he couldn't get any air. So we asked him, 'Michael, what's wrong?' Well, he recovered pretty quickly...but he told us that, for a moment, he felt as though he was being attacked by something he couldn't see. It was as if an invisible pair of hands was tightening around his throat. Interestingly, it was when he walked past this table, right over here. This just happens to be the very table we used to set the Ouija board on years ago. He would have liked to be here tonight but he had a party to go to in New Hampshire."

Brian, Carl, Sandra and I shared a look with each other. Carl then suggested, "Well, now that Keith and Sandra know the complete background of the case perhaps we should proceed with the blessing."

Everyone agreed. Sandra asked me, "Where would you like to start?"

"I think the basement would be as good a place as any," I said.

Carl said, "Brian has something of a game plan, from what I understand."

We all glanced at Brian, who said, "While you're starting with the blessing, I might start doing some invocation of my own up on the second and third floor. If anything goes down while you guys are in the basement, just give me a shout and I'll be right there."

"Sure thing, Brian," said Carl. "But keep in mind, as Keith mentioned before, it might be a good idea to maintain a detached state of mind. You should avoid any serious provoking, especially while you're alone."

"That's right," I emphasized. "Whatever you do, Brian, try not to turn this into a personal confrontation."

"Oh, no, I'm certainly not gonna try any serious provocation by myself," Brian assured us.

Carl then requested, "Keith, before we separate and go off in different directions, would you like to lead us in a brief prayer of protection?"

"Of course," I said. "Let's gather in a circle for a moment."

After we'd joined hands, I prayed, "Heavenly Father, we ask for Your protection in our endeavor this evening. We ask that You send the Holy Spirit upon us and that You also send mighty and holy angels to be with us. In the words of the Psalmist, 'Touch not my prophets, nor do my anointed ones harm. In Your holy name, we pray. Amen."

"Amen," everyone echoed in unison.

"Thank you, Keith," said Cheryl. "And I'd like to thank both you and Sandra, again, for being so kind and patient with Druscilla while she was here."

"Oh, no problem," said Sandra. "She was a sweetie."

Carl, amused, looked at Sandra, "And she certainly took a liking to you."

Sandra, Carl and I returned to the basement to begin the blessing. As Sandra followed me with the camcorder, I began by saying a prayer for any restless spirits that may be present to be at peace. I then spayed a liberal amount of holy water in each section of the basement and anointed each of the doors and windows with blessed oil. Meanwhile, Carl was monitoring the ambient temperature in the basement with a digital thermometer. At one point, as he was standing in the vicinity of the well, Carl announced, "The temperature over here just dropped six degrees, from seventy-four to sixty-eight."

Approaching the area where Carl was standing, with Sandra still videotaping beside me, I said, "In the name of Jesus Christ, Beatrice was and is a child of God. Buffy is also a child of God." I then threw some holy water onto the surface of the sealed well. "May all restless, wandering spirits be sent to the presence of Jesus," I said, holding a wooden cross over the well.

Immediately, Sandra said, "I just saw two white particles shoot straight up from that exact spot. Interesting…this is quite close to where I captured the large, shooting orb with the camcorder."

Carl informed us, "By the way, the room temperature in this area has just now returned to seventy-four degrees."

"This concludes the blessing of the basement," I told Carl and Sandra. "Let's head back upstairs and begin the blessing of the first floor.

Once we had returned to the kitchen area, Brian excitedly reported to us that he'd been conducting some provocation up on the third floor. Carl reminded him, "Brian, remember what we talked about earlier. You really shouldn't be turning this into a personal conflict; it's better to remain as non-confrontational as possible."

"Oh yeah, I know that," Brian quickly responded. "Trust me; I wouldn't do anything that would endanger either myself or Cheryl and her family."

Sandra and I then commenced with the blessing of the first floor, with both Carl and Brian accompanying us…paying special attention to Druscilla's bedroom. At my request, Sandra once again read aloud from the Gospel of Mark, Chapter 10 verses 13-16. We also thoroughly blessed the hallway just outside of her bedroom. When we were done, I approached Cheryl and told her, "Your daughter's bedroom and the hallway have both been cleansed. Everything should be alright there for her now."

"Again, I can't thank you enough," said Cheryl, tears filling her eyes. "I've just been so worried about her lately, with all that's been going on in this house."

"We understand," said Sandra. "And both you and your daughter certainly have a God-given right to live at peace in your own home."

We were about to proceed upstairs, to begin the blessing of the second floor, when a strange feeling came over me. Seeing that I appeared to be a little short of breath, Sandra became concerned. "Keith, are you all right?" she asked me.

"I'm just feeling a tad queasy all of a sudden," I said.

Carl said, "Seems somewhat similar to what happened to Chris Finch the last time we were here."

Sandra asked, "Do you feel that you're being spiritually oppressed?"

"Yes… yes, I suppose I do," I replied. "But I think I just need to take a break for a few minutes and then hopefully I'll be okay."

After resting up a bit and once again praying for angelic protection, I was ready to continue. Brian asked me, "Keith, are you sure you're up to this?"

"Oh yes, I'm fine now," I assured him.

Before we continued on up to the second floor rooms, Carl said, "I'll just let Cheryl and Barbara know that we're about to make our way upstairs." Brian offered to accompany him.

When Carl and Brian stepped into the parlor, they found Cheryl seated on the sofa. She was lightly dabbing her eyes with a tissue, her cousin Barbara seated close beside her. In Cheryl's lap was a recent school photo of her daughter Druscilla. Carl apologized, "Oh, I'm sorry. I didn't mean to interrupt."

"It's okay," said Cheryl. "We were just discussing all that's been going on here over the past months and how frightened Druscilla's been lately. I'm just concerned about her, that's all."

"That's totally understandable," Carl assured her. "I'm just letting you know that Keith and Sandra are about to start the blessing of the second floor rooms now."

"Thank you," Cheryl said with a small sniffle. "Your being here tonight already seems to have made such a difference, especially with my daughter."

Barbara added, "Yes, thank you again for all you're doing here tonight and for all that you guys have been doing for us."

Brian smiled at them, "No problem. It's what we do."

Cheryl managed a small smile at Brian before returning her glance back to the photo that rested on her lap.

The four of us had ascended the stairs to the second floor when we noticed that Brian was unusually quiet. Carl asked, "Is something wrong, Brian?"

"I'm just really pissed off at whatever's been doing this to Cheryl and her daughter," Brian replied. "Listen, while you guys are blessing the second floor rooms, I'm going up to the third floor bedroom again. I've got a little score to settle."

Seeing that Brian was determined, Carl said, "Alright then. I'm going with you, man."

With a nod, Brian turned and began making his way up to the third floor. Before following after him, Carl told us, ""I'll do my best, to see that he stays out of trouble. At least this time they'll be two of us up there."

"Go for it," I said.

After Carl had joined Brian in the third floor bedroom, Sandra and I proceeded to bless the rooms on the second floor without incident. From immediately above us, we could overhear the muffled sounds of moving about and shouting. Brian was attempting to provoke whatever entity might be present out of hiding.

After about twenty minutes, Carl and Brian returned to the second floor. Brian appeared a little the worse for wear. He was visibly shaken and his face was gleaming with perspiration. "Brian?" Sandra asked. "Are you alright?"

With a sigh, Brian replied, "Yeah…for the most part."

"What just happened up there?" I asked.

Carl told us, "Brian just had an encounter with whatever entity makes its home on the third floor; presumably an entity of non-human origin. Fortunately, this time I was up there with him."

Brian explained, "I knew that it was up there in the bedroom with us because my eyes started watering, which is always a sure sign to me that there's an inhuman presence around. So, I started cussing it out and telling it, 'You son of a bitch, I know you're up here with us! You're pretty brave attacking women and a little girl in this house, so why not try attacking me? Now's your chance 'cause here I am, a walking, talking monkey! C'mon, show me what you got!' And then, all of a sudden, I felt the back of my left leg getting hit from behind. And right after that I was slapped on the back of my head."

"He really looked as though he was being knocked around up there," Carl verified.

"Alright," I said to everyone, "at least it's been sufficiently provoked into revealing its presence." I looked at Brian, and said,

"Fortunately, you weren't attacked more seriously. Are you done provoking it for the night?"

"Yeah, I've definitely had enough for now," said Brian. From the looks of him, he seemed sincere.

Carl asked, "Did either of you experience any activity here on the second floor?"

"No, not at all," said Sandra. "In fact, it seemed unusually quiet all throughout the blessing of these rooms."

Carl said, "So, would the rest of you agree that the entity now seems confined to the third floor of this house?"

"Yes, it seems to be," I said. "Everything appears to be tranquil throughout the rest of the house now. I guess all that's left is the blessing of the third floor rooms. Naturally, we'll save the main third floor bedroom for last. We'll try to corner it in there and then perform the final expulsion."

"Alright," said Carl. "I think we should go downstairs and let Cheryl and Barbara know that we're about to take the final step here."

Upon returning to the downstairs area, we informed Cheryl and Barbara what had just happened with Brian. "Oh no!" said Cheryl. "Are you alright now, Brian?"

"Yeah, I'm okay," he said. However, Brian still appeared somewhat shaken from the experience.

In fact, by now we were all anxious to conclude things for the evening. Since all that remained was the blessing of the third floor rooms – including the infamous bedroom, which had previously belonged to Cheryl's father – we reasoned that whatever demonic entity was present in this house would now be contained up on the third floor. Also, because the entity also seemed to be considerably weakened at this point, we all agreed that we should now conclude the blessing without delay.

Both Cheryl and Barbara decided they wanted to accompany us upstairs for the final part of the blessing. "Fair enough," said Brian.

"Just as long as no one's alone up there at any time until the all the third floor rooms have been blessed."

After thoroughly blessing most of the third floor rooms, including the "infested" closet, Sandra and I rejoined Carl, Brian, Cheryl and Barbara in the large main bedroom. With a sigh, Brian said, "Well, this is it, guys. It's down to this room. If anything's gonna happen, I hope it happens now while we're all together."

With the lights in the bedroom lowered, Sandra and I sat on a small sofa several feet from the bed while Brian, Carl, Cheryl and Barbara sat in seats directly in front of us. Following about twenty or so seconds of silence, I asked, "In the name of Jesus Christ, without harming anyone, can you make your presence known to us?"

We waited for about thirty seconds with no response. Carl added, "This may be your last chance to communicate with us before expulsion is pronounced."

Sandra said, "For the last time, is there any way we might be able to help you?"

Again, we waited in silence.

Cheryl asked, "What is it that you want from us?"

"What have we ever done to you?" asked Barbara. "Why do you seem to hate us so much?"

Brian asked, "Why do you persist in tormenting this family?"

Following a wait of perhaps another thirty seconds or so, I suggested that we play the conversation back, which I'd been recording. When we did so, no trace of EVP was evident. "Alright," I said to the others, "it doesn't seem that this entity has any intention of communicating with us. Let's continue with the final part of the blessing."

As we sat there in the semi-darkened bedroom for the last time, I commenced with the prayers of expulsion. Immediately after I'd finished leading everyone in a recitation of the Lord's Prayer, Brian, who happened to be facing Sandra and me, said, "Keith... it's right behind you."

I paused for only a couple of seconds before continuing with the session by saying, "In the name of Jesus Christ, we are under the protection of the Holy Spirit, as well as mighty and holy warrior angels.' Then, suddenly jumping to my feet, I whipped around and tossed holy water into the shadows directly behind me. I commanded, "In the name of Jesus Christ, may you be nullified and driven from this house!"

Brian told me, "It came walking up right behind you after we started praying. I saw something like a reflection, like from a mirror. And while we were praying, it started walking from over by the bed all the way through the room."

Still standing, I said, "We do not ask this under our own authority, but under the authority of Jesus Christ. May the Holy Spirit rest upon this room and upon this entire house. And now, in the name of Jesus Christ, I ask for a sign of your departure."

Within moments, there seemed to be a noticeable lightening of the atmosphere in the room, which everyone present commented upon. Cheryl said, "I can definitely feel the change in here. It's as if the oppressive feeling has suddenly lifted."

"I can feel it, too," Barbara agreed. "It certainly feels as though a tremendous weight has suddenly been lifted in this room."

I then finished up with a reading of the 23rd Psalm.

Carl spoke into the tape recorder, "Time check... it is now approximately eleven forty-four PM. Keith has just completed the blessing of the third floor."

Turning to Brian, I asked, "You actually saw the thing manifesting just now?"

"Oh yes, it was coming right up behind you," he said. "My eyes became watery and everything. Then it just completely vanished, as soon as you tossed the holy water."

Carl grinned, "Keith was like a spiritual Doc Holiday with the holy water."

Barbara laughed and said, "I know, he was like Quick-draw McGraw, there!"

Noticing that Brian now appeared to be both physically and emotionally drained, I approached him and asked, "Brian, would you mind if I anointed you?"

"It's probably a good idea if you did," said Brian. After I'd prayed over Brian and anointed him with blessed oil, he said, "Thanks, man. I really appreciate it."

Back downstairs, as Carl, Brian, Sandra and I were getting ready to leave, Cheryl insisted on packing sandwiches and soda pop for us to take with us for our trip home. Embracing each of us in turn she said, "Once again, I can't thank you all enough for all that you've done for us here."

"Yes, thank you all so much," said her cousin Barbara also embracing each of us. "And please be sure to thank Jason and Grant and the rest of the TAPS team for us, too."

"Will do," Brian assured her. "Which reminds me, we've got quite a report to submit to Jason, especially after tonight."

Looking on the verge of tears, Cheryl told us, "Because of you people, my daughter Druscilla will be returning to a much more peaceful environment. And I feel it will be a safer environment for us as well."

"So glad to meet you both," said Sandra. "And please give Druscilla a big hug for me when she gets home."

"I certainly will," said Cheryl. "And please do come and visit us again real soon. I know that Druscilla would be so excited for you to come back for a visit, especially when she doesn't have to leave for the night."

Carl reminded them, "In the meantime, please keep in mind that we're only a phone call away, twenty-four/seven, if you need us."

Taking Carl's hand in hers, Cheryl smiled and said, "We know... and we're grateful for that."

Outside in front of the three-story brownstone house I said a final payer of protection, asking that God's holy angels continue to keep watch over all those who dwelt within. I also prayed for our own protection, that nothing would follow us home. Carl agreed to stay with the family for the remainder of the night, before driving back in the morning, just to make certain they'd be all right. Sandra and I then climbed into Brian's car and the three of us set out for the return trip from Brooklyn to back to Rhode Island.

As Brian once again neared the Brooklyn Bridge, he said, "Well, hopefully we've brought closure to this case and we can call it a success. Like Cheryl told us, her daughter will be coming back into a much more peaceful environment."

"Yes," said Sandra. "I hope she notices the change in the atmosphere in the house, just like the rest of us did."

"Yeah, I hope so," Brian said with a yawn. "It certainly was an exhausting night."

"Not that we didn't have our share of excitement," I reminded him.

"Well, I admit I did break a few rules tonight. But the provocation did eventually get the spirit to manifest itself."

"Well," I said, "at least I've also prayed that nothing unholy be allowed to follow us."

Sandra said, "Yes, thank you for remembering to do that."

"Yeah, thanks, Keith," said Brian. "We don't need any demons following us home."

After passing over the Brooklyn Bridge, we continued on in silence, feeling relatively relaxed. Several minutes had passed when I suddenly broke the silence by pulling a tissue from my pocket and blowing my nose.

"What the hell was that??" Brian asked, snapping to sudden alertness.

"Oh, that was just me, blowing my nose," I said.

"Jeez!" Brian exclaimed. "Warn me before you do that next time, will ya, dude? I thought that something in the car just blew out."

"Sorry, Brian. I'll be sure to give you advance notice next time." I then turned to Sandra in the back seat, who was trying unsuccessfully to stifle her laughter, and winked.

Chapter 8

Walkin' Rosie

In the rural town of Monroeville, Pennsylvania, there is a quaint historic cemetery, ironically named Restland... in which the inhabitants are rumored to be anything but restful. Known for its beautiful monuments, the cemetery attracts its share of local pedestrians, who come there in pleasant weather to walk through the cemetery grounds while enjoying the area and the statuary. Over the years, there have also been numerous reported sightings in Restland Cemetery of the specter of a young woman who walks among the headstones at night. As an odd twist, this specter is said to closely resemble one of the life-like statues within the cemetery. Some of the local people in the Monroeville community - who refer to this mysterious figure as "Walkin' Rosie" - believe that the monument itself comes to life at night and wanders through the moonlit cemetery grounds. Others claim to have actually witnessed the figure of a young woman attired in a white, antiquated ball gown listlessly wandering among the headstones either at fading twilight or by the light of the full moon. The exact identity of this ghostly young woman remains a mystery, as well as the reason her restless spirit may still be wandering.

There is a local tradition, however, which may perhaps be based on truth. As the story goes, one evening in the late 1930's, a lovely young teenage woman named Rose was on her way home from a prom with her escort and another teenage couple. Somehow, the young man who was driving lost control of the car and they crashed right outside of the cemetery gates. Young Rose was killed instantly. Over the years, it is said that the apparition of this woman continues to walk the cemetery grounds in search of her boyfriend, not realizing that she herself is no longer alive or that decades have elapsed. Although many individuals have reported encountering this lovely yet elusive apparition, no one has, as yet, succeeded in communicating with her.

One such encounter took place in the late 1970's. Bill, a resident of Monroeville and a high school student at the time, had been told by his buddy Jim about the legend of "Walkin' Rosie." Early one summer evening just before sunset, the two of them took Jim's 1967 Rambler for a little cruise over to Restland Cemetery. They had spent some time driving through the extremely winding and narrow roads of the cemetery and had driven up an incline…when they suddenly spotted a woman wearing a long white dress standing some distance ahead on the right side of the road. As they continued to approach, she seemed to "glide" over to the left side of the road. "Holy cow!" Bill exclaimed. "It's her! Jim, you were right!"

However, there may have been a plausible explanation for their sighting. Sure enough, there was a white memorial statue of a woman in a white dress in front of one of the graves near the road. Although the statue was located on the left side of the road, Jim explained that as a car approaches, it at first appears to be on the right side due to the way the road is curved. As you continue along the turn, the statue appears to move to the left side of the car, although it's actually the car that's moving. "Certainly at night with just the headlights for illumination," says Bill, "this must have been one spooky sight!"

And yet, reported sightings of a mysterious young woman in white wandering the grounds of Restland Cemetery persist to this day. She has even been spotted at the cemetery gate pacing back and forth in an agitated manner, as if still waiting for her boyfriend who never arrives. Whenever someone pulls their car over or gets too close, she vanishes. Unfortunately, the head of the statue of "Rosie" is now missing, presumably broken off and stolen by vandals. It is for this reason that the cemetery is now closed to the public each night after sunset.

Perhaps someday the wandering spirit which is seemingly bound to Restland cemetery will find peace. Or at the very least, it is hoped that her true identity will be uncovered. If anyone should, by chance, have any further information regarding these sightings or know the possible identity of this mysterious young woman, please feel free to contact us at New England Anomalies Research. Your input will be greatly appreciated. For now, rest assured that the legend of "Walkin' Rosie" is alive and well in Monroeville, PA.

Chapter 9

Followed Home

(The names of the family members involved have been altered to protect their anonymity.)

Quite often Sandra and I are asked the question: "In the course of your investigations, do you ever have something follow you home?" By this, they are of course referring to whether or not unwelcome spirits ever follow us home from a paranormal investigation. The answer to the question is that, by the grace of God, we have been very successful in preventing negative entities from accompanying us when leaving allegedly haunted locations. We do take specific precautions in these situations, such as reading aloud from the Book of Ephesians in the New Testament, Chapter 6, where the spiritual armor of God is described. Also, when leaving a location, I make it my practice to pray something along these lines: "We came to this place in peace and we leave in peace, taking nothing unholy with us, only that which is of God. In the Lord's name, we ask that a holy angel of God accompany us as we leave and guide us safely home. Amen."

However, it is sometimes an unfortunate reality that someone will visit a haunted location, perhaps to investigate out of innocent curiosity, only to find that they have gotten more than they bargained for. Soon afterward, they discover that an unwanted entity has somehow attached itself to them and has hitched a free ride back home with them, so to speak. Quite often when this happens, this parasitic entity will refuse to leave unless it is forced into doing so. The following true account is what I feel is a good example of someone having unwittingly invited an entity to follow her home, which is why I have chosen to include it here.

It was in early August of 2003 that TAPS Case Manager Brian Harnois received an urgent message from a woman in Marlboro, Massachusetts, who claimed that she was being violently attacked by a spirit within her apartment. She also suspected that this spirit had somehow attached itself to her when she, her teenage son and her son's best friend recently conducted an amateur paranormal investigation at a local mental asylum.

At our weekly meeting of TAPS, Brian presented the particulars of the case to us and explained, "The client's name is Barbara Baxter and she's desperate for someone to help her. She claims that she's being both physically and psychically attacked and she's terrified of what might happen if this keeps up. So, my suggestion is that we make this case a priority."

TAPS founder Jason Hawes gave Brian the go-ahead to set up the case and arrange for an initial investigation. Although neither Jason nor Grant would be attending this one, they told Brian he could feel free to assemble a small investigation team consisting of no more than five members, tops. From what the client described, her second floor apartment was relatively small and somewhat cramped.

For the initial investigation, because this case might potentially involve inhuman spirits, Brian chose Sandra, myself and Carl to accompany him. He had also originally wanted to include Chris Angelo. However, Chris was still away on a temporary leave of absence involving a family matter, and would therefore be unavailable.

The four of us arrived at the Marlboro location early on a seasonably warm August evening, while we still had some daylight. While unloading our equipment from our parked cars, we observed that the apartment building where Barbara Baxter lived happened to be located almost directly across from a small electrical power station. Sandra commented, "That's not exactly the healthiest of living conditions, to be so close to a power station."

"Tell me about it," Brian agreed, while lifting his equipment case out from the trunk of his car.

Barbara Baxter, a pleasant-looking, dark-hared single mother, welcomed us into her second floor apartment. Upon meeting her, Carl pointed out her remarkable resemblance to Canadian singer, Ann Wilson, of the rock band Heart. Barbara thanked him for the compliment and introduced us to her teenage son Justin, his best friend Jesse and their friend Marisa, who was in her early twenties.

Once the introductions had been made, Barbara and Justin showed us their two pet ferrets, which were both frisky and quite lively. They seemed to naturally take to Brian right away. Sandra asked, "Do they seem to be affected by the activity here?"

Barbara's son Justin replied, "Sometimes, but it's hard to tell since they're naturally hyper most of the time anyway."

Carl volunteered to be the interviewer this evening. After taking out a copy of the case file, he recorded the date – August 9th, 2003 – and began by confirming some of the background of the case. Both Justin and Jesse had been conducting amateur paranormal investigations, purely as a hobby, for the past couple of years. Occasionally Justin's mom, Barbara, would join them on these investigations since she also took an interest in the paranormal. Several months ago Justin and Jesse began investigating an asylum for the mentally ill in Waltham, Massachusetts, which was still functioning yet partially abandoned. Since it was located less than ten minutes from their apartment, it was a convenient place for them to investigate. They, of course, only went there at night and only explored the abandoned section. While there, Justin and Jesse did take multiple photos, several of which displayed what seemed to be anomalous distortions. (Justin presented these to us to examine.) One night while visiting there, Justin had peeped into one of the side windows and had briefly glimpsed what appeared to be an older man sitting in a wheelchair. This was particularly unusual considering the fact that this section of the building had been shut down for years and was in a dilapidated condition. When Jason took a second look to try and get a picture, the old man in the wheelchair had vanished.

Then, that past January, both Barbara and Marisa had accompanied Justin and Jesse to the old asylum. It was soon after this that Barbara and her son began realizing that something was not right in their apartment and that the activity seemed to be centering mainly on

Barbara. They soon began to strongly suspect that something had followed them home from the asylum that night.

Carl said, "Let's go over some of the history of this asylum you visited. Apparently, from what you've been able to research, a certain amount of government subsidized experimentation took place there. Also, the prophylactic sterilization of inmates was carried out in this institution... perhaps even illegally and without their consent."

"That's right," said Barbara. "I'm sure a lot of these inmates were deprived of their legal rights."

Brian commented, "This sounds very similar to the Ladd Center in Exeter, Rhode Island, which we investigated."

Carl said, "And then there are these pictures you took at the asylum that seem to have some anomalies in them. They seem to look like gaseous formations that don't look like vapor or to have any natural source."

Marisa added, "And the first time I was there with them, there was a bluish-white light in one of the upper rooms. But on our next visit the whole upstairs section was lit up, even though that entire section is completely deserted."

Since their family friend Marisa had also reportedly witnessed some activity, Carl began questioning her as well. "Marisa, I understand that you live out of state?" Carl asked.

"I live in New Hampshire," she said. "But I'm down here to visit with Barbara quite frequently."

"And you also experienced something while at the asylum?" asked Carl.

"Yes, I did," said Marisa. "I didn't want to go at first because I was afraid the police might be there, you know, guarding the place. But I finally agreed to go. And then, while I was there, I suddenly felt like I was walking into a freezing blast of air. I know that it was January and cold, as it was, but it was suddenly really, unusually cold."

Justin said, "Yeah, I felt it too, in this one particular section we were walking through."

"You mean like suddenly walking into a meat locker?" asked Carl.

"Yes, exactly!" said Marisa.

I asked, "Now, was this outside of the building or inside of it?"

"It was outside," said Justin. "We never actually went inside."

"I'm certainly glad to hear that," I said.

Marisa continued, "So right when we walked into the blast of cold air, I also felt a hand on my shoulder, pushing me, as if it wanted me to get out of there."

Justin said, "And another thing that happened when we were there with my mom is that the batteries in our cameras kept draining. Even when we put fresh batteries in, we'd take about two pictures and that would be it."

Marisa also informed us that while they were there, both she and Barbara suddenly felt numb on one side of their bodies. I asked, "Was it on the left side?"

Barbara and Marisa glanced at each other in surprise. "Yes, it was," Barbara replied. "Why, what does that mean?"

"Well, it could be significant in that certain entities function in a contrary manner, from left to right," I explained. "But please continue with what happened next."

Marisa said, "Right after we felt the numb sensation, we began hearing voices that were talking to us. But they weren't real voices like someone speaking out loud; they were more like inside our heads. The voice I heard sounded to me like a female voice, telling me, "Please don't bring me back!"

Barbara said, "And the voice I heard was more like a male's voice telling me, "Take her back there."

Sandra asked, "And did you wind up going back there?"

Marisa replied, "Yes, we did go back that same night. But there was a cop parked in front of the building and he made us leave."

Justin added, "The strange thing was, even though we didn't get out of the car, as soon as we left there were what looked like children's hand prints all over the back windshield. It was only when we were driving away that we noticed them."

"That's interesting," said Sandra. "In fact, it reminds me of that case out west where a group of children were killed while riding on a school bus. As the story goes, when someone stops their car at the location where the accident took place, the car will move as if being pushed. Then the driver will supposedly find children's hand prints on the car's bumper, as if the car has been pushed away from danger."

Brian asked, "Has anyone else besides you experienced activity there that you know of?"

"Oh, yes," Barbara replied. "There's a website Justin goes on where he recently read about a psychic who visited there. She had a vision of the entire upstairs section being covered in blood. The psychic also reported hearing what sounded like a metal pipe being banged from inside the building. We heard the same exact sound while we were there. It sounded to us like metal banging against metal."

Carl asked Justin, "How does being at the asylum affect you personally, Justin?"

Justin replied, "Oh, it never really bothers me that much. In fact, I'm kind of used to it by now."

"Oh, yeah?" Marisa asked him teasingly. "Then what about that time you started crying because there was a raccoon there?"

Justin smirked and glanced downward, blushing with embarrassment. We all shared a brief laugh.

Carl said, "Okay, let's go over some of the things you people have been experiencing here, which you feel may represent something that's followed you from the asylum. You say the activity started shortly after your visit there in January?"

Barbara explained, "Yes, I've actually been physically assaulted by something unseen within this apartment. In fact, there have been times when I've been having dreams where I'm being attacked and choked by something. I'll actually wake up with bruises and gasping for breath."

"So you'd describe them as very lucid dreams?" Carl asked.

"Oh, yes, definitely," said Barbara.

Referring to the large unsightly bruise that happened to be on the upper section of Barbara's right arm, Carl asked, "When did that bruise on your arm first appear?"

"This past Monday," said Barbara. "I actually woke up with it."

"Is it painful?" asked Carl.

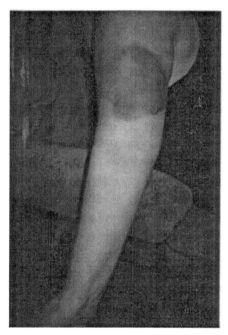

Bruise which appeared on a client's arm in Marlboro, MA.

Barbara said, "Yes, very. It's very sensitive to the touch."

Carl asked, "Would you mind if my brother Keith took a picture of it?"

"No, not at all," said Barbara.

I stepped forward with my camera and snapped a photo of the large bruise on Barbara's arm.

Checking his notes, Carl asked her, "And you say you've also woken up with finger marks on you?"

"Yes, after I had a dream that I was being forcibly dragged into an institution," said Barbara. "I woke up with bruise marks on my chest that ended in scratches at the end, as if somebody's fingernails slipped."

"So, how do you account for the bruises?" asked Carl.

"I have no idea," said Barbara. "I mean, like I said, I do have pretty vivid bad dreams sometimes."

Carl asked, "By the way, what are your particular religious beliefs?"

Barbara replied, "We're Catholic, although we haven't been to church in a long time."

Marisa said, "I don't go to church but I do pray to God, every day. And I'm probably more spiritual than a lot of people who do attend church."

"Is there anything else you'd like to tell us about the activity?" asked Carl.

Barbara said, "One night, we heard a clawing sound coming from inside our refrigerator. And when we went to investigate we saw our dog, which had passed away, sitting there in the kitchen."

"Oh, really?" asked Carl.

Justin said, "Yes, I saw him too. He was just there for a moment, sort of in the shadows, and then he was gone. But we definitely recognized that it was him."

Barbara, Justin and Marisa also told us that they'd recently been seeing a dark gray, shadowy form appearing in the apartment, which all three of them had witnessed on more than one occasion. Carl asked, "Does this gray mass ever coalesce into human form?"

Barbara replied, "No, it's just a smoky form. But for the past month or so, I'll be watching TV in my bedroom and all of a sudden I'll get this feeling like I'm being watched. And I'll look over at the doorway and I'll see it there for just a moment before it disappears."

Justin and Marisa described seeing the same exact thing, while sitting in the parlor and watching TV. Justin said, "We both suddenly saw it in the doorway leading to Barbara's room and we looked at each other and started asking, 'Did you just see that?' And then there was the time that my mom saw a red ball of light floating in her bedroom at night."

Humorously, Marisa said, "Yes, it's all Justin's fault, for taking his mother to investigate the asylum in the first place."

I then decided to approach another topic and said, "Now, Barbara, Brian has also informed us that you felt as though you might be in danger of possession. What can you tell us about that?"

Barbara said, "Oh yes, there were a couple of times when I suddenly went into some kind of trance. But I don't really have any memory of it, so you'll have to ask Marisa about exactly what happened."

We all looked to Marisa, who explained, "It happened twice, where all of a sudden Barbara seemed to go into some sort of a trance while she was sitting in the parlor here, and she just started mumbling. And she had this strange look to her eyes, like they became kind of glazed."

"And what did she say?" I asked.

Marisa said, "She wasn't really saying anything that we could understand, she just started mumbling to herself. And it took her awhile to snap out of it."

(We of course asked Barbara if she'd ever experienced epilepsy or been tested for it. The answer was no. We also questioned her about taking any medications that might possibly account for her sudden trance-like state. Again, she answered no.)

Barbara added, "But really, after I came out of it, I didn't remember anything about going into a trance or what I'd said. All I remember is sitting here in the parlor and Marisa and Justin telling me to snap out of it."

Carl asked, "Barbara, do you have any history in your family of precognition or of family members being sensitive or psychic?"

"No, not that I'm aware of," said Barbara.

With a smile, Carl said, "Well perhaps you could be the first. After all, this seems to be concentrating on you and maybe that's because you can perceive it."

When the interview was concluded, Barbara asked us, "So, what do you think this is?"

Carl replied, "One theory is that intense emotions can make an impression, like a snapshot. And then after time has passed and conditions have changed, it remains and seeks a resolution. It takes on a quasi-consciousness of its own."

"And do you think that's what may have happened at the asylum, and why it followed us home?" asked Barbara.

"Well, that's just one theory," said Carl. "There's also what we refer to as a 'residual haunt,' which is something like an imprint of energy or emotion simply replaying itself. That could account for you and Justin seeing your deceased dog in the kitchen."

I asked, "Barbara, what exactly did you experience when the voice was speaking to you? I mean, how did it make you feel?"

Barbara said, "Well, even though the male voice was speaking to me, it was like I could also feel the girl's spirit somehow reaching out to me. It was as if she was trying to communicate her suffering to me. And I suddenly felt filled with sadness and compassion for her."

"And did you communicate back?" I asked.

"Yeah, I did," said Barbara. "I communicated back to her that she could come to me and I'd try to help her. That was the wrong thing to do, wasn't it?"

I gently explained to Barbara, "Well, certain entities will sometimes pretend to be something they're not and will prey upon a person's sympathy as a ploy to gain acceptance. So you may have inadvertently given it permission to follow you."

Looking downcast, Barbara said, "Stupid me, I should've known better."

"No, these spirits can be very deceptive," I said. "Sometimes they'll project an emotion of overwhelming sorrow or sometimes even terror."

Brian told her, "Trust me, Barbara; I've made the same mistake myself."

Barbara asked, "But if it's something that wants us to help it then why would it hurt us?"

Carl said, "Well, it could be more than one entity at work here. One could be crying out for help, while another may be trying to counteract that and trying to prevent you from helping."

Sandra asked Barbara, "Are you looking to end the activity that's here or are you just curious to find out what it is?"

"Oh, we definitely want it to end," replied Barbara. "We want you to take it with you."

With a lighthearted laugh, Sandra said, "Well, I don't know if we exactly want to take it with us."

Brian added, "That's right, we're not Ghost Busters."

After we'd all shared a laugh, Barbara said, "Well, I think we all have a curiosity of what it is and why it's so angry up there at the asylum. And I have this nagging feeling that 'someone' wants us to go back up there to show us something."

Sandra asked, "You're not planning on going back there, are you?"

"Well, actually we have plans to go back there next Tuesday night," Barbara replied. "For some reason I feel I have to go up there to help someone but I don't know what to do."

Carl cautioned them "If you do wind up going there, one thing I would advise you NOT to do - especially you, Barbara - is to leave your mind as open and receptive as the last time. In other words, you shouldn't say, 'Whatever is here, please give me an inner message.' Keep a strong sense of yourself."

Sandra added, "In fact, I'd advise against going there again at all, at least until your situation here is somewhat resolved."

Fortunately, Barbara and the others saw our point. Even Justin and Jesse agreed not to return to the asylum for the time being.

For the remainder of our visit that evening, we conducted an investigation in the small apartment. Our EMF detectors displayed some slightly high fluctuations in the kitchen, in Barbara's bedroom and in the bathroom. Inside Justin's bedroom, the teenager explained that a poster of Justin Timberlake on his wall had suddenly been scratched, with no explanation. "I just came in to the bedroom and it was like that," he told us, indicating the long scratch on the poster.

Before leaving, I also anointed each member of the family, as well as Marisa and Jesse, and said a special prayer of protection over Barbara. They sincerely thanked us for coming and expressed how much they appreciated our help. Barbara asked us, "So, after this I should have no more problems, right?"

We of course explained that there were no absolutes or guarantees. However, we did explain that the blessing we performed should be effective in at least lessening the activity and preventing it from increasing. We also advised them on some methods of spiritually protecting themselves and reminded them that it would be in their best interest to refrain from visiting the asylum again for the time being. Brian assured Barbara that we'd be in touch within a week with the results of our findings. He encouraged her to contact TAPS again should she or anyone else experience any further activity in the meantime.

    We did contact Barbara, a few days later, with an update on her case. She was pleased to learn that aside from the slightly high EMF readings we'd obtained, our investigation had revealed nothing that would be considered as paranormal activity in her apartment. Barbara again thanked us for the help and understanding we'd given her and for not thinking she was crazy. She was both pleased and relieved to inform us that, since our visit, things were now very peaceful in her apartment. She also assured us that she, Justin, Jesse and Marisa had been staying clear of the Waltham asylum.

    We of course discussed our findings and our conclusions at the next TAPS meeting. Much of what Barbara, her teenage son and their two friends had been experiencing at the apartment could be explained by natural means. Since Barbara was a single mother, and from what she'd told us, not currently involved in a relationship, we decided to take her word for it that she was not being physically abused. However, since she'd been experiencing some very disturbing dreams after visiting the asylum, it was entirely possible that she was self-inflicting these bruises and scratches upon herself, perhaps without even realizing it. Barbara's son, Justin, had admittedly found her choking herself in her sleep on at least one occasion. There was also the question of Barbara's trance-like state. It was actually suggested that she perhaps be tested at a sleep clinic or have other neurological testing, especially if the problems persisted.

    The EMF fluctuations we'd gauged could very likely be attributed to the fact that the apartment building was located almost directly across the street from a small power station.

    Some of the other reported activity was not as readily explained, such as the grayish shadowy figure, the appearance of the deceased dog, the glowing red light, etc. However, according to Barbara, nothing unusual had been happening in her apartment since our visit. What was most important was the fact that we'd been able to bring some measure of comfort and reassurance to another family who might otherwise feel that they had nowhere to turn for help.

A little over two months later, TAPS was contacted once again by Barbara Baxter. She informed us that the activity in her apartment had again begun to pick up, this time with renewed intensity. Since she was desperate for us to come back and help her, we agreed to a return visit...this time with the intention of performing a thorough and complete blessing following our investigation.

With this being the midst of the Halloween season, it was naturally a busy time for us as paranormal investigators, especially since we were just beginning to become rather well known. On Halloween, which fell on a Friday, Jason and I had a radio interview to do together. On Saturday, November 1st, TAPS was scheduled to be guest speakers at the Cumberland Library. Nevertheless, because this case was now priority status, we scheduled our follow-up investigation for that weekend, on Saturday evening.

The TAPS team this time consisted of Brian, Sandra and myself, along with our new Systems Manager Brian Bell, and his girlfriend Kristin Allen, who was an investigator in training. Since neither Brian Bell nor Kristin had ever experienced a case of this possible magnitude before, they were pleased to be included. Carl was unavailable this time due to a prior commitment. We had also hoped to include TAPS member Chris Angelo on this investigation. Chris had just returned from a military leave of absence and was anxious to begin investigating once again. Also, he had some experience in dealing with hauntings involving inhuman spirits, which made him very valuable on a case such as this. Unfortunately, a close friend of his had previously committed him to an important social occasion, so Chris regrettably would also be unavailable.

We again arrived at Barbara's apartment in Marlboro in the early evening. After being welcomed in, we introduced Brian Bell and Kristin to Barbara, her son Justin and Justin's friend, Jesse. Barbara informed us that Marisa, their friend in New Hampshire, was busy with her family this weekend and therefore would not be joining us.

As we sat in the parlor for the interview, we explained to Barbara that Brian Bell and Kristin had already been filled in on the background of her case and what had transpired on our previous investigation. All we needed to discuss was how the activity had recently begun to pick up once again.

Brian Harnois began the interview by saying, "Alright, first question… have any of you been back to the asylum in Waltham since our last visit?"

Justin replied, "No, and I'm not going back there. At least not until this situation has been resolved."

Barbara said, "And I sure as hell have no intentions of going back there either."

Reaching down and petting one of the two pet ferrets, Brian asked, "By the way, how have the little guys been?"

Justin said, "They've been hyper as usual, maybe even a little more so lately. I think even they can sense a presence in here."

Barbara and Justin then related to us how over the past few weeks, activity had been rapidly picking up within the apartment. Barbara's nightmares had increased. She'd also experienced two more instances of being "attacked" in her sleep, which again resulted in unsightly bruises. Barbara and Justin, as well as Jesse and Marisa, had all seen the grayish form again, hovering in the doorways…only now it seemed to have become thicker and more condensed, taking on more of a smoky, grayish-black appearance.

I then asked Barbara if she had experienced any more episodes of going into a trance-like state. She instantly replied, "Yes, and in a way, that's what frightens me the most. Of course, I don't remember any of this. But one afternoon I was on the phone with Marisa, who had called me from New Hampshire. Now I do remember talking with her. But apparently, from what she told me later, all of a sudden I started talking in a strange voice that wasn't even my own. And according to Marisa, I was saying something about going back to the asylum...but I wasn't talking about myself. I was saying, 'She's going back there, I'm taking her back and you're not stopping her.' And I supposedly just kept saying that, until Marisa said firmly, 'I want to talk to Barbara now.' And that was when she said that I suddenly snapped out of it."

When our interview concluded, Sandra asked Barbara and Justin if there was anything they'd like to add. Barbara said, "We just want it to stop, once and for all. Like I've mentioned before, if this was something physical that I could plainly see and touch, then I could fight it. But this is just taking away my peace of mind."

We assured Barbara and Jason that, while we of course could make no guarantees, we'd do everything we could to quell the activity in their apartment.

The two Brians quickly began setting up their equipment inside of Barbara's bedroom, since this was where Barbara was allegedly being attacked. Once everything was set up, Kristin and Sandra and I joined them in the bedroom. We saw that Brian Bell had Barbara's bedroom television set switched to a neutral, or "white noise" channel, while Brian Harnois was positioning his video camera on a tripod. Brian H. explained to us, "The video camera will be recording the TV and creating a mirror image. It's actually supposed to be the same frequency that ghosts operate on. So, hopefully, it may even capture the image of an actual ghost. What I'd like to do now is turn off all the lights and just talk about it."

I said, "Oh yes, in other words, you want to give the entity recognition."

"Exactly, Keith," said Brian. "And we'll be recording audio with both your and my tape recorders and we'll see if anything happens."

We shut the bedroom door and switched off the lights so that the only illumination in the room came from the soft glow of the TV screen. Brian Bell began by asking, "If there is a presence in this room, could you give us a sign that you are here?" After a wait of several seconds, Brian also encouraged his girlfriend Kristin to try asking some questions.

Kristin asked, "Why are you here?" She paused before asking, "Are you from the asylum in Waltham?"

"Why are you bothering this family?" asked Sandra.

Kristin asked, "Do you mean harm to Barbara or Justin?"

A somewhat peculiar distortion suddenly appeared on the TV screen, creating what looked like a "looping" effect. "Look at that!" Brian Bell exclaimed, calling it to our attention.

"That sure is weird," Brian Harnois commented. He then suggested, "Keith, try some religious provocation."

"In the name of Jesus Christ," I said, "if you are here, give us a sign of your presence."

There was no immediate reaction. "Keep going, Keith," said Brian. "Everyone continue asking questions to see if we can get some kind of a response."

We asked several more questions but there were no further distortions on the TV screen. Brian H. said, "I'm not getting anything significant on video, either. What we saw before may just have been some random interference that was picked up."

We then took a short break to listen for any possible EVPs we may have captured. However, there were none that we could detect.

Then we came back out to the parlor and rejoined the family. Barbara somewhat nervously asked us, "So, how's it going, guys? Did you find anything in my bedroom?"

Brian Bell answered, "No, nothing definite. We did get some distortions on the TV monitor but, so far, our results are inconclusive."

Looking a bit worried, Barbara asked, "So now do I have to be afraid of watching TV in my bedroom?"

"Oh, no, not at all," Brian B. said with a laugh. "We just had the monitor hooked up and facing the video, to create a mirror image. But like I said, so far there's nothing conclusive."

"Well, in a way I guess that's a relief," said Barbara. "Hey, anyway, guys, I was thinking of ordering a pizza for us all since you were kind enough to come all the way out here again to help."

Brian H. said, "Hey that sounds great to me! Thanks, I sure could go for some pizza right about now." The rest of us were all in agreement.

While we were enjoying refreshments, I asked Justin and Jesse, "By the way, guys, how's your own ghost hunting going? Have you investigated any interesting places lately?"

Justin replied, "Actually we just recently went to Spider Gates Cemetery in Leicester."

Brian H. perked up. "Oh, really?" he asked, while munching on a slice of pizza." "How'd it go?"

"Not too good," said Jesse. "The police got us almost as soon as we walked in."

"They did?" I asked. "Did you guys go there at night?"

Justin said, "No, we went there while it was still daylight, in the afternoon. But the police got us and searched us, even after we explained to them that we were just there to take pictures. And they told us that the cemetery was off limits because of all the vandalism that's gone on there."

(Considering the black clad, Goth-style appearance of these two teenage lads I wasn't all that surprised that the local police had denied them access, even in the daylight. Because of repeated vandalism and cult activity, the police were now really cracking down on people in general entering this particular cemetery.)

We resumed our investigation by, once again, taking EMF readings in each of the rooms. Just as last time, there were somewhat high fluctuations in both the kitchen and in the bathroom. This time, however, there were also unusually high readings within Justin's bedroom. We noted that each of these three rooms were located on the west side of the building, which was the side of the building that was nearest to the small electrical power station across the street.

Meanwhile, Brian Bell and Kristin were continuing to monitor the TV screen inside of Barbara's still darkened bedroom. From the parlor, Brian H. called out, "You getting anything in there, Brian?"

"Nothing," Brian B. called back.

A thought then occurred to Brian H., that the use of ultra-violet light could be used to repel negative inhuman spirits. Although it was of course only a theory, two other friends of ours in the field – Al Tyas and Barry Fitzgerald – had both recently been utilizing ultra-violet lights in an attempt to "flush out" inhuman entities. After discussing this theory with the rest of us, Brian also explained to Barbara, Justin and Jesse, "Sometime, I'd like to try working with ultra-violet light in a case where inhuman spirits may be present. It seems that inhumans do not like florescent light, especially ultra-violet, like with a black light. And as we were just discussing, a couple of friends of ours have been working on this theory. They've experimented by placing black lights in a certain room and, according to them, an inhuman entity will completely bypass that room. It seemingly has worked in some cases."

I added, "It could be that it exposes them, too."

"Yes, that's another possibility" Brian agreed. "Now, if we were to do this here, it could be that we'd actually see something manifest."

Barbara said, "Well, if that happened, then I'd be outta here."

Brian quickly told her, "Oh, no, we don't even have a blacklight with us. I was just saying what might happen if we did use one."

Barbara thought for a moment, and then reconsidered. "Justin has one, underneath his bed," she informed us. "If it'll help to get whatever's in here out, then maybe you should use it."

Brian Bell asked Justin if we could borrow his blacklight, to which he agreed. As soon as we had it set up inside Barbara's bedroom, Brian Harnois suggested to Sandra and myself, "Maybe it's time we should start the blessing, and afterward start wrapping things up. What do you think?"

Sandra and I both agreed. We were both beginning to feel a bit drowsy, due to the hectic schedule of the past week. Sandra decided that while I was conducting the religious cleansing in Barbara's bedroom, she'd set up our own video camera on a tripod in the parlor, in an attempt to monitor any possible activity.

Before the blessing commenced, we conferred with Barbara, Justin and Jesse, and asked if they had any questions. Barbara said, "Yes. At the end of this, you'll take it with you, right?"

Brian Harnois said, "Well, no. Like we explained to you last time, we can't simply capture a spirit, and we certainly don't want it following us home."

"That's exactly right," said Sandra. "If this is actually a spirit form we're dealing with, then it can't be physically contained. But when Keith does his blessing, we're hoping to coerce it into moving on, and then he'll be inviting positive spirits in to take fill the void. In other words, he'll be introducing positive energy to take the place of the negative."

Brian Bell added, "You see, Barbara, a spirit form is composed of energy, and it's not something that can be contained in a physical sense. In fact, we were just discussing the possibility that whatever static electricity is being given off by that power station across the street, could be contributing to some of the activity here."

Barbara asked, "You mean it's feeding off the energy?"

"Yes, in a manner of speaking," said Brian. "At least, that's a theory that we have to take into account."

Kristin said, "But you can be sure, Barbara, that we're going to do everything in our power to lessen the negative activity in here."

Barbara appeared somewhat reassured, and said, "Well, I'd of course be extremely grateful, if you could help bring back our peace of mind here. I really can't afford to move, and besides, I don't like the idea of being chased out of my apartment. Especially by a spirit!"

"That's the right attitude to have," Brian Bell told her.

With tears suddenly filling her eyes, Barbara said, "I feel as though this is really all my fault... because when it first contacted me, I told it that it could come to me, and I'd help it."

Sandra placed a hand on Barbara's shoulder and said, "But you did so out of compassion, which means you simply reacted as you naturally would. It may have even sensed your maternal instincts."

Just before beginning the blessing, I again anointed Barbara, tracing the sign of the cross on her forehead with blessed oil while reciting Psalm 105, verse 15: "Do not touch My anointed ones, and do My prophets no harm." I also anointed Justin and Jesse, as well as Sandra and my other teammates. Sandra, in turn, anointed me with the blessed oil.

Brian Harnois placed his tape recorder in the parlor near the entrance to the kitchen, while I placed my tape recorder in the parlor beside where Sandra was recording video. Brian Bell and Kristin Allen were continuing to monitor the TV and the video within Barbara's bedroom, as I entered to begin the blessing. I asked Brian and Kristin, "Excuse me, will it interfere with your evidence if I begin the religious cleansing in here?"

"No, not at all," said Brian. "In fact, I haven't been getting any activity on the screen at all, so maybe it'll help to stir something up."

While I was concluding the blessing inside of Barbara's bedroom, I invoked the name of Jesus Christ to expel any negative spiritual influences from the room. "In the name of Jesus Christ," I said, "if there are any unholy spirits within this room, give us a sign of your presence, or depart."

At that same moment, while Sandra was monitoring our own camcorder, she suddenly saw what appeared to be two anomalies flit by near the ceiling. "Holy cow," she said to herself.

"What is it, Sandra?" asked Brian Harnois, who was taking readings nearby.

Sandra replied, "I think I just saw something really significant fly by the camera lens. There were two of them. They looked something like orbs, but they also seemed to have a fluttering motion."

When I was done blessing the bedroom, Sandra called my attention over to her, and said, "Keith, I want you to take a look at this. I was recording at the moment you pronounced the expulsion within the bedroom, and this is what came out. This wasn't visible to the naked eye. Let me know what you think."

Sandra replayed the footage for me. As I watched, what looked like two anomalies suddenly flitted by the camera lens, near the parlor ceiling. Although they only appeared for about two seconds, they were rather solid looking, and even had a fluttering bat-like quality to them. Sandra asked, "What the heck are they? I've never seen anything exactly like them before, have you?"

"No, never," I said. "They seem to have kind of a metallic gold color to them."

Sandra said, "Yes, that's exactly what I was thinking, just like liquid metal. And if you look closely enough, you can see that the two anomalies are solid enough to even cast a shadow."

We called our fellow investigators over to also get their opinions. Brian Bell said, "They sure are bizarre looking anomalies. At first I thought they were orbs, but they're a little too solid looking, even casting a shadow. Plus the fact that they're that liquid gold color, and the way they zipped past the camera lens at an arched angle is unlike any orb activity I've ever seen."

"That's exactly what I thought," said Sandra. "They didn't look small and white like most genuine orbs tend to. In fact, they actually looked more like 'rods' to me, especially with that fluttering motion."

We also showed the anomalies Sandra had captured on video to Barbara, Justin and Jesse. Although they were impressed, Barbara was also somewhat unnerved by what she saw. "What did you do?" Barbara asked me.

"I asked for a sign of its presence," I replied.

"What'd you do that for??" she asked, sounding alarmed.

Sandra explained to her, "Keith did some holy provocation in your bedroom, and that's when the two gold orbs appeared from the left direction, almost as if they just flew out. And of course, we had Justin's blacklight set up in your bedroom as well."

Before continuing with the blessing, we also briefly reviewed our audio recordings. While my magnetic recording happened to reveal nothing unusual this time, Brian Harnois' digital recording had picked up a rather clear EVP. It was a male voice whispering, "Please forgive me." We speculated as to what this may have meant. Barbara and Justin took it to mean that the entity may have been feeling remorseful, for having caused them so much discomfort over the past several months.

Brian was elated at having captured his first EVP using his digital recorder. "This is the first time I've gotten an EVP on this," he proudly announced. "I've actually had this thing on the side of Keith's, recording at the same time. I usually won't get anything, and his tape recorder will pick up all the damn EVPs. I'll be like, 'It's not fair!'" He then gave a laugh.

The cleansing within Justin's bedroom, the kitchen and the bathroom went without incident. Now all that remained was the parlor itself. Barbara, Justin and Jesse joined the rest of us. Brian Harnois suggested that the family attempt to communicate with whatever spirits might be present, and let them know, politely yet firmly, that they were not welcome here. Brian also suggested to the family that they try to make peace with the spirits, by apologizing for having disturbed them in the first place. "After all," Brian explained, "they may have felt as if you were invading their territory."

Since Barbara felt too uncomfortable to directly address the spirits, Justin volunteered to do so. After he was seated in a cushioned chair, he looked at his mom, and then at his best friend Jesse, who gave Justin the thumbs up as a vote of encouragement. Brian Harnois then gave Justin the go-ahead. "Would you please leave?" Justin asked the spirits. "We'd appreciate it. We don't feel safe at home with you here. We're sorry if we disturbed you in any way; we didn't mean harm to you. Could you please leave?"

When Justin was finished addressing the spirits, I continued the blessing within the parlor. Knowing that Barbara was still very unnerved by the prospect of a demonic entity visually or audibly manifesting itself, I instead asked for a sign of angelic presence. Sandra, who was again monitoring the video camera, said, "That's freaky. As soon as Keith asked for an angelic sign, I just saw what looked like some sort of glitter falling down around him, as if from the ceiling."

We all gathered round as Sandra rewound and played back the footage that she'd just taken. Sure enough, the moment I asked for a sign of angelic presence, a brief shower of sparkles cascaded down around me... with Brian Harnois munching on a slice of pizza in the background.

Barbara, Justin and James all remarked to us on just how much lighter the atmosphere within the parlor suddenly felt. Both Sandra and Kristin commented on it as well. Barbara asked us, "Does this mean that it's gone from here? For good?"

Brian Bell replied, "Well, only time will tell that for sure. Like we said before, there are no real certainties or guarantees. But, Keith's blessing did seem to have a positive effect."

Sandra added, "In the meantime, you have our contact info, and you're certainly welcome to keep in touch with us."

"Thanks, I'll do that," said Barbara. "And believe me, if the activity starts up again, I'll be in touch right away."

"Please do so," I said. "And again, I'd certainly advise everyone to stay clear of the Waltham Asylum, especially for the present. You don't want to risk reactivating anything."

"Oh, don't worry, I'm not going back to that place, ever!" Barbara assured us.

That's certainly a step in the right direction," I said.

As we were packing up our equipment, "Barbara told us, "Again, I want to thank you guys so much, for everything."

Brian H. said, "You're welcome. And thanks for the pizza, it was delicious!"

"Yes, it really hit the spot," Sandra agreed. "Thank you, Barbara."

Our hostess gave us each a big hug, and promised to stay in touch with us, to keep us informed of how she and her family were doing.

Fortunately, the religious cleansing which was performed inside of the apartment did seem to have a positive effect. Barbara Baxter periodically remained in touch with us over the following year, and let us know that her problems with the paranormal were continuing to be held in check. Although she, her son Justin and their two best friends Jesse and Marisa did continue to occasionally investigate cemeteries and other haunted locations as a hobby, they took our advice by grounding themselves beforehand. Also, they made certain to never again "invite" spirit attachment, by falling for the ploy of sympathy projected by a deceptive spirit.

On a tragic note, it was on the weekend of our second investigation in Marlboro that we lost our close friend and fellow TAPS member Chris Angelo to a car accident. Chris was driving his friend's car along a dark rural road in Smithfield, when he apparently missed a turn causing the car to careen off the road, hitting a tree. The report was that Chris had been killed instantly. He was 22 years old. Chris Angelo will of course always be missed. But more than this, his inspiration as a dear friend and fellow paranormal investigator will always remain with us.

Chapter 10

A Visit from Ted?

Although my sister Cynthia has pretty much had a life-long interest in true crime stories and famous serial killers, some years ago she developed a particular fascination for American serial killer Ted Bundy. Perhaps it was the outward personal charm that Ted Bundy managed to exude, combined with his complex psychological profile. As Cynthia herself put it, "I was very into Ted Bundy. I read every book and watched every documentary, and studied him." Although Ted Bundy had never been one of my personal studies, I did eventually develop somewhat of an interest in him, having mainly been influenced by my sister's captivation with this infamous persona in the annals of American crime.

Ted Bundy was born Theodore Robert Cowell on Nov. 24, 1946 in Burlington, Vermont. His childhood was difficult to say the least. Ted's mother Eleanor had been abandoned by his father when he found out she was pregnant, and Ted grew up being led to believe that his maternal grandparents, Samuel and Eleanor Cowell, were actually his parents and that his mother was his older sister. He was frequently picked on and ostracized by other students during his school years, and he did not share a close relationship with his stepparents. However, despite these obstacles, Ted was apparently highly intelligent, which enabled him to successfully complete a college career. He was also able to develop impressive social skills, and was seemingly capable of maintaining some seemingly normal relationships with women. Ted even briefly pursued a promising career in politics.

Ted Bundy was also secretly strangling and mutilating female victims, often utilizing his personal charm and wit to gain their trust. He embarked upon a career as a serial killer and rapist, eventually becoming one of the most notorious criminals in American history.

Between 1974 and 1978 he sexually assaulted and murdered several young women in the states of Colorado, Florida, Oregon, Utah and Washington. Although he may indeed have been responsible for a great many more homicides – perhaps well over a hundred - Bundy eventually confessed to 28 murders. He received a death sentence in 1979 for the murder of two college students, and received another one in 1980 when he was convicted of the rape and murder of a 12-year-old girl. Ted Bundy was executed by electrocution in Starke, Florida, on January 24, 1989.

Both during his lifetime and afterward, Ted Bundy gained fame, celebrity, and notoriety, particularly during his much-publicized trial. His intelligence and personal charm attracted a great amount of public attention. Ted Bundy's story has been the subject of numerous books, as well as TV films and documentaries. Despite his horrific crimes, some view Bundy as a strangely romantic figure, while to others he remains a mystery; the quintessential doomed misanthrope. And still to others, especially to those who lost innocent love ones to his crimes, Ted Bundy is viewed as the personification of evil itself.

However, what personally interested me the most in reference to Ted Bundy, was the fact that my sister Cynthia's fascination with him may have culminated in an otherworldly visit, of sorts.

Cynthia detailed her experience to me: "Well, one time, one night, I was lying in bed reading one of my new books I bought on Ted Bundy. And there was a documentary that I was recording on the TV about him at the same exact time. Now I don't know if this was so much of a force from me thinking about him with these two things going on at once, between me reading the book and the documentary being on the TV, but suddenly my bed shook. It was down at the bottom of the foot of the bed. It was only for a minute, but there was a definite shaking. It was frightening! And I think it might possibly have had something to do with his presence, with me being so involved with reading about him at the time, along with watching and studying him. Like, I had been researching him for months. So I think all the energy in the room might possibly have attracted something. I even wonder if Ted Bundy may have been letting me know he was there. Why would my bed shake like that?"

Cynthia was adamant that she wasn't exaggerating, and I tend to believe her. Certainly there were no earth tremors reported in our area at that moment. Whether it was actually the spirit of Ted Bundy, however, remains questionable. Just as there are deceptive people, it is my personal belief that there are also many deceptive entities within the spirit realm. Without doubt, I would agree with Cynthia that this was indeed the Law of Attraction at work. And even if this was not the actual spiritual essence of Ted Bundy himself, misery certainly tends to attract company!

To be on the safe side, my wife Sandra and I prayed for my sister's protection, specifically asking through prayer and supplication that whatever negative entity may have been activated in my sister's house, it would now be removed, and that in its place an angelic spirit would be invited in. We also prayed that whatever lost or wandering spirits might have been present, they would now be placed at rest, and sent to their proper abode.

Fortunately, since the prayer vigil, my sister's bed shaking incident has not been repeated. However, her fascination with serial killer Ted Bundy remains.

Chapter 11

Oakie Pokie

Okay, so many other parts of the world at large can admittedly boast their own personalized "cryptids" (or, mysterious, largely unproven and unclassified creatures of the fantastic and unknown). Some of these creatures – especially the legendary water creatures - have even attained local celebrity status. There are those that have affectionately been given personalized pet names. Yes, Loch Ness in Scotland boasts "Nessie," Lake Chaplain of the Great Lakes has "Champ," Lake Okanagan in Canada has "Ogopogo," and Margate in South Africa was allegedly once visited by the mysterious, unidentified creature known as "Trunko." What might not be so publicly well known, is the fact that we here in "Little Rhody" have our own indigenous cryptozological creatures. And this even includes a possible lesser known relative to the more famous water monsters.

Of course, since sightings of this creature have been reported in the bay waters bordering the City of Warwick, it's technically more of a sea creature than a lake monster, as are some of its more famous cousins. And because this sea creature has been spotted lurking primarily in the waters of Oakland Beach, the locals have affectionately given it the name of "Oakie Pokie." (Alright, truth be told it was actually one local in particular who coined the name, and that is yours truly. I just figured it was an appropriate enough take-off on the name "Ogopogo.")

The very first occasion I heard of this elusive local creature was in the late 1980's, while I was employed at a nursing facility located in Smithfield, Rhode Island. It was during our lunch break early one afternoon in the cafeteria, when a young woman named Margaret, who worked as dietary staff, began telling us about a strange experience she and her boyfriend recently had. According to Margaret, they were out on a date together one recent evening, and had decided to park at

Oakland Beach in Warwick for a while. The boyfriend parked his car in front of the stone seawall that separates the parking lot from the beach area, then shut off the headlights and the engine. He and Margaret had been there for perhaps forty-five minutes or so, when Margaret noticed something moving over behind the seawall in front of them. She alerted her boyfriend, who also peered through his car windshield at the darkened shape. At first, they thought it might be a large dog walking along the edge of the wall, wagging its uplifted tail. However, it soon became apparent that this was no large dog they were seeing.

What they were both looking at appeared to be a long, dark, snake-like creature, apparently also eying them from the other side of the wall. Although they could see no body, the long neck protruded at least a good seven or eight feel over the wall, and was slightly swaying. "What the hell IS that thing??" Margaret's boyfriend asked in astonishment.

From what Margaret could make out in the darkness, the creature's small, snake-like head seemed to have two small projections on top. They looked something like small horns, expect they were blunted, not pointed. After twenty seconds or so of observing this creature, Margaret's boyfriend thought to switch the car headlights back on, thereby illuminating it. The sudden burst of light must have startled the serpentine creature, for within seconds it had slunk out of sight. Before it disappeared, however, they had both gotten a good enough look at it, to plainly see its two reptilian-looking eyes, and its glistening black color. They knew for certain that they had not been imagining it, nor could it possibly have been a trick of the light! At Margaret's urgings, her boyfriend then started his car, and they quickly left.

When Margaret concluded her story, she told us, "I don't care if nobody believes me, either. I know what my boyfriend and I saw, and it happened exactly like I just said!"

She certainly seemed to be sincere. And while Margaret had been sharing her experience with us, I had also been sketching the creature she described on a piece of scrap paper. "Does this look like the creature you saw?" I asked when done, holding the sketch up to her.

Margaret's eyes widened. "Yes, that looks exactly like it!" she said.

I then conducted a mini-interview with her, as the others at the table listened. "So, you didn't see any part of the body at all, just the neck and the head?"

"No, we couldn't see any of the body at all," she said. "We figured it must've just slunk back unto the water when it disappeared, and out of our sight."

"Were there any other witnesses, or other cars there at Oakland Beach that night?" I asked.

Margaret replied, "Oh, yeah, there were other cars there. Probably some other people must've seen it too."

"Did any of the other people there get out of their cars, or was there any sort of commotion going on?" I asked.

"No, at least not that we saw," said Margaret. "But, like I said, we were in a hurry to get out of there."

"Have you and your boyfriend been back there since?" I asked.

Margaret said with a laugh, "No, we haven't quite worked up the nerve. But if we do go back, we're definitely bringing a camera with us!"

During the remaining minutes of our lunch break, I asked Margaret several more general questions. She obviously appreciated the fact that I displayed more than a casual interest in her story, and that I also took her seriously.

Of course, I myself had visited the Oakland Beach area on numerous occasions, both in the daytime and at night, but never before had I seen or heard of anything remotely unusual being sighted there. I also asked our family friend Al Brown, who was a long time private shell fisherman in the area, if he'd ever seen anything unusual in the waters of the Oakland and Conimicut beaches. He replied that no, he hadn't. So, I simply kept Margaret's account of the Oakland Beach serpent sighting in the back of my mind, as an interesting yet unverifiable story.

In fact, I hadn't even given it much thought at all until one afternoon several months later, when my wife Sandra and I were taking some classes at the CCRI Knight Campus in Warwick. While waiting for Sandra to get out of class I was seated in the cafeteria, when I happened to strike up a casual conversation with a young male student who was sitting at the same table. It turned out that he was also a resident of the city of Warwick. We were chatting about various locations in Warwick, when all of a sudden he mentioned, "You know, there's been some unusual things spotted in the waters of Oakland Beach."

"Oh, really?" I asked, my interest perking up. "Like what?"

He replied, "Well, for instance, there's a strange creature with a long, snake-like neck that's been seen at night at Oakland Beach. I know this sounds crazy, but I also know that it's true, because I've actually seen this creature myself with my own eyes."

Intrigued, I asked him if he could describe this creature in detail. And, without me filling in anything for him, he described the same exact creature in every detail that Margaret had also described... blackish in color, long snake-like neck at least several feet in length, and a head with two small bumps, or mini-antlers on top. He also mentioned that the creature has been known to pull itself up to the shoreline and extend it's neck up over the stone seawall separating Oakland Beach from the parking lot, to briefly gaze at people parked there, which was what it was doing when he witnessed it.

Only then did I tell him about my co-worker Margaret, who several months earlier had described seeing the exact same type of creature at Oakland Beach, along with her boyfriend. I even asked if he possibly knew anyone named Margaret who lived in Smithfield, but he replied that he didn't. "Living in Warwick I don't even know anyone who lives in Smithfield, certainly no one named Margaret," he told me.

When Sandra arrived in the Knight Campus cafeteria, I introduced her to the student I'd just been chatting with, and asked him to quickly fill her in on what he'd just told me. Sandra was also quite intrigued, especially since it corroborated exactly with the story I'd heard from Margaret several months earlier.

During my very next lunch break at the nursing facility, I was naturally very anxious to inform Margaret that I'd just met another eyewitness to the creature that she and her boyfriend had seen at Oakland Beach in Warwick, and that his description had identically matched hers. Although Margaret hadn't mentioned her sighting since she'd first told us about it several months earlier, I assumed that she'd be excited to hear that someone else had seen the same creature at the same location. However, to my surprise, Margaret now seemed extremely uncomfortable when I brought the subject up. She became hesitant, and even evasive, saying, "Well, I'm not sure exactly what I saw that night. It could have been anything."

I reminded her, "Yes, but you said that your boyfriend saw it too, and the guy I was talking with yesterday gave the same exact description of the creature that you did. And I remember you saying that you and your boyfriend had even raced out of the Oakland Beach parking lot that night."

Margaret said, "Yeah, but I-I'm not sure that's what we were really seeing. It coulda' just been a trick of the light, because it was dark out."

I was about to remind Margaret about her and her boyfriend seeing the creature illuminated by the headlights, but because she now seemed so embarrassed about the topic, I decided to drop it. Most likely she'd told the story to one too many people, and had been ridiculed for it. Besides, from my own past experiences over the years, I knew that if I kept pursuing the subject, I risked being ridiculed myself, for believing in sea monsters.

And so, I was left with two intriguing yet unverifiable eyewitness accounts of the creature I eventually dubbed "Oakie Pokie." It was interesting to note the similarities between the way this creature was described, and the descriptions of some of the more famed lake and sea monsters. In fact, "Oakie Pokie," or the "Oakland Beach Monster" seemed almost to be a smaller version of Champ, Nessie, or Ogopogo. And of course, my two "eyewitness" friends could easily have taken their descriptions from these creatures. The only thing that lent any possible credibility to the story was the fact that two entirely different people from two different parts of the state came up with the same exact description and location, combined with the fact that they both seemed completely sincere. Otherwise, there was simply nothing else at all to go on. And the story simply did not seem to be wide spread enough, to be considered a local urban legend.

Yes, I confess to having occasionally strolled along or driven by Oakland Beach during the evening hours, inwardly wondering if I might catch perhaps just a fleeting glimpse of a serpentine head and neck peering at me over the stone wall. I'd even determined that if I did spot the creature, I was going to immediately glance over the wall myself (at least at a safe enough distance from the creature) to rule out any possibility of a hoax.

Years after hearing the original "eyewitness" stories, I would often take my young son, Keith Jr. on daytime excursions to Oakland Beach, especially on hot summer days, playfully telling him, "Let's go down to the beach to get some ice cream, and maybe even see Oakie Pokie!" Of course, we never did run into Oakie Pokie, and my son never really seemed to take me seriously, as his primary interest was always in the ice cream. Eventually I did hear from at least one other Warwick resident that there was something strange rumored to be lurking in the waters of Oakland Beach... but again, this account offered nothing conclusive.

Keith Johnson Jr. points to one of the spots where the mysterious creature known as Oakie Pokie has been sighted at Oakland Beach in Warwick, RI.

It was on a summer afternoon in the mid-1990's, at a time when I'd certainly thought I'd heard the last of any strange creature inhabiting the local waters, that there was suddenly a slight commotion going on outside in our local neighborhood. Several of my neighbors were scurrying about in their swim trunks and denim shorts, grabbing up floatation devices. I quickly caught up with one of them, whose name was Doug, and asked him what was going on. He told me, "There's something really big swimming down in the bay, like a big black whale or something. We don't know what it is, but we're going down there!"

I told Doug I'd meet them there, and then rushed inside to get a camera. As I grabbed my camera and rushed passed Sandra, she asked me what all the excitement was about. Glancing back at her, I said, "We just might have a genuine 'Oakie Pokie' sighting down at the bay, and I want to try and get a picture!"

"Good luck," she called after me.

As I hurriedly sprinted in the direction of the bay to catch up with the others, my own excitement mounted. After all, the bay was directly connected to the waters of Oakland Beach. There was always the slim chance that the reports of some mysterious, heretofore unknown creature might finally be verified, with multiple witnesses and photographs. And even if this did turn out to be a small pilot whale, or something of that nature, that in itself would certainly be newsworthy. Also, if it was conclusively identified as some other known species, such as a large sturgeon-type fish (however unlikely that may be in these waters), then at least we would finally have some explanation as to the previously reported sightings of a large, mysterious aquatic creature.

Unfortunately, by the time we arrived on the scene, whatever was there in the bay had by now eluded us. A couple of my neighbors swiftly began paddling out on the floatation devices they'd brought along, but the bay appeared as calm and serene as usual. I did question two of the actual eyewitnesses as to what they'd seen. Still hyperventilating with the thrill of it, the young couple explained that they'd been swimming in the bay, when they'd suddenly seen this huge, glistening black creature gliding through the bay about a hundred feet or so away from them. They couldn't see any fins, head or neck, just the top of some long black body, and it was swimming at a good speed. So they'd gotten out of the water as fast as they could, and run to get more witnesses. There were also at least a few other people there at the bay who had seen the same exact thing, and had stayed their watching it, until it disappeared underneath the water and never resurfaced.

"Could it have possibly bee a large seal?" I asked them, since after all, a seal had recently been spotted at Oakland Beach.

But they were all adamant, that this creature was far too large to have possibly been a seal.

And so, at the end of the day we were simply left with another mystery, nothing that would even rate the local six o'clock TV news.

Having been a resident of the City of Warwick for approximately two decades now, I will still every now and then overhear someone mentioning something about a mysterious large, unidentified serpent-like creature being sighted lurking in the waters of Oakland Beach... or, less frequently, at nearby Conimicut Beach. And I will never miss an opportunity to join in the conversation and ask for any specific details. Sometimes these people are eyewitness. More often, they have either heard the story from a relative or from "a friend of a friend," who swears it is true and isn't the type of person to make these things up. However, one problem is, that I never seem to hear tell of any strange creature in these waters from experienced local fishermen, quahogers (clammers) or lobstermen.

For my own part, all I can say is that over the years, I've received enough verbal reports of supposed encounters with this creature to make the subject of at least some passing interest to me. I've even speculated that because there was a rat infestation at Oakland Beach at the time of the original sightings, then the creature - if it did indeed exist - may perhaps have been coming close enough to feed off the rats that were scurrying along the stone seawall. And it was only after the beach area had been thoroughly cleaned up, that the sightings at Oakland Beach seemed to diminish.

But, like so many other reports of this nature, until something more conclusive comes my way, the legend of "Oakie Pokie" remains just that to me... a legend. And at least this legend is one of the more entertaining ones!

Sandra, Keith Age and Keith at the Mid-South Paranormal Convention.

Lisa Dowaliby investigates a haunted location.

Paranormal Realities II

Christopher Finch disposes of a tainted Ouija board.

Psychic mist captured on film inside a house in Foster, RI.

Plasma light inside of the Farns-worth House, Gettysburg, PA.

Chapter 12

The Maine Possession Case – Part 1

(The names of the family members involved have been altered to protect their privacy.)

This case originated during the first week of January in 2004. Ironically, Sandra, my brother Carl, Christopher Finch and I (all members of the Atlantic Paranormal Society at the time) had just been investigating an alleged case of possession in RI, when our friends Bill and Nancy Washell of Maine Paranormal contacted Sandra and me. Because of our personal experience with inhuman entities, they wished us to assist them with another case they were currently working on, in Lewiston, Maine... this one involving a case of possible demonic possession. "What a way to start out the New Year," we though to ourselves. Here it was only the 3rd of January, and we were already dealing with our second possession case of the year!

It was late afternoon on January 3rd that a TAPS team consisting of Sandra and I, along with Brian Harnois and Jill Raczelowski started out on the trip from Warwick, RI to Lewiston, ME. Unfortunately, Brian had suddenly and unexpectedly been hit by a feeling of fatigue and illness. By the time we set out, he was indeed looking quite green around the gills. Despite this fact, he insisted on making the trip anyway, and asked me to take over driving his car.
Upon our arrival in Lewiston that evening some hours later, we found the roads to be completely iced over, making driving conditions extremely treacherous... not to mention that Brian's condition had progressively worsened along the way. After stopping at several different locations, however, we finally arrived at the correct residence, known as Pine Hills.

Bill and Nancy Washell were already there, along with another member of their investigation team named Harold. After greeting us, Bill and Nancy introduced us to the clients, who from the start appeared to be a loveable, grandparent-type older couple, of French Canadian descent. "Luis and Marjorie," said Bill, "these are our friends from TAPS, Keith and his wife Sandra, and Brian... and Jill, who I'm meeting for the first time. Guys, this is Luis and Marjorie Ray."

"Very nice meeting you," said Luis, shaking our hands.

"Yes, thank you for coming all this way on a winter night," said Marjorie. "Bill and Nancy speak very highly of you."

"And it's such a pleasure to meet you people as well," I said. Sandra, Brian and Jill said likewise.

After the introductions had been made and everyone was seated, we were served hunks of homemade peanut butter fudge and soda. (Brian, still feeling queasy, declined the refreshments with thanks.) Also present in the room was Lisa, the fiancée of Luis and Marjorie's son Clayton. As soon as Sandra had readied our video cam, the interview commenced.

As had been previously told to us by Bill and Nancy, the family had moved into this condo in Lewiston a little over two years ago. When they'd first moved in, however, they'd discovered various satanic-looking symbols and inscriptions painted on the walls of the basement, as well as on the walls of some of the upstairs rooms...particularly the room that their son Clayton always kept padlocked, so they informed us. I asked, "Why does he keep it padlocked?"

Lisa replied, "Well, Clayton feels that's where most of the evil spirits are in this house. And he's afraid that if we open up the room, they'll get out and do something terrible to us, probably kill us all."

"From what I've been told, some rather frightening things have already been happening here," I commented.

Right after moving in, the family had painted over the satanic inscriptions on the upstairs and basement walls. It was shortly after this that they were informed by neighbors that a group of young guys, who were practicing members of a local satanic coven, had previously occupied their apartment, and that they'd been known to hold rituals there prior to being evicted. In fact, there was even a rumor that these cult members had robbed a grave of a French Canadian man from a local cemetery for ritualistic purposes, and then buried his remains underneath the basement! (This was according to a psychic named Vickie who had recently visited the Ray family.)

It was also shortly after moving in, that Luis, Marjorie and the rest of the family began being met with one seemingly inexplicable mishap after another, almost as if a dark cloud of misfortune was following them everywhere they went. To make matters even worse, over the past several months Marjorie herself would periodically go into a trance-like state, where her normally gentle personality seemed to be completely taken over by some sort of malicious entity. Supposedly, this was the spirit of the French Canadian gentleman whose remains were rumored to be buried in their basement.

Nancy told us, "This is why we asked you guys to consult with us on this case. Whenever this personality overtakes her, she certainly doesn't seem to be Marjorie. It really seems as though Marjorie temporarily leaves, and something else takes over that's completely alien to her personality."

Bill interjected, "Nan and I have both been here to witness it when it happens to her. In fact, the last time this happened, I was holding Marjorie's hand, and all of a sudden she started squeezing my hand with a strength I couldn't believe. I cried out and was practically sinking down to the floor on my knees... and you know I'm not exactly what you'd call a small guy!"

"And her eyes change, too; they get very dark and sinister looking," said Nancy. She then added, "Wait a minute, I just realized something. Marjorie, every time you're about to go under, you always take your glasses off. That's one sign that it's about to happen."

"Do I?" asked Marjorie. "I don't really seem to remember much of anything afterwards, I just seem to sort of blank out. I guess I'm not really possessed though, like in 'The Exorcist', because I'm not like that all the time."

"Well," I explained, "in most cases of actual spirit possession, the afflicted individual is their normal self most of the time, meaning that the possession is transitory. The person usually only experiences temporary episodes of not being him or herself. Total possession is extremely rare."

"Really?" asked Marjorie. "Well, when it happens, I usually have to have other people tell me what I did. I know that one time my sister was over here visiting and I guess I scared her pretty badly. They say I suddenly looked up at her with this real mean-looking face, and I growled at her. She didn't want to stay around me too long after that, so she high-tailed it outta here!" Marjorie chuckled, and we all shared a momentary laugh.

"And how often do these episodes happen to you, Marjorie?" I asked her.

"Well, for awhile it was happening to me at least two or three time a week," she replied. "But, it hasn't happened for about two weeks now, so I don't think it's gonna happen tonight."

I asked, "Now, to your knowledge has this place ever been blessed?"

Marjorie replied, "Yes, a few months ago. We called in our local priest, and he did a general blessing of the house."

"Did he bless every room in here?" I asked.

"Well, I'm not sure," said Marjorie. She asked her husband Luis, who wasn't sure either. She then added, "I know he couldn't get into that upstairs bedroom, which Clayton keeps locked all the time."

"Oh, I see," I said. "Well, is there anything else you'd like to add?"

"Yes," said Marjorie. "It was a few weeks ago now, in the middle of the night while Luis and I were upstairs in bed, that all of a sudden we heard this big boom, or banging sound. So Luis turned over, and in the doorway, was what looked like a strange man, standing there looking at him! And that's when I fell out of the bed, and I banged my head when I fell. I wasn't seriously injured, but it sure shook me up!"

I asked Luis, "What did this man you saw look like?"

Luis explained, "Well, it was in the dark, so I couldn't really get a good look at his face or anything. But, from what I could see, he sorta' looked like an Indian fella. That's how I'd describe him."

"Could you see if he was wearing buckskin?" I asked.

"Yes, I think he was," said Luis. "And his face was very dark. He just stood there looking in on me for a few seconds, and then he was gone. And I had to make sure Marjorie was alright."

Sandra asked, "Did you see him too, Marjorie?"

"No, I didn't see him, just Luis did," she replied.

As our interview with the family concluded, I told them, "Now, I know that you've already had this house at least partially blessed. But Bill and Nancy have informed me that you'd like us to conduct a more thorough blessing of your house. Is this still your desire?"

"Yes," Marjorie replied without hesitation. "Another one certainly couldn't hurt."

Luis added, "We really would appreciate it,"

"Good, I'll be glad to conduct a blessing," I said. Looking at my fellow investigators, I suggested, "Well, maybe we should start in the basement?"

"Sounds good to me," Brian agreed.

"How're you feeling, Bro'?" I asked him. "You sure you're up to this?"

"Oh, yeah, I'm sure a lot feeling better than I was earlier," he assured me.

Before we ventured downstairs, Marjorie briefly spoke to us about the beautiful, ornate statue of the Blessed Mother, encased in glass, which was displayed in her parlor. "It's temporarily on loan to us from the church," she explained.

"I was noticing how beautiful it is," Sandra commented. "I mean, it looks almost like it's alive."

Nancy agreed, "Yeah, doesn't it, though?"

Brian also indicated a framed picture that hung on the wall, which we passed by on our way to the basement. "See that, Keith? It's Padre Pio."

"Yes," I said, "Padre Pio was quite a guy, very kind and loving to children. And he was also a stigmatic, of course."

"He certainly was," said Brian. "He also had the ability to bio-locate. Padre Pio truly was a saint."

We then made our way downstairs as a group to the basement, with Marjorie, Luis and Lisa accompanying us. As Sandra was setting up the camcorder, Marjorie reminded us, "It was on the walls over there that we found a lot of those symbols and strange writings, left over from those devil worshipers who lived here."

Brian commented, "No wonder there's so much negative energy here."

"We'll begin with an 'Our Father'," I announced to all who were present. "Our Father, who art in Heaven, hallowed be Thy name..."

Marjorie devoutly joined in the Our Father, while holding onto the Rosary beads that she'd brought with her.

After the recitation of prayers and the reading of selected Psalms and various other Scriptures, Brian and I proceeded to anoint the basement with blessed water and blessed oil. Suddenly Marjorie began to react, becoming noticeably short of breath and stooping over. "Marjorie, what's wrong??" asked Nancy, naturally concerned for the older woman.

Marjorie replied, "I...I don't think I can... stay down here for this any longer. I think… I'd better go upstairs now."

I asked Marjorie, "Are you going to be alright? Maybe we should discontinue for now."

"No, I-I'll be alright," Marjorie insisted. "I just have to go upstairs, and sit down for awhile...that's all." Her husband and Lisa then assisted Marjorie up the basement stairs, followed by Nancy Washell.

Brian also excused himself, saying that he and Jill were just going upstairs for a moment to make certain Marjorie was all right, and that they'd be right back down. Realizing they would let me know if there was an actual emergency, I continued blessing the basement, assisted by Sandra.

Immediately after the blessing of the basement area was concluded, Bill's assistant Harold, who also had extensive construction experience, took this opportunity to inspect the area of the basement floor where the remains of the French Canadian gentleman were rumored to have been buried. Shaking his head, Harold commented, "From what I can see, it just doesn't seem as though there'd be any way a body could be buried underneath here. There'd simply be more evidence of a recent disruption in the floor, plus the area's just not big enough."

"I hear ya," said Bill. "So, probably it was just a rumor after all."

Suddenly, Brian's voice called down to us from upstairs: "Keith! Keith, get up here quick, we need you!!"

Instantly I dashed upstairs, followed close behind by the others. "What is it?" I asked Brian.

"Marjorie's starting to go under!" he said.

In the parlor Marjorie was seated in her favorite chair, her chin slumped upon her chest, screeching out something in French. I asked

Sandra to recommence videotaping, as I quickly switched my small audio recorder on.

Nancy quickly explained to me, "Marjorie speaks almost entirely in French when this happens, which is her second language...although sometimes she uses some kind of garbled speech which we can't understand, that sounds like it could be Native American."

Nancy then rushed over and knelt beside Marjorie's chair. Handing Marjorie her cherished Rosary beads, she began telling her, "Marjorie...'Hail Mary'... 'Hail Mary'..."

Uncharacteristically, Marjorie disdainfully flung her cherished Rosary beads to the floor, as if the very touch of them was painful to her.

As Nancy had earlier pointed out, Marjorie had removed her eyeglasses when she'd began going under. Observing her physiognomy, I noticed that Marjorie's narrowed eyes did indeed appear very black and serpentine, and that her head continually swayed back and forth as she spoke. (This was a look that I myself had seen before, when confronting a possessed individual.)

I glanced over at Sandra and caught her eye. She was still holding the camcorder, and switching camera angles, as the situation became more intense. Although Sandra was as always the picture of calm professionalism, I knew what she was thinking...that at any moment, all pandemonium could suddenly break loose.

Taking a seat on the right side of Marjorie, her husband Luis began acting as translator for her.

"What is your name?" asked Nancy.

Marjorie continued screeching and shouting, until Luis deliberately asked her in French to give us her name.

"Edwaaaaard," Marjorie replied.

"Edward who?" Nancy asked through Luis.

"Pelletier," she said in a heavy French accent.

In my own rudimentary high school French, I asked her age. "Quel age avez-vous?"

In French, she replied harshly, "Quatre-vingts." ("Eighty.")

"Why are you here?" asked Nancy. "What do you want, Edward? You need to speak English to us."

Marjorie responded, and Luis translated: "She don't know how to say it in English."

Hesitantly, as if with an effort, Marjorie said, "I-I... don't...know." She then began loudly spouting in French again. As she spoke, Marjorie's breathing became increasingly labored, and she began to salivate profusely over her mouth and down her chin.

"Edward, did you live in Lewiston?" asked Nancy. "Are you from Lewiston?"

Marjorie slowly shook her head no.

"Where are you from?" Nancy asked again, and Luis translated.

"Canada," Marjorie replied.

"Where in Canada?"

"Montreal."

"Montreal?"

Marjorie slowly nodded, and began to cough.

I said ,"Ask him if he's sick."

"Edward, are you ill?" asked Nancy.

Catching her breath, Marjorie emphatically replied, "Yes! Oui!"

Nancy asked, "How did you get sick? What happened?"

Marjorie made no reply, but simply continued to choke and breathe in a labored fashion.

"What's wrong with you?" Nancy persisted.

"Ask him if he's alive," I suggested.

"Are you alive?" Nancy asked her.

"No. No!" she replied. (She again began to cough, as if suffering from lung disorder.)

"Why do you cough?" asked Nancy. "Why do you cough?"

When Marjorie did not answer, I decided to begin subtly leading the questioning into another direction. "Ask if he's on the other side," I said.

"Are you on the other side?" asked Nancy.

Marjorie hesitated before replying in French.

"She don't understand," said Luis.

"Where is your body?" asked Nancy. "Where is your earthly body?"

Marjorie motioned downward with her right hand, presumably indicating the basement. Luis said, "Right... here."

"Ask him if he sees other people there," I said.

"Do you see others where you are?" asked Nancy. "Do you see other people?"

Marjorie slowly nodded.

"Yes? Who do you see?" asked Nancy. "Do you see your family?"

Marjorie coughed, then replied in French. "She don't know that," Luis translated.

I then subtly began leading the line of questioning into religious provocation. "Ask him if he sees angels."

"Do you see angels?" asked Nancy. (No reply.) "What do you see? Tell us, what do you see?"

Marjorie shook her head, and again began to cough.

"She don't know," said Luis.

"Edward, you don't have this affliction any longer," said Nancy, as Marjorie continued to cough. "You don't need to cough."

Addressing this personality directly, I asked, "Do you ever see Jesus?" (The coughing abruptly ceased.) "Is Jesus there with you on the other side?"

"No...no," Marjorie replied,

"Who's there?" asked Nancy.

Marjorie sighed, and then replied in French, sounding increasingly distressed.

"Leave me alone," Luis translated. "Leave me alone, leave me alone."

Marjorie then began to loudly whimper, and writhe as if in pain.

"Edward, you need to move on," said Nancy. "You're hurting Marjorie, why are you doing this? What do you want?" (No reply.)

Now coming over to stand directly beside Nancy and Marjorie, I said, "Can you call upon the name of Jesus? Maybe Jesus will help you. Jesus shed His blood for the remission of sins." (Still no reply.) "We look to Jesus for the hope of the resurrection, and the life of the world to come. Jesus shed His blood for the remission of sins; the blood of Jesus, which was shed on Calvary. Jesus has the power to heal." (Marjorie gasped loudly, and again began to writhe as if in pain, her teeth bared.) "Marjorie is a child of God. Marjorie is a child of Jesus."

Marjorie then seemed to be quietly struggling to say the name of Jesus, but could not quite get the word out. "Je... Je...uh-uh... Jes...

deh... desus. Desus"

"How do you know Marjorie?" asked Nancy. "Where do you know her from?"

I asked, "In the name of Jesus Christ, where do you know Marjorie from?"

Without hesitation this time, Marjorie suddenly replied in a low, ominous tone: "I like her. I NEED her."

"In the name of Jesus Christ," I asked, "are you human? Are you a human spirit?"

"No," she softly replied. "No."

"In the name of Jesus Christ, what kind of a spirit are you?" I asked.

Marjorie then emitted a low, almost imperceptible laugh, seemingly more to herself than to us.

"Tell us," I persisted.

"THE DEVIL!!" she suddenly shrieked defiantly. "Deeeevil!"

Nancy turned to look at us with a shocked expression.

Now in a husky and combative tone, Marjorie began shouting at us in French, as her husband translated: "'Get the devil away from me! Get out of here!' That's what she's saying."

I then said, "The word of God according to the Psalmist: 'Touch not my prophets, nor do my anointed ones harm.'"

Realizing how unusually quiet Brian had been throughout this, I momentarily turned to look at him. There was a hint of green to his pallor. He was obviously still feeling somewhat ill, and seemed disconnected from what was occurring around him. As for Jill, she remained silently seated beside Brian on the sofa, saucer-eyed. Although Brian had been personally training her, this was the first time she'd encountered something like this on an investigation.

Meanwhile, Sandra continued to monitor the camcorder as the dialogue shifted from one person to the next, with Bill, Harold and Lisa standing directly behind her.

"Marjorie is a child of God, and you cannot remain in her," I said.

Now enraged, Marjorie gave a deep-throated growl, followed by guttural gurgling sounds, while thrashing about in her chair.

"You realize this?" I asked. She responded with more gurgling sounds.

I asked, "In the name of Jesus, how did you enter Marjorie?"

She coughed, and continued swaying her head from side to side.

"In the name of Jesus Christ, answer," I commanded. "How did you enter?"

Marjorie then began to protest loudly in French. Luis attempted to translate but was unable to keep up with her.

"In the name of Jesus, is your name really Edward?" I asked.

When she did not reply, Nancy questioningly looked up at me from her position on the floor next to Marjorie's chair.

I tried again. "In the name of Jesus Christ, what is your name?"

Marjorie replied in French. Luis translated, "She could give you all kinds of names."

"In the name of Jesus Christ, what name do you choose to go by?" I asked.

Although Marjorie did give some sort of a name, it was difficult to understand. At first she seemed to be saying "Mort" (meaning "Dead" in French). However, when I asked her to clarify, it sounded more to be a two-syllable name... possibly "Mu-el". She then began making loud, pathetic weeping sounds.

"You are suffering, aren't you?" I asked. "In the name of Jesus, why are you suffering?"

She replied in French, and Luis translated, "She says you won't leave her alone."

"In the name of Jesus Christ, Marjorie is a child of God," I said. "In the name of Jesus, what do you want?"

She then launched into a verbal tirade directed at me, screeching furiously in a mix of English and French. Her cursing was intermingled with enraged, animalistic growls and gurgling noises: "OW!! Leave me alone!" (Then in French): "Go to the Devil! Get the devil away from me!! GRRRRRRRR!! AAAAAAARRRRRR!! YEEEEEEEEEECCCHHH!!"

Throughout this barrage, Nancy had continued to hold onto Marjorie's hand, in an effort to comfort her and maintain communication. At one point, however, Nancy's eyes suddenly widened and her mouth opened in pain, as Marjorie began tightening her hold on Nancy's hand in a vice-like grip. Fortunately, I was able to momentarily distract Marjorie and quickly pry her fingers off in a matter of seconds.

Marjorie now began thrashing violently in her chair, growling and gnashing her teeth in frustration, as if somehow seemingly restrained by unseen bonds. Looking up at me with tears of concern in his eyes for his wife of so many years, Luis said quietly, "She's been through enough."

"Yes," I had to agree with him.

My heart went out with compassion for this older couple...especially for Luis, having to see his beloved partner in life reduced to such a bestial level. Although I sensed that the entity might have been weakening its grip on Marjorie, there was simply no way under the present circumstances, that I could submit her to anymore of this physical strain. Placing my right hand gently on her shoulder, I said, "In the name of Jesus Christ, you may go down now. In the name of Jesus Christ, go down, until you are called forth again. Marjorie, be at peace. Marjorie, be at peace."

Marjorie's growling began tapering off as I spoke, replaced by a quiet whimpering. Her eyes closed, and with a sigh, her glistening chin slowly slumped down to her chest. When she again looked up and opened her eyes, they'd returned to their normal hazel hue.

However, when Marjorie's own personality had fully returned to us, she was anything but at peace. Sobbing, she now once again held onto her cherished Rosary beads, which Nancy had handed back to her. "Mary," she said though her tears. "'Hail Mary, full of grace, the Lord is with thee.'" (Luis, Nancy and I all gathered around Marjorie in an effort to provide solace.) "'Blessed art thou among women, and blessed is the fruit of thy womb Jesus. Holy Mary, Mother of God, pray for us sinners, now and at the hour of our death. Amen.'"

"Amen," we all said.

When Marjorie had finished her prayer, she held out her arms in supplication to the life-like statue of the Blessed Mother across the room, and called out though her tears: "Mary! I love you, Mary! I don't want to go with him, Mary! I don't want to go with that devil! Please, I don't want to go with him; I want to go with you!"

I tried reassuring her, "You don't have to go with him, Marjorie. I swear, you never will."

Marjorie continued imploring the statue of the Blessed Mother. "Mary...you can make miracles. That's why they brought you here.

Make one now. Take him away, Mary! Help me, please, Mary. Give me a sign that he won't come back!"

Over the next twenty minutes, Marjorie gradually regained her composure. There was some talk about her perhaps going to the nearest hospital because of the difficulty in breathing she'd experienced, although she and her family later decided this was unnecessary. During this time, her son Clayton also arrived home. He was a dark haired young man somewhere in his thirties, about average height, with a stocky build. When his girlfriend Lisa came over to join him, I introduced myself, the other TAPS investigators, and Harold of Maine Paranormal. (Clayton was, of course, already acquainted with Bill and Nancy.) We then briefed him in on what had just taken place during his absence.

Clayton seemed delighted to have us there. When we'd finished our brief explanation of what had occurred over the past few hours, he commented, "Yeah, I heard you guys from Rhode Island were coming tonight; I was hoping you'd still be here when I got back." Glancing around at us, he then asked, "So, which one of you is the psychic?"

Brian, Jill, Sandra and I all exchanged glances with each other, before Sandra replied, "Well, we're not really 'psychics' per se. We're basically just paranormal researchers."

"Oh, really?" asked Clayton. "I was hoping that at least one of you would be psychic, so I could get your impression of what's down in the basement. There used to be some kind of witches or Satanists that lived here before we did, 'cause we found all of these strange writings and drawings on the basement walls when we first moved in."

"Yes, so we've been informed," I said.

Clayton persisted, "Are you sure you didn't get any impressions down there? Because we had a psychic over here before, and she got this impression that there's the body of some French Canadian guy named Edward buried in the basement, and that he's at unrest because his grave was robbed."

I asked, "And this is supposedly his spirit that takes over your mother's personality sometimes, correct?"

"Yeah, it is," said Clayton. "And I guess you guys got to see it happen to her tonight, from what you've told me, right? I was beginning to think no one would believe us, an' that everyone would think we were crazy! I know Bill and Nancy have seen it happen before, too."

"Well, we certainly don't think you're crazy," I assured him. "And as far as impressions go, I did get a very oppressive feeling while we were in the basement."

"Oh yeah?" asked Clayton, with anticipation in his voice.

"Yes, most definitely," I replied. "However, when I was questioning your mother while she was taken over by this personality, I used some religious provocation...and we found out that it might actually be an inhuman entity, which is masquerading as the spirit of someone named Edward."

"Oh-really??" Clayton asked in astonishment.

"From what she said, and the way that she reacted, we feel this may be a possibility," I told him. "But, what we'd like to do next tonight, is to complete the blessing here. We've already done the basement. Is that alright with you?"

"Yeah...sure, fine with me," said Clayton. "I'd really appreciate that. Maybe I'd be able to get some sleep here at night for a change!"

"Good," I said. "Now, I understand that there's a particular bedroom upstairs..."

"Oh yeah," said Clayton, shooting an apprehensive glance at me. "All except for that bedroom. I keep that room locked. I haven't even been in it myself since right after we moved in."

Brian asked, "Why? What's in it?"

"Uh, nothin.' It's just an empty room," Clayton quickly replied. "There's just some kind of an evil presence in there. That's why I always keep it locked."

I explained, "Yes, but that's why we're here, to try to remedy that situation. So I'd really need access to that room as well, to complete the entire blessing of the house."

Lisa interjected, "Clayton, these people are here to help. They know what they're doing. Then you wouldn't have to worry about that room no more."

"Trust me," said Brian, "letting us into that room so Keith can bless it wouldn't do any harm. In fact, it would expel whatever negativity is in there."

The more we attempted to persuade him, however, the more emotionally agitated Clayton became. It was apparent that he had some deep, personal issues concerning that locked bedroom upstairs. "No. No," said Clayton, becoming increasingly paranoid. "I-I can't...not now, not tonight. Maybe someday, but, I'm just not ready to take that chance yet."

Seeing that we were not about to make any further progress in persuading Clayton, we decided to simply continue with the blessing of the rest of the residence. After we'd completed a thorough blessing of the kitchen and the rest of the rooms in the downstairs area, all that remained were the staircase and the upstairs rooms... with the exception of the one bedroom that Clayton kept securely padlocked, of course.

Brian and Keith in Lewiston, ME.

Lisa volunteered to lead us through the upstairs area. As Lisa, Sandra, Jill, Brian and I slowly ascended the stairs, I recited a prayer for protection, while Brian followed up by anointing the stairwell with blessed water. Then, in each of the open rooms in the upstairs area, I recited the Lord's Prayer, followed by a reading of Psalm 23, as well as various other prayers and petitions for our protection, and the protection of the family living there. Brian followed by spraying blessed water in each corner of the room, while I anointed the doors and windows with blessed oil.

We then came to the padlocked bedroom door. After briefly examining the lock, Brian commented, "Well, there's obviously no way we're getting in there tonight."

"You're right," I agreed with him. "I suppose the best we can do is anoint the door itself."

Leaning close and cautiously whispering to us, Lisa said, "Clayton doesn't want anyone even touching the door. But, what he doesn't know..."

"What he doesn't know, won't hurt him," I said.

"Exactly," said Lisa.

Brian suggested, "Maybe we can spray some holy water underneath the crack at the bottom of the door. That might do some good."

While Sandra videotaped, I again led everyone in the Lord's Prayer, then followed up by anointing the padlocked door with blessed oil in the form of a cross.

As she continued to videotape, Sandra commented, "Holy cow! When Keith just did that, I could see two large anomalies shoot out from underneath the door."

Jill asked, "What do you think they were, Sandra?"

Sandra replied, "I'm not sure. I mean, they could've been nothing more than large dust orbs, but they seemed to be brightly illuminated. It just startled me for an instant."

Brian then proceeded to spray a generous amount of holy water underneath the padlocked door... the premise being that hopefully, enough of the positive vibrations would permeate into the room to counteract whatever negativity the room harbored. (Privately, I could not help but wonder what Clayton's reaction would be, when he noticed the cross-shaped smear from the anointing oil that I'd left on the locked bedroom door!)

When we returned back downstairs, I announced to the family that the blessing of their residence was now complete. Marjorie smiled and told us, "Thank you so much. Somehow, it does feel a little more peaceful in here."

"Yes, thank you," said Luis. "We appreciate everything you've done for us."

Sandra asked, "How are you feeling now, Marjorie? Physically, I mean."

"Oh, much better now, dear," she replied, although she still seemed somewhat weakened by her earlier experience.

Clayton asked us, "So, are the spirits gone now? I remember the psychic said that there are at least two other spirits trapped here, besides the one named Edward, whose body is buried in the basement."

I explained, "They may not be completely gone, but I feel that the activity will be considerably lessened. I've also attempted to introduce positive energy into the rooms of this house to counteract the negative, through prayer and by anointing the rooms with blessed water and blessed oil. And while we were upstairs just now, we said a special prayer outside of the locked bedroom, that the Holy Spirit will enter and keep everyone safe from harm."

Sandra added, "Through your faith, and by maintaining a positive attitude, I believe you'll be able to keep whatever negative spirits that may be here at bay. We've also prayed for angelic protection over everyone who lives here."

"God bless you for that," said Marjorie. Clayton also appeared to be at least somewhat relieved.

As we were conferring with the members of Maine Paranormal over our findings and theirs, Bill told us, "I think there's something you guys may want to see. I took this digital snapshot while you guys were in there blessing the kitchen area. Take a look at this large aquamarine colored orb which appeared on the back of Sandra's neck."

Sure enough, there in the digital snapshot of Sandra and myself, with Sandra's back inclined toward the camera, was a large bluish-green oval shape on the nape of her neck.

Sandra seemed a little uncomfortable. "I don't like the look of that," she said.

I asked her, "Did you feel anything at the time, like maybe a tingling sensation on the back of your neck?"

"No, not at all, which is a relief, " she replied.

Bill added, "It looks as though it's riding piggy-back on her!"

"It sure does," I agreed. I then explained the possible significance. "Although this could just be a camera glitch, the nape of the neck is sometimes considered to be an entry point for demonic spirits. But there is no cause for alarm; since Sandra didn't feel anything at the time. It seems more to have been probing her for a weakness it didn't find. Wasn't this taken soon after Marjorie had come out of her state of possession?"

"You're right, it was right afterward," Sandra recollected.

I added, "I've been in a situation involving demonic possession, where the spirit was systematically probing other individuals in the room at this exact spot. They all actually felt a tingling sensation but it wasn't able enter. So just to be on the safe side, I think I'd better anoint Sandra with some oil."

"Yes, I'd very much appreciate that," said Sandra.

I anointed the back of Sandra's neck with oil and recited a brief prayer of protection for her.

She turned to me, smiled and said, "Thank you, I do feel safer now."

Once again, the family expressed their heartfelt gratitude to us. Bill and Nancy of Maine Paranormal also thanked us for driving the distance to Lewiston on this icy, early January night to confer with them on their investigation. Bill told us "If there're any updates in the situation, we'll be sure to get in touch with you and let you know. Thanks again for everything, guys!"

Before leaving, I took the precaution of performing a general blessing upon everyone involved, to make certain that none of us would be "followed home" by anything negative.

During the return trip to Rhode Island, Sandra offered to take the first shift driving Brian's car (also affectionately dubbed the "Bro'-mobile"), while Brian himself passed out in the back seat next to Jill. "Thank you again for anointing the back of my neck with the blessed oil," Sandra told me. "It's somewhat disturbing to think something may have been searching for weakness in a possible entry point of the demonic. I'm glad it didn't find any."

(Although the anomaly in the photo which appeared on the back of Sandra' neck may also have simply been a light reflection, Sandra was still pleased that I'd taken no chances.)

Sandra turned around to look at Brian in the back seat and commented, "So, it was quite an interesting case tonight, right, Bro'?"

Brian groaned and shifted position so that his head was in Jill's lap, but didn't answer.

Jill said, "He's obviously still really out of it. So anyway, guys, what will happen to the family, now?"

Knowing this was all somewhat new territory for Jill, I explained, "What I attempted to do, in this case, was to move the existing negativity into a dormant state. In other words, I may have temporarily put it down, but I didn't completely drive it out. It's the best we could do with the limited time we had. However, I have a feeling that we'll be returning to Lewiston."

Sandra agreed with me.

Chapter 13

The Maine Possession Case - Part 2

It was on a seasonably hot and humid mid-morning in August of 2004, that Jason Hawes, Grant Wilson, Carl and myself, Brian Harnois, Steve Gonsalves and Andy Andrews, along with several production members of Pilgrim Films, set out for the vicinity of Lewiston, Maine. There were actually two "possible possession" cases to be documented and filmed as segments that weekend, the first being on the way to Lewiston... and both cases required my participation. (Unfortunately my wife Sandra would not be able to join us this time. This factor caused me to feel quite depressed, to say the least.)

Several days before, I had spoken at length over the telephone with Carol, our first client who we'd be dealing with, who'd contacted us complaining of spiritual problems which were seriously affecting her ability to function normally in everyday life. The very next day both Carl and Brian had arrived at her house during their day trip to Maine (prior to their visit with Marjorie Ray), and had conducted a lengthy preliminary interview with her. Carol was a slim, attractive woman in her early forties who'd been divorced a number of years. Although she lived alone, she kept in touch regularly with her teenage and young adult children, who often came there for extended visits. For the past five or so years this woman had been troubled by predominately male voices in her head. Recently, these male voices had assumed a harsh quality and increased the frequency of communication with her, to the point where it was now almost constant. As a result, Carol had become convinced that she was now under "possession" by these intrusive entities. She'd also willingly agreed to the idea of having a film crew present during our upcoming investigation.

When we arrived at her home just outside of Lewiston that afternoon, Carol cordially welcomed us in. After the film crew had set up their equipment in her parlor, Carl and Grant conducted an official interview. After this I asked the woman a series of questions related to the supposition that her psyche was being invaded and partially manipulated by spirits. At the conclusion of my own interview with her, I recited certain select Scripture passages, and then asked her to please join with me in prayer, which she did.

Suffice it to say, we found no overt or convincing evidence to indicate Carol was experiencing actual episodes of possession, demonic or otherwise. She seemed painfully sincere, and I believe she may have truly been experiencing these intrusive male voices, which lately had been practically denying her a moment of peace. However, when I asked Carol if she had experienced any loss of self or episodes of time unaccounted for, her answer was no. There was no reaction at all to religious inference. She may indeed have been undergoing some level of spiritual oppression, for which I did pray with her. Then again, she may also have been suffering from some sort of mental affliction. We explored a number of possibilities with her, off camera and confidentially. At any rate, our function as paranormal investigators in any given situation was to look for possible evidence of paranormal activity, and to honestly and objectively evaluate our findings. After subsequently evaluating our data in this case, we came up negative.

However, this of course does not mean we simply abandoned our client. Rather, Grant and Carl and I spent a good amount of time personally reassuring her that no matter what she may be experiencing, we were still only a phone call away, day or night. We did ascertain that Carol had previously been undergoing professional counseling, and we strongly advised her to continue with this.

It was then time for us to set out for our next destination.

A rain shower had begun to fall by the time we arrived at Pine Hills in Lewiston. Marjorie Ray's son Clayton, who was attired casually in a checkered shirt, hunting cap and faded jeans, welcomed Brian and Carl and me in first. "Hi, guys" he said, shaking hands with us. "Thanks for coming all this way again."

Clayton's girlfriend Lisa was there to greet us as well. "Hey, it's really nice to see you guys again!" she said, giving us each a hug.

Luis, dressed in his customary rumpled white shirt, suspenders and black trousers, was also delighted to see us. Luis explained to us that although Marjorie had not been feeling well earlier that day, she had by now recovered, and was certainly anticipating our visit.

When Marjorie did slowly enter the parlor to greet and welcome us, she was wearing a violet colored housecoat over a nightgown, and slippers. "Thank you so much for coming," she told me. "Now… you're not the brother who was here several days ago?"

"No, that was my brother Carl over here," I said. "He was here with Brian."

"My goodness, you and your brother do look alike," she said with a chuckle. "So you're the one who was here back in January."

"Yes, that's right," I said.

I then introduced the others as they entered. "Marjorie, I'd like to introduce Jason Hawes and Grant Wilson, the founder and co-founder of TAPS."

"It's a pleasure to meet you, Marjorie," said Jason.

"Yes, it's indeed a pleasure, Marjorie," said Grant, adding, "Keith has certainly told us a lot about you, and we've been looking forward to finally meeting you in person."

Marjorie apologized, "You'll have to excuse the housecoat. I'm afraid I'm not properly dressed to be meeting you people, but I'm sure my family's told you, I wasn't feeling well earlier."

"That's quite alright," Jason assured her. "I just hope you're feeling up to our visit today."

"Oh, I'll be okay," Marjorie said with a slight wave of dismissal. "Besides, I've been looking forward to your visit. I guess now I'd better go upstairs and make myself look presentable."

I asked her, "Marjorie, are you sure you're feeling up to this today?"

"Oh, yes… just give me a few minutes, and I'll be back downstairs," she replied. Marjorie then shuffled over to the staircase, and began slowly ascending the stairs while holding onto the railing for support.

Lisa rushed over and asked Marjorie is she needed assistance, but she assured Lisa she'd be fine.

One thing I noticed right away was that the ornate statue of the Blessed Virgin, which had been displayed during our last visit, was no longer there in the parlor. When I inquired about it, Lisa explained that the statue had been returned to their local parish church, which it had been on loan from.

By the time the production crew had set up most of their equipment, Marjorie had come back downstairs, now looking freshened with her hair done nicely, and wearing an attractive flowered dress. "Oh, you look very nice, Marjorie," I complimented her.

Brian agreed, "Yes, you certainly do, Marjorie."

"Oh, thank you," she told us. "I wanted to look at least halfway presentable. Sorry I wasn't fixed up when you first arrived."

"Oh, by the way, Marjorie, this is Andy Andrews," I said, introducing him.

"Hi, Andy," she said, shaking his hand. "Welcome to my humble abode."

"It's a pleasure to meet you, Marjorie; I've heard so much about you," said Andy.

After we'd introduced the members of the production crew to Marjorie, we of course expressed our sincere sympathies to both her and her husband Luis, on the loss of their youngest son. They both thanked us very much for our concern, explaining that Bobby had been the unfortunate victim of a fatal altercation with the local police, in which illegal drugs had been involved.

Marjorie added, "I suppose you've been told, that Bobby recently appeared to me, standing right over there on the stairs."

"Yes, so Carl and Brian informed us," I said gently. "Exactly how long ago was this?"

"I'd say about two weeks ago now," she replied.

Andy wanted to know, "Now, when you saw him, Marjorie, did he say anything to you, or attempt to communicate in anyway?"

"No, he didn't say anything at all," said Marjorie. "He just stood there looking at me for a moment, and then he was gone."

Brian asked me, "Residual, maybe?"

I replied, "Perhaps this was what's sometimes referred to as a crises, or transition apparition, especially if he was intentionally making eye contact with her. This suggests that he was probably aware of her presence."

"Good point," Brian agreed.

Meanwhile, neighbors from across the parking lot had somehow received word that the "Ghost Busters" had arrived. Having managed to momentarily catch Steve Gonsalves' attention while he was outside in the rain unloading equipment, a young woman had waved him over, calling out, "Hey! We need help over here!"

After quickly alerting Jason and Grant to the situation, Steve and Brian, both responded to the cry for assistance. Upon returning several minutes later, Steve informed us that it had turned out to be nothing more than a ruse apparently intended to lure him into the apartment. "There was a woman sprawled on the sofa, obviously completely stoned out of her mind," Steve explained. "She could hardly even hold her head up, let alone talk straight. And she and some girl, who I assume was her teenage daughter, were telling me to come inside and help them out, because they had ghosts. They said their neighbor from the next condo over had told them that a group of 'ghost busters' were here!"

With the cameras, sound and lighting equipment now in place, we were ready to commence the initial on-camera interview with Marjorie. Jason and Grant proved very adept at putting the older woman at ease, as she sat comfortably in her favorite chair and related the chain of bizarre events, which she and her family had experienced since moving into their present location. "I know that the rest of my family has still been experiencing things in here," Marjorie told them. "We always get an uncomfortable feeling down in the basement. Of course, Luis and I don't go down there much anymore, especially since it's so difficult for us to make it up and down those basement stairs. But one time we had a psychic over here, whose name was Vickie, to see if she could pick up on anything... and this psychic told my son Clayton that there's a man whose body is buried down in the cellar. And I suppose if it's true, then he could be one of the spirits that are here."

Jason and Grant then approached the topic of Marjorie's episodes of suspected demonic possession. After she'd related the basic details to them, Grant asked, "And when this happens to you, how much of it do you actually recall, once you've come out of it?"

"Well, not too much," she explained. "Most of it's hazy, and some of it I don't really remember at all. I have to rely on other people to tell me afterwards everything I said and did. I've been told that my eyes become real dark, and mean looking,"

Jason asked, "When was the last time you experienced one of these episodes, Marjorie?"

"Well, it hasn't happened in quite awhile now," said Marjorie. "But, I don't feel that it's completely left. I still get the feeling sometimes that I'm not alone, and that it's still with me... inside of me sometimes."

When it came to the rather sensitive subject of Marjorie's sighting of her late son's apparition, Grant respectfully asked, "Marjorie, would you mind sharing with us about the recent sighting which you experienced on the staircase? The one involving your late son Bobby?"

Marjorie replied, "Well, it was one night just about a couple of weeks ago, I was coming around the corner intending to go upstairs, when all of a sudden, I saw my deceased son, Bobby, standing right there on the stairs in front of me. He didn't say anything, but just stood there looking right at me, and then he was gone."

"Did you attempt to communicate with him at all?" asked Grant.

"No. I was just too shocked, it all happened so fast," said Marjorie. "One moment he was there, and the next, he wasn't."

Jason asked, "Did he look like he did in life?"

"Yes, exactly, except that he didn't have any facial expression, just a blank stare," Marjorie replied.

Gently, Grant asked her, "Do you feel as though he was trying to tell you something?"

With a sigh, Marjorie said, "Well, I don't know. He died so suddenly. Maybe he's still here, or... or maybe he just came back, to say good bye." She paused to dab the corners of her eyes with a tissue.

"Thank you, Marjorie," said Grant. "Now in conclusion, I'd like to ask, what would you personally like to see accomplished from our visit here today?"

Reflectively, Marjorie replied, "Well, for one thing, I guess I hope you find some proof that these things are really going on here, and that we're not all nuts." (They all shared a laugh.) "And, I hope that whatever spirits are here can finally be put to rest, and that if there is still a spirit inside of me, it can be gotten rid of once and for all."

"Well," said Jason with his reassuring smile, "that's what we have Keith here with us for."

"Oh, yes. I like Keith, very much," said Marjorie.

Next on the agenda would be a tour of the house itself, which Lisa would lead us on, starting with the basement. As the members of the production crew were repositioning their equipment, Marjorie asked me, "By the way, Keith, where is your lovely wife, today? Isn't she with you this time?" Luis and Lisa wanted to know as well.

"Unfortunately, Sandra couldn't make it this time," I replied. "I really miss her being by my side."

"Oh, that's such a shame! She's so sweet," said Marjorie.

"Yes, she is," I agreed.

Luis added, "You just make sure you come up to visit us again, and that you bring Sandra with ya! Okay?"

"It's a deal, Luis," I assured the kindly older gentleman with a smile.

Downstairs in the basement, the atmosphere did feel rather thick and oppressive, although I was certain that the added humidity was at least partly responsible. After making a methodical sweep throughout the basement with a digital thermometer, Steve announced, "The temperature down here seems to be holding steady, at seventy-four degrees…except over here near the stairs, where it goes down to seventy-two."

Brian and I pointed out the small section of the basement floor, where the visiting psychic had claimed to sense the presence of human remains. I explained to everyone else, "One of the members of Maine Paranormal who was here has extensive experience in laying foundations. And after examining this area, he claimed that it's extremely doubtful, if not impossible, that a complete body could be buried underneath here. There's certainly no sign of the concrete recently being disturbed."

Brian held his Gauss meter over the area, which indicated only a slight energy spike. "Could even be a minor electrical current under here, although nothing to write home about," he concluded.

Next, Lisa led us to the upstairs area where the bedrooms were, including the room that Clayton kept securely locked. Turning to Jason and Grant, Brian announced, "So, guys, this is the infamous locked bedroom door."

"That it is," Jason agreed, examining the padlock.

Huddling closer to us, Lisa whispered, "Clayton would have a bird, if he knew we were even up here touching the lock."

In a lowered voice, Jason asked her, "So, Clayton's had this door locked ever since he and his family first moved in here?"

"Yes, almost right after they first moved in, I'd say in the first week," Lisa confirmed in her hushed tone.

"Lisa's right about Clayton," said Carl. "He's completely obsessed, and adamant about keeping this room securely locked at all times, for fear of what's inside."

"A proverbial 'Pandora's Box'," I added.

Grant asked, "Well, what the hell IS inside?"

I said, "According to Clayton, it's completely empty."

Nervously, Lisa began urging us on, saying, "We better not stay up here too long, or Clayton might start getting suspicious."

Ignoring her, Brian swept his Gauss meter along the crack underneath the door. Turning to Jason, he commented, "I'm definitely getting some spikes from underneath here, dude!"

"Yeah, but that could be anything," said Jason. "I mean, we can't even get inside the damn room to investigate."

"That's right," Grant agreed. "And what's more, we definitely need access to that room, for Keith to properly conduct a thorough blessing."

Jason said, "Well, all I can say is, we'll have to cross that bridge when we come to it." We then moved away from the padlocked door and continued on our tour of the upstairs area, causing Lisa to breathe a temporary sigh of relief.

Back downstairs it was almost time for me to begin the deliverance session with Marjorie. Before we began, Andy and two members of the production crew asked me if I could explain to them why Marjorie's eyes had appeared to "black out" when she'd been under apparent possession. I said, "When a person is in a full state of possession, the eyes will often be wide and staring, with what could be described as a wild, unearthly look of hatred. However, there are also times where the afflicted individual's eyelids with be narrowed, and the eyes themselves will assume a darkened, almost serpentine appearance, which was apparently the case with Marjorie while she was under. At other times, the person's eyes will simply roll upward until only the whites of the sclera are visible. Or, the eyes will roll around wildly, as if in spasm. Grant has also witnessed this in the eyes of the possessed. Now, the reason for this is that the possessing entity is deliberately attempting to avoid eye contact. If someone is conducting any sort of deliverance over a possessed individual, direct eye contact seems to lend greater control to the person performing the deliverance."

They thanked me for my explanation. I then excused myself and retired to the kitchen area, where I began reading Scripture in preparation for what was ahead.

Minutes later, glancing up from my open Bible which rested on the kitchen table in front of me, I saw both Jason and Grant approaching. "So, you ready for this, Buddy?" Jason asked me. "Everything's all set up in the parlor."

"Ready as I'll ever be," I said, rising from my seat.

"I know you can do this," said Jason, reassuringly placing a hand on my shoulder. "We've been through a lot together, and I have total confidence in you."

Grant added, "We'll both be right there in the room with you, my friend."

"Thank you, guys," I told them with a smile. "That means a lot to me, and I'm glad you'll both be there. I really appreciate your support."

We were now ready to begin. With Marjorie once again seated comfortably in her cushioned parlor chair, I was positioned in one of the smaller chairs beside her to the immediate right, allowing me to face her. Luis was seated nearby, in case he was needed to translate for Marjorie like the last time.

After checking with Dave who was manning the camera, sound technician Frank announced, "We're good to go."

"Whenever you're ready, Keith," said Jason.

"Alright, Marjorie," I began, "I understand you haven't had an episode of being completely taken over for awhile now, is that correct?"

"That's right, I haven't," she replied. "At least not completely, the way it used to happen,"

"But, you personally feel as though it's still with you, oppressing you?"

"Yes, I definitely feel that it's still with me. I don't know if it's just been laying low for awhile, or what."

"And you'd like me to help you to rid yourself of it, and stop it from further oppressing you?"

"Yes, if possible, I'd like you to."

"Very well, Marjorie. If you would, please join with me in prayer. Let's begin with an 'Our Father'." Noticing that she was holding onto her Rosary beads in her right hand, I gently took hold of her free hand, and began reciting the Lord's Prayer. Marjorie closed her eyes, bowed her head, and prayed along with me.

At the conclusion of this prayer, Marjorie looked back up at me, with her accustomed peaceful expression. "Now, Marjorie, I'd like to read some Scripture, from the New Testament," I said. Turning in my Bible to the Book of Hebrews, Chapter 9, I read verses 11 through 14 out loud: "When Christ came as high priest of the good things that are already here, he went through the greater and more perfect tabernacle that is not man-made, that is to say, not a part of this creation. He did not enter by means of the blood of goats and calves; but he entered the Most Holy Place once for all by his own blood, having obtained eternal redemption. The blood of goats and bulls and the ashes of a heifer sprinkled on those who are ceremonially unclean sanctify them so that they are outwardly clean. How much more, then, will the blood of Christ, who through the eternal Spirit offered himself unblemished to God, cleanse our consciences from acts that lead to death, so that we may serve the living God!"

When I was done reading, I asked her, "How are you feeling?"

"Alright," she said quietly. (Although there was a somewhat distant look to her eyes, no dramatic change was apparent. Also, one indication that Marjorie would be about to go under was that she'd remove her glasses. But since she was not now wearing her glasses, I could not use this as a warning sign.)

"Now, Marjorie, I'd like to pray over you." Placing my right hand lightly on her shoulder, I began an invocation. "In the name of our Lord and Savior Jesus Christ, whose blood was shed for us at Calvary for the remission of our sins, we ask that if there be any unholy spirit inside of Marjorie, it reveal its presence to us now. In the name of Jesus, we ask that, without harming Marjorie or anyone else in this room, this invading spirit give us a sign of its presence. Amen."

Still, Marjorie displayed no overt reaction. Deciding that this might be a good time to attempt a direct confrontation with the entity, I said,

"Marjorie, I'd now like for you to maintain eye contact with me. I'm going to try to bring the spirit forward now. Do you understand?"

"Yes... I understand," she replied almost dreamily.

"Good," I said. As a precaution, I first quoted the Psalmist: "'Touch not my prophets, nor do my anointed ones harm.'" Gazing intently into her eyes, I then said, "In the name of Jesus Christ, I am now addressing the unclean spirit inside of Marjorie. Come forward, now. By the authority of the shed blood of Jesus Christ, come up to the surface, and reveal yourself."

For a moment, Marjorie's gaze slowly began to drift away from me. "Please continue to look at me," I said. (She did as instructed, her eyes now appearing vague and slightly clouded.) "In the name of Jesus Christ, let that which is unholy, and not a part of Marjorie Ray, come forth." (A pause.) "Come forth out of hiding now, and reveal yourself to us."

Almost imperceptibly, Marjorie's eyes began to narrow, and her upper lip curled into a slight sneer. Sensing that I was now making progress, I continued: "In the name of Jesus, are you the spirit who has been oppressing Marjorie, and invading her body?"

When she did not reply, I asked again, "In the name of Jesus Christ, are you the unclean spirit who has been oppressing Marjorie, and taking over her personality?"

"Yeeeees... yeeeees," she answered.

"What is your name?" I asked. "In the name of Jesus, identify yourself."

"I...don't... know," she said quietly.

Recalling the two garbled names she's given me back in January, I asked, "In the name of Jesus Christ, is your name 'Mort'?"

"No," she replied.

"Do you go by the name of 'Mu-el'?" I asked.

She slowly shook her head no.

"But you are the spirit who has been residing inside of Marjorie? In the name of Jesus, answer truthfully."

"Yes," she replied without expression.

Now positioning my right hand slightly above Marjorie's head, while maintaining close eye contact, I said, "Then in the name of Jesus Christ, I declare that you must leave Marjorie, now! Depart from this temple of God. In the name of Jesus, may you now be cast out of Marjorie, never to return to her!"

Marjorie's eyes closed for a moment, then reopened, still with that somewhat vacant look. I asked, "In the name of Jesus Christ, who are you?"

"Marjorie," she replied quietly, almost as if hypnotized.

"In the name of Jesus Christ, are there any unclean spirits still inside of you?" I asked.

"No," she said flatly.

"Marjorie, how do you feel now?"

"Peaceful," she replied in the same flat tone. "I feel at peace now."

"Do you feel that the oppressing spirit is now gone from you?" I asked her.

"Yes... I feel it's gone from me now. Thank you, very much," she said quietly.

"I'm so glad, Marjorie," I told her, resting my hand on her shoulder. "God bless you."

All through this, Clayton had been sitting upon the parlor sofa, observing in silence. Although he made no comment now, Lisa - who'd been standing by the stairs - approached us and said, "For a moment there, Marjorie, I saw your face starting to turn mean, just like it used to. Right then I thought that you were gonna start freaking out again!"

"It did?" Marjorie asked her with a light chuckle.

"Yes, I noticed it too," said Carl, also coming forward.

"Well, I guess this time I wasn't as wild acting as usual," said Marjorie, in a subdued tone.

Grant asked, "But you do feel better, Marjorie?"

"Oh, yes, much better," she replied. "Just a little tired, that's all."

"Well, that's understandable," said Grant, rising from his seat. "Well done, Keith!"

"Yes, great job, Keith!" said Jason, also rising from his seat.

"Thank you, guys," I said. "And thank you for being here."

"Not a problem," Jason assured me.

Luis suggested, "Maybe you'd like to go upstairs and take a nap for awhile, Marjorie?"

"Oh, no, I think I'll just sit here for awhile," she said.

Coming over to me, Carl said, "Yes, that was extremely well done, Keith. How are you feeling now?"

I told him "Oh, I'm fine. Just a little drained, I suppose, but otherwise all right."

Jason then announced, "I think we could all use a little breather. How about we take a few, and allow Keith a chance to get his second wind? Then afterward, Keith can start blessing the house before we leave." Addressing Marjorie and Luis, Jason verified, "That is what you people would like, right?"

"Oh, yes, we certainly would," replied Marjorie.

"Yes, definitely," confirmed Luis. "Keith does a good job at that."

Glancing over at Clayton, I noticed him flinch slightly.

As Carl and I sat together at the kitchen table, Lisa came over with two large glasses of soda, with plenty of ice, and set them down before us. "Here ya go, guys," she said pleasantly.

"Thank you, Lisa," said Carl. "These will sure go down well right about now."

"Yes, thank you very much, Lisa," I told her.

"You're welcome, guys," she said with a smile.

As soon as she'd walked away, I leaned toward Carl and whispered, "The thing is, I need Sandra to be here with me now; I need her support, as well as her experience with this case."

"Yes, I know, and I sympathize, Keith," Carl whispered back. "Just remember, after filming this case there shouldn't be any reason why you should ever have to be on an investigation without Sandra by your side."

I nodded agreeably.

Very quietly, Carl then asked me, "What did you think of the way Marjorie reacted, during your deliverance session with her?"

Leaning closer to him, I whispered, "Well, it certainly wasn't like when we were here back in January, when she went off. I mean, there were no bells and whistles this time, so to speak... no blackening out of her eyes, no cussing me out in French, no labored breathing, and no excessive salivating. I mean, in a way it's fortunate that it wasn't as traumatic, especially since she wasn't feeling well earlier."

"Yes, I noticed that she was considerably more subdued than on the video," Carl agreed. "And how would you account for that? You think the fact that it's daytime might have limited the spirit's ability to function?"

"Yes, I suppose that could have had something to do with it," I said. "Possibly it's the atmosphere in here today, too, with so many unfamiliar people here. But, remember when Marjorie's facial expression started to change for just a moment?"

"And she briefly took on that sinister look? Yes, I noticed," said Carl.

I said, "Well, right after that, when I was actually addressing the entity, I had the impression that the spirit personality was only partly coming through... and that Marjorie's personality was also present, simultaneously. It hadn't completely taken over her, like it has in the past. You know what I mean?"

"You're suggesting she may have only been in a state of 'partial possession'," said Carl.

"Exactly," I whispered. "Or, maybe even oppression. That's why I could really have used the assistance someone with of the full spiritual gift of Discernment."

"Well," said Carl, "as you know, my personal belief is that in cases of severe oppression, when an actual spirit entity is involved... and this also goes for cases of possession... there's almost invariably a psychological factor involved as well, regarding the afflicted individual. There has to be some psychological or emotional vulnerability, to allow an incorporeal intelligence to invade the psyche. In fact, in the majority of cases I believe it's ninety-eight percent psychology, and two per cent parapsychology."

"Hmm-hmm," I acknowledged. "I'm of the same opinion. And we can only hope and pray that Marjorie's affliction doesn't reoccur, especially since we don't happen to have a psychoanalyst available."

Adding some levity, Carl said, "Well, at least we've got Brian. Next best thing."

Following refreshments, Jason, Grant, Brian, Steve, Andy, Carl and I gathered around the kitchen table and reviewed a possible EVP I'd captured on audiotape while in the basement, during our initial investigation back in January. Basically it was undecipherable, although it definitely sounded like a male voice briefly whispering some sort of chant. There was also the photo taken by Bill Washell of my wife Sandra, with the aquamarine colored orb seemingly riding piggyback, as he'd put it, on the nape of her neck. After each of us had closely examined the enlarged print of the photo, we still had to admit that it was inconclusive.

One of the cameramen named Dave then approached me, along with Frank the soundman, and asked if I could elaborate on camera about the two names I'd mentioned, when trying to identity the spirit inside of Marjorie. "Sure," I said. "During our initial investigation several months ago, while I was performing my original session with Marjorie, she'd given two names while under possession, which were what sounded like 'Mort' and 'Mu-el'. Now, 'Mort' is a French word meaning 'Dead,' while 'Mu-el' sounded as if it could be an angelic name, because of the 'el' connotation at the end, meaning 'of God', since angels are messengers of God… such as the archangels Michael and Gabriel, for example. However, after the first investigation, my wife Sandra and I did a search for the name 'Mu-el', but we were unable to find it. Of course, that doesn't necessarily mean that this was the entity's actual name."

"Thanks Keith, very much," Dave said when I'd concluded.

A minute or so later, Jason came over to me and asked, "So, you doing okay Buddy?"

"Sure. Ready to start the blessing, whenever you'd like," I said.

"Listen, before we start the blessing, I'm going outside for a cigarette and to chill for a moment. How about joining me?" asked Jason.

"Sure, I could use a breath of fresh air right about now," I replied.

Outside the rain had tapered off to light drizzle, as Jason and I leaned our forearms on the metal railing outside on the front steps. Casually glancing around the parking lot, Jason said, "So, like I said before, you and me have sure been through a lot together over the past several years. And we've certainly come a long way."

"You said it," I agreed. "And again, I'd like to say how much it meant to me, to have both you and Grant in the room there with me, while I was going through the session with Marjorie. Now, I guess all we have to do is the cleansing of the house from room to room, before we wrap things up for the day."

"Yeah," said Jason. "Speaking of which, we've really got to try and convince Marjorie's son Clayton that we positively, absolutely need to have access into that locked bedroom, if we're going to complete what we came here to do."

"Well, that won't be easy, knowing how paranoid Clayton is about keeping that room locked," I said. "And both Luis and Marjorie have given Clayton final say about that room, so they certainly won't dare to override him."

Jason said, "Well, then we'll just have to work on Clayton. Anyway, getting back to the session with Marjorie, how did you feel about that, the way she was reacting, and how she came out of it?"

"To be honest, it all seemed a bit too easy," I said. "First of all, she didn't put up as much resistance as she did back in January. And also, this time she didn't really seem to have totally gone under, like she did last time. And she didn't seem to have fully come out of it, either. She seemed like she was dazed or something, both during and after."

"Yeah, I noticed that too," said Jason. "And you're right, it did seem to go a little too easy this time. So, are you wondering the same thing I am?"

Glancing over at him, I asked, "That perhaps the entity only pretended to leave Marjorie, and it could still be inside of her?"

"That's exactly what I'm thinking," said Jason, now turning to face me as well. "Something just didn't feel right about it."

"Well, that certainly is a demonic strategy," I said. "It does happen sometimes, in cases of possession. A spirit only pretends to leave at first, hoping that if it simply hides itself for awhile, everyone will naturally just assume it's gone."

"And you and I have been around these sort of things too long, to simply give up and leave without a fight, if we're not totally convinced the situation's been taken care of," Jason reminded me. "Plus there's also the fact that we have an episode to wrap up filming today. So, if you're feeling up to it, I think we should ask Marjorie if she'd mind you trying one final test, just to make certain that everything's totally gone. What do you think?"

"You don't have to ask twice, Jason," I told him. "I'll just announce to her that it's simply something we normally do in such situations, just as a final precaution."

"Alright, Buddy!" said Jason, smiling and slapping me on the shoulder. "Like I said before, I have total confidence in you. Hopefully we'll be able to wrap things up and get out of here within the next few hours. I know you're anxious to get home, and so am I. Now let's go back in there and do this."

Actually, I was presently feeling even more drained of energy than before and depressed over Sandra not being there with me. Although Jason and Grant had earlier been singing my praises to Marjorie and her family, I was certainly not feeling very adequate at the moment. What was more, I would now be performing an impromptu exorcism with the cameras rolling. Nonetheless, I realized that it was now or never, and this family desperately needed our help. It was for this reason, I believed, that the Lord had led us here.

After praying for success in this endeavor, as well as for the protection of everyone involved, I approached Marjorie and explained to her that I would like to do one brief, final prayer session with her. "This is just a standard precaution we take, to make certain once and for all that the invading spirit is completely gone. Would you be agreeable to this?" I asked her.

"Oh yes, that seems like it would be a good idea," Marjorie readily agreed.

"Good," I said with a smile. "Then let's all gather around exactly like we did before. This shouldn't take long at all."

(Indeed, beforehand I had resolved that this would be over as quickly as possible. For one thing, owing to Marjorie's weakened condition, I had no intention of putting her though the ordeal of a prolonged struggle, as had happened back in January. For another thing, if I could succeed in provoking the demonic personality to manifest, I was determined that this time, it would not elude me before I'd dealt with it.)

After once again taking my seat beside her, as she sat comfortably in her large, cushioned easy chair, I said, "Alright, Marjorie, we'll begin with an 'Our Father,' just like we did before. Please pray along with me, as we recite the prayer, which Jesus gave to us: 'Our Father, who art in Heaven, Hallowed be Thy name...'"

Again holding her Rosary beads in her right hand, Marjorie prayed along with me flawlessly. "Amen," we said together, at the conclusion of the Lord's Prayer.

Then turning to the New Testament, I announced, "Next will be a reading from the Gospel of Luke, Chapter Ten, verses seventeen through twenty: 'The seventy-two returned with joy and said, 'Lord, even the demons submit to us in your name.' He replied, 'I saw Satan fall like lightening from heaven. I have given you authority to trample on snakes and scorpions and to overcome all the power of the enemy; nothing will harm you. However, do not rejoice that the spirits submit to you, but rejoice that your names are written in heaven.'"

Next, I chose to once again read from the ninth chapter of Hebrews, making certain to place emphasis on the sections where the blood of Christ was mentioned. "'How much more then, will the blood of Christ, who through the eternal Spirit offered himself unblemished to God, cleanse our consciences from acts that lead to death, so that we may serve the living God!'"

Closing my Bible at the end of this Scripture reading, I looked up and smiled pleasantly, at the same time making certain to closely scrutinize Marjorie's facial expression. Just as I'd hoped, there was the barely perceptible, glazed look of unrest to her eyes. "And now, Marjorie, I'd like to pray with you again," I said. "Jesus, our Lord and Savior, in Your name we ask for angelic intervention. In Your name, we ask that this daughter of Abraham be set free from any unclean spirit, which may be oppressing her. Send Your Spirit down upon Marjorie, Lord, and touch her with Your healing power. May she be covered with Your blood, which was shed for us on Calvary. Amen."

Although Marjorie's eyes did not black out, they had now become quite glossy. "The blood of Christ be upon you, Marjorie," I said. "The blood of Christ be upon you."

Marjorie's breathing suddenly became noticeably labored. The sneering expression returned to her face, and she dropped her Rosary beads onto her lap. "In the name of Jesus Christ, are you Marjorie?" I asked her.

"No," she replied in a husky voice, between intakes of breath.

"In the name of Jesus Christ, who are you?"

"Edward."

"Edward who?"

"Pelletier."

"Where are you, Edward?"

"Down," she wheezed, motioning downward with her left hand in a clawed position. "Down... there."

Refusing to further indulge these delay tactics, I then asked directly, "In the name of Jesus Christ, is your name really Edward?"

She cast her glance downward, and began to turn away.

"Look at me," I said firmly. "In the name of Jesus Christ, are you really Edward? Are you a human spirit?"

"No," she grudgingly replied.

"In the same of Jesus Christ... what kind of spirit are you?"

She again averted her glance. "In the name of Jesus Christ," I repeated, "What kind of spirit are you? Speak truthfully."

"A devil!" she hissed with an air of defiance.

"So, just like before, we have again established that you are not Edward, but that you are instead a spirit of Perdition," I said. "Why are you doing this to Marjorie? Why are you inside of her?"

"I like her," the entity replied as before. "I need her."

"In the name of Jesus Christ, do you have a legal right to be inside of Marjorie?" I asked pointedly.

After a moment's pause, she reluctantly replied, "No."

"Then why are you inside of her?" I asked.

"I need her body, to live through," she replied.

Noticing that her breathing was now slightly less labored, I decided to briefly pursue this line of interrogation. "But by staying in her, you're also inflicting great discomfort on Marjorie. Why are you doing this to her? In the name of Jesus, answer truthfully."

"Because...because of...because..." she murmured, her voice trailing off. She then began to cough.

"Because of what?" I asked as soon as she'd caught her breath. "Answer, in the name of Jesus Christ."

She then replied, "Because of… Clayton."

"Because of Clayton? What about Clayton??" I asked.

"Because… she cares about Clayton. Marjorie loves Clayton, and cares about him. And-I-want-her-all-for-myself!" the entity declared.

(So, Marjorie's emotional attachment to her son Clayton seemed to be the key! The theory Carl and I shared about the psychological/emotional vulnerability factor had proven correct.)

"In the name of Jesus Christ, do you have any connection to the bedroom which Clayton keeps locked upstairs?" I asked.

"Noooo," she replied.

"Are you ever in that upstairs bedroom?"

"Noooo."

"On the authority of Jesus Christ, is there more than one of you inside of Marjorie?"

"No. I'm the only one."

"On the authority of Jesus Christ, is there ever more than one of you inside of Marjorie?"

"No. Only me."

For a moment, I suddenly discerned that the entity was once again beginning to retreat. "In the name of Jesus Christ," I said quickly, "on the authority of His shed blood, do not go down! How did you first enter Marjorie?"

"I just entered her," the spirit reluctantly answered.

Marjorie again began to avert her gaze. "Look at me," I directed. "In the name of Jesus–"

"I HATE YOU!!" she suddenly shot back, now turning to face me again.

"You hate me?" I asked. "Well, the time has come, and you are now going to have to leave this child of God. And when you leave, in the name of Jesus Christ, you will give me a sign of your departure."

With a sigh she again began to turn away. "Look at me," I said, commanding the entity's attention. "By the power of Jesus Christ, you are now compelled to leave this child of God. You will go to Jesus, to be dealt with as He will. Let the Holy Spirit now descend, and free this daughter of Abraham."

"I'm strong!" the entity said, in an effort to intimidate.

"You may be strong, but the power of Jesus Christ is ultimately stronger," I said.

Gritting her teeth, Marjorie began to writhe, although the intense ferocity she'd previously exhibited was no longer apparent.

"In the name of God the Father, God the Son, and God the Holy Spirit," I prayed, "let Marjorie be covered in the precious shed blood of Jesus Christ. Covered by the blood, covered by the blood, covered by the blood. May a mighty warrior angel of God be present with us, Lord, and may Your servant Marjorie be set free…"

Suddenly closing her eyes and throwing her head back, Marjorie let out a long, baleful cry: "AAAAAAAAAWWW!!" She then slowly raised her head, opened her eyes and blinked.

"Marjorie?" I asked. "Marjorie, are you alright?"

The look in her eyes and the tone of her voice were now altogether different, as she quietly replied, "Yes…yes, I'm alright." She then smiled at me, with such an expression of serenity to her face that she truly seemed to be free of her oppression.

"How do you feel now, Marjorie?" I asked her.

"I feel very peaceful, and relaxed," she replied.

As a final precaution, I handed Marjorie back her Rosary beads and said an additional prayer, asking in the name of Jesus that if any oppressing spirit remained, it reveal its presence. Since Marjorie demonstrated no adverse reaction whatsoever, I asked her to join me in a prayer of thanksgiving." Joining hands with her, I prayed: "Almighty God we praise and thank You, that through Your divine mercy, Your servant Marjorie has been delivered from the captivity of this spirit of darkness. Let the precious blood of Your Son Jesus continue to cover her, and the Holy Spirit continue to dwell within her. In Your holy name we pray with thanksgiving... amen."

"Amen!" Marjorie repeated with conviction.

Grant then asked, "So, Marjorie, how are you feeling? Better?"

"Yes, I'm actually feeling much better," she replied. "It does feel something like a weight off of me."

Smiling delightedly, her husband Luis remarked on just how clear her eyes now appeared.

Grant agreed. "Yes, Marjorie, your eyes do look so sparkling and clear!"

"There's even a certain radiance to them," I added.

Marjorie blushed slightly, and chuckled with embarrassment at all the sudden compliments she was receiving.

As my brother Carl and I began to prepare for the final blessing of the residence, both Jason and Grant pulled their chairs up in front of Marjorie to further interview her. Jason asked, "So, you're feeling better now than you did before, Marjorie?"

"Oh, yes, so much better," she replied.

On my way into the kitchen area to join Carl, I happened to glance at Clayton, who was seated on the sofa with Lisa beside him. Because he'd been in and out of the house a few times over the last hour, I really had no idea just how much of the deliverance session he'd paid attention to. However, since he'd now removed his hunting cap and his jacket, it appeared as if he planned on remaining inside for now.

When both Brian and Steve then emerged from the basement after having taken some EMF readings, they paused for a moment to converse with each other in hushed tones. At one point, I overheard Brian quietly mention the words "upstairs, next"... which Clayton had apparently also overheard, since his head instantly turned to their direction.

Because Jason and Grant were presently being filmed interviewing Marjorie in the parlor, it was arranged that cameraman Dave would accompany Carl and I down into the basement. Once the three of us were in the basement, Dave commented, "It's hard to breathe down here; the air's really thick." He then asked us, "Are you guys feeling anything unusual down here?"

"There is a noticeable heaviness to the atmosphere in this basement," Carl agreed. "How about you, Keith? Are you feeling anything?"

"Yes, it does feel somewhat oppressive," I said. Turning to Dave, I explained, "When Marjorie and her family first moved into this place, they found satanic writings on the walls down here. There were references to satanic worship, the number '666' and all sorts of blasphemies and anti-religious symbols. So, presumably, the people who lived here just before they moved in were involved in satanic worship of some sort, and they obviously introduced negative energy into this place."

"So, it's really focused down here?" asked Dave. "You're feeling it really heavy?"

"I feel it very heavily right now," said Carl. "And I sense it may be with us down here now, although sometimes these things do tend to be elusive."

I added, "One thing about inhuman demonic entities, is once they've been invited in, they're hard as hell to get rid of. They don't necessarily leave when you tell them to. They're generally easier to bring in than they are to expel."

Dave then wanted to know exactly what I happened to be experiencing at that precise moment. "I'm feeling pressure around me," I said. "A little difficulty in breathing… the air down here seems quite heavy. It's as though whatever's here is issuing a warning for us to proceed no further, that we're infringing upon its territory. We have no right to be here. That's the impression I'm getting, very heavily, right now." Since I already had my tape recorder going, I said, "I'm asking that if anyone has any messages, please give them now."

Standing at a certain spot near the center of the room, Carl commented, "You know, I like to consider myself not given to fancy, or suggestion. But right here, it's palpable, electric. It doesn't feel so much evil or oppressive to me right now, but as soon as I stepped into this radius here, a sensation like an electrical current went down through my thorax, and through my left arm."

I asked Carl, "Are you feeling the heaviness too, like a weight?"

"I'm not feeling that; it was more like a tingling sensation," said Carl.

In a further attempt to possibly obtain an EVP, I asked, "Is there something you'd like to say?" After a pause, I asked, "Does the name Edward mean anything to you? Please give a message or some sort of sign, now."

Upon reviewing the audiotape, however, the EVP session yielded nothing definitive.

When we were prepared to commence with the blessing of the basement, Dave asked, "What have you got there, Carl?"

"I'm going to pass Keith the cross he uses to conduct a blessing," Carl explained. "He'll also be using holy water and blessed oil."

"Thank you," I said as Carl passed these items to me.

Carl said, "If you don't mind, Keith, I'll be following you around with the digital recorder."

For some reason, I was now getting the distinct impression that whatever unseen force might be down here in the basement with us was now moving about. Focusing upon the area directly over the floor where human remains were rumored to have been deposited, I held the cross in my right hand, ready to proceed with the blessing. Suddenly, my brother Carl began to appear a bit unsteady. As Dave and I both shot a questioning glance in his direction, Carl explained, "Now I feel it... that sensation of electricity; I feel that so strongly right through my legs, making my knees weak..."

Realizing that I'd never seen Carl react in quite this manner before, I rushed over to offer him assistance. Carl then became so off balance, his knees began to buckle. Dave instantly grabbed a nearby aluminum chair and slid it over to us. Leaning upon my arm for support, Carl apologized and said, "I'll tell ya, Keith, I've never felt anything just like this."

"No?' I asked, easing him down into the chair.

"No, it's... it's just since I moved into that radius, where you were feeling oppressed before," replied Carl.

"It seems to be moving around, and building," I remarked.

"What do you mean by 'building'?" Dave wanted to know.

"The energy seems to be building," I replied. "It's almost as if it's getting ready to do something, even if it's just to keep in motion."

"It's like a surge of electrical energy," Carl reiterated. "And I agree, it does seem to be moving, almost as though it's playing a game of cat and mouse with us."

I then announced, "In the name of Jesus Christ, I bind you to the framework of this cellar, and command that you will not leave, until you are dealt with according to His divine justice!"

As Dave readied his camera, I then began the blessing of the basement area by reciting Psalm 23. "The Lord in my shepherd; I shall not want. He maketh me to lie down in green pastures..."

When the blessing of the entire basement had been completed, we returned upstairs, whereupon Jason and Grant called all TAPS members together outside for a private meeting. The seven of us all gathered in a group outside by our parked vehicles. Leaning against the TAPS van, Jason told us, "Alright, guys, here's the scoop: Obviously, as much as we like these people, we don't want to wind up having to make a trip back up here every other month. But, in order to wrap things up properly here today, we positively need access into that padlocked bedroom. Now, I don't know if you're all aware of the situation, but Marjorie's and Luis's son Clayton was just on the verge of freaking out in there, because he's absolutely terrified about opening the door and letting us in there. And his girlfriend Lisa isn't helping matters any."

Andy asked, "Excuse me Jason, but, what exactly is he afraid will happen if he does open it for us?"

"Oh, he probably thinks he's got Satan himself locked up in that bedroom, and Armageddon will be unleashed if he opens it!" said Jason.

Straight-faced, Steve suggested, "Of course, we could always just kick the door in, and tell them it was an accident."

Brian chimed in, "Believe me, dude, that thought crossed my mind!"

"There's the cop in you speaking up, guy," Grant told Steve with a smile.

"Which brings me to a point," said Jason. "Me and Grant have been discussing our possible options, and this is what we've come up with. Steve, as part of your police tactical training, you've had to be trained in negotiations, haven't you?"

Waxing serious, Steve affirmed, "Yes, that is part of required training at the police academy."

"Good," said Jason. "So what I need from you, Steve, is to use your negotiating skills, to try and convince Clayton into letting us into that room. Would you be willing to do this?"

"Absolutely," Steve replied without hesitation. "I'll certainly give it my best shot."

"Excellent, Steve," said Jason. Turning to me, he added, "Keith, I'd like you to be with Steve when he talks with Clayton, since you tend to have a calming effect on people."

"Will do, Jason," I assured him.

Turning to the others, Jason said, "Andy and Carl, I'd like the two of you to keep both Luis's and Marjorie's attention diverted away from what's going on with Clayton, as much as possible. Just keep them focused on discussing their situation and what's being done about it, or whatever. Meanwhile, since we can't be sure exactly how Clayton will react, Grant and Brian and I will be keeping a close watch over everything that's going on, including making sure the film crew's out of harm's way should he suddenly freak out." Sweeping a serious glance over each of us, he asked, "Alright, is everyone clear on exactly what his position is?"

We all agreed that Jason's instructions were perfectly clear. Each one of us understood exactly what was expected.

"Alright then, guys…let's go in there as a team, and take care of this situation once and for all," Jason told us.

"Let's do this, guys," added Grant, giving us a double thumbs-up. He and Jason then led us back inside the condo.

As soon as Andy and Carl had successfully managed to engage both Luis and Marjorie in conversation, Steve and I approached Clayton, who was seated beside Lisa on the sofa at the other end of the parlor. Smiling politely, Steve asked, "Hi, Clayton. Would you mind if we just had a word with you for a few minutes?"

"Uh, sure, no problem," he replied.

"Good," said Steve, as we both pulled up chairs in front of him. "So, how're you doing, Clayton?"

"Oh, I'm doin' okay, just fine," Clayton replied.

Glancing at Steve's arms, Lisa smiled and commented, "Say, those are some pretty neat tattoos you got there!"

"Thank you," said Steve.

"Yeah, I was just noticing them too," said Clayton, who was obviously also impressed.

"What exactly are they of?" asked Lisa.

"Mostly Star Wars illustrations," said Steve, holding out his arms to enable both Clayton and Lisa a closer inspection.

"Wow! Did you get 'em all at once?" Lisa asked.

"No, this was actually over the course of three years," Steve explained. Casually folding his hands together, he then said, "So, Clayton, would you mind if I asked you a question, about that upstairs bedroom?"

"Uh…no, I wouldn't mind," he said.

"Why do you feel that it's necessary to keep it padlocked?" asked Steve.

Hesitantly, Clayton replied, "Uh...um... for everyone's safety."

"Why for everyone's safety? I don't quite understand," said Steve.

"Because there's evil in there," said Clayton.

"Why, what exactly is in that room?" asked Steve.

"Nothing, really. Just a bed, and some cardboard boxes. That's all," said Clayton.

"So, what's so evil about that?" asked Steve.

"There's evil spirits in there," explained Clayton. "That's why I keep it locked all the time, so they can't get out."

"But you still have a key to that padlock, right?" asked Steve.

Shifting uncomfortably in his seat, Clayton replied, "Yeah, but I never use it. I haven't been in there myself for over a year now, y'know?"

"Hmm... must need some serious dusting in there by now, wouldn't you think?" asked Steve, with his pleasant smile.

However, Steve's light-hearted tension breaker was lost on Clayton. "But you have to understand, I never go in there anymore, for any reason, ever," he said.

"Well, I do understand that you keep that bedroom off-limits to everyone," said Steve. "But, you know, Clayton, just because you keep the door padlocked, that doesn't necessarily mean that whatever spirits may be in that room can't still effect you and your family. Now, Keith's pretty much blessed the rest of the entire house here. And I feel that if you were to let him in to bless that one bedroom that's left, it might take care of the problem once and for all."

Becoming defensive, Clayton said, "But if I open that door, that'll allow 'em to escape."

"Allow what to escape, Clayton?" asked Steve.

"The evil spirits," Clayton replied. "I'm afraid that they'll get out, and then they'll kill us all!"

"But I'm telling you, Clayton, that Keith's had years of experience doing this, and you can trust him to handle the situation safely," said Steve.

I also tried to assure him by saying, "That's right, Clayton, this can be handled safely. You wouldn't even have to be right there, if you don't want to. In fact, if you'd prefer, one of us could unlock the door, and it would take less than ten minutes for me to properly bless the room. It's up to you."

Clayton glanced apprehensively from me, to Steve, and then to Lisa for support. "Listen to them, Clay," Lisa gently urged him. "They're only trying to do what's best for you and your family. Then you wouldn't have to worry about that room up there no more, honey."

"No... no, I'm not ready to open that bedroom door yet," he told us. "Maybe I'll be ready next time you guys come over here."

Steve attempted to reason, "But why not let us do it today while we're all here, and get it over with? Like Lisa said, then you wouldn't have to worry about the spirits escaping from the bedroom anymore."

"That's right," I said. "Then I could spiritually seal the room, through prayers and with blessed oil."

"So what do you say, scout?" asked Steve, lightly patting Clayton's arm in a friendly manner.

"I... I say, I don't think I'm ready for this right now," he replied, becoming visibly more agitated. "Next week, I'm supposed to start seeing a new doctor, so hopefully she'll be able to help me. Then maybe I'll be ready to unlock the door."

"You were seeing a doctor regularly before?" Steve asked him.

"Yes," said Clayton. "I used to be on tranquilizers, for hypertension."

"But you're not taking any medications now?" asked Steve.

"No. But, I'm pretty sure my new doctor will prescribe some new medication for me. So next time, I should be ready to unlock the door for you guys," Clayton explained.

Steve reiterated, "Clayton, there's no guarantee that there will be a next time. So, that's why we feel it's imperative that you grant us access to that room before we leave today. So, if I might offer another suggestion, do you think that maybe you'd feel more comfortable, if you just gave us the key to the lock, and you and Lisa waited outside the house while Keith blessed the room?"

"No," Clayton was adamant. "Because then the evil spirits would be loose in the house when we came back in."

Steve asked, "What if Keith and I were to give you a guarantee, that the spirits would be completely gone by the time you came back inside?"

"Well, no," said Clayton, "because they might come back in and attack us after you guys have left!"

"That wouldn't happen, Clayton," said Steve. "Not if Keith does his job thoroughly, which I know he will. You see, I've been with Keith when he's done these types of spiritual cleansings before. That's how Keith and I first met, when I asked for his assistance in a case which involved evil spirits."

"So please, Clayton," I implored him. "Your mother and father want this to happen, so they can sleep peacefully at night. Lisa wants this to happen. And I promise that none of you will be attacked while I'm doing this, or after we leave. The most that will happen is that the spirits will simply move on to someplace else. So, what do you say?"

Steve said, "It's just up to you now, Clayton, to give us the go-ahead."

Now beginning to stammer and hyperventilate, Clayton replied, "N-No, I canna-no do that! Next time you guys come down here - or up here - I'll probably feel more comfortable about lettin' you in that bedroom!"

Steve then instructed, "Alright, Clayton, listen to me. Right now, I just want you to take a deep breath. Can you do that for me, Clayton? Just take a deep breath, and then let it out slowly. Okay?"

"Okay... okay," Clayton panted.

Demonstrating mutual support, both Steve and I breathed in deeply along with Clayton, held it for a moment, and then slowly exhaled together. "Very good, Clayton," Steve told him. "Now, are you feeling any better? Any more relaxed?"

Appearing slightly less agitated, he replied, "Yeah…I'm feelin' a little more relaxed now."

"Good," said Steve. "Now, without getting upset, I just want you to calmly consider what we've been discussing, about possibly allowing us access into that bedroom upstairs."

However, as soon as the locked upstairs bedroom door was mentioned again, Clayton's paranoia returned with full intensity, this time accompanied by whining and wheezing sounds between intakes of breath. In fact, he appeared completely and utterly terrified, as if he were about to be led to his own execution. Realizing that Clayton was now on the threshold of a potentially violent panic attack, Steve and I finally relinquished our attempts to coerce him into permitting us access into the upstairs bedroom.

"It's alright, Clayton," I told him, lightly patting his shoulder. "Just forget about it for now. No one's going to force you into anything. Be calm, be still." Gently taking hold of Lisa's hand and placing it into Clayton's, I added, "You have someone right here who loves you, and you're among family, and friends. It's alright now."

"Thanks, Keith," said Clayton, his breathing gradually becoming slightly less labored, although he was still noticeably trembling.

Lisa then clasped his hand in both of hers, and told him, "It's okay now, honey. It's okay."

Upstairs once again, with Carl assisting me, I began the blessing of the bedrooms and the hallway with the 23rd Psalm, followed by Psalm 91. At the top of the stairway, I also recited a prayer for the spirits of the deceased: "Merciful Jesus, who takes away the sins of the world, grant them rest. Merciful Jesus, who takes away the sins of the world, grant them rest. Lamb of God, who takes away the sins of the world, grant them rest eternal. Amen."

There was then nothing left, but the padlocked bedroom door in front of us. Carl commented, "It seems the best that you can do, Keith, is to simply anoint the outside of the door, and hope it takes effect. Unfortunately, I guess we'll never know the exact cause of Brian's EMF reading of one-point-nine, although the explanation was most likely mundane."

"Yes, most likely," I agreed with a sigh. "Well, we may as well commence, and then the blessing of the condo will be completed, as far as we can go."

Smearing the blessed oil onto the front of the door in the shape of a large cross, I said, "In the name of the Father, and of the Son, and of the Holy Spirit, we bless and seal this door, declaring that anything unholy which may be connected with it be nullified, and rendered inactive." After also anointing all four corners of the door, and all along the edges, I tossed some holy water underneath the door, as far into the room as it could possibly reach. "In the name of Jesus," I said, "may anything unholy which dwells within this room be cast out. And in its place, we ask that an angel of God be sent to watch over this room, and to guard against any evil presence which may attempt to dwell within."

By now, I was feeling emotionally spent and overwhelmed with frustration over being denied access to the locked bedroom. This was combined with the fact that I was acutely missing having Sandra by my side, to lend her support and professionalism. Leaning both my hands against the bedroom door, I began pushing against it, as if it would somehow automatically open for me this way. Carl, sensing that I was about to collapse from exhaustion, placed his hands on my shoulders and told me, "Keith, you've done all that you can. It's over now."

After lowering my head and nodding in agreement, I slowly backed away from the door.

When Carl and I had returned downstairs to the first floor once again, we reported to Jason and Grant and the others that the blessing of the upstairs area was now complete. "At least, to the extent that we were allowed," I added. (Still seated upon the sofa beside Lisa, Clayton appeared greatly relieved.)

Grant then told us, "Listen, before we wrap things up, I'd just like to go downstairs into the basement for a few minutes, by myself, off camera. It's a personalized type of blessing I'd like to perform, which I believe will help."

"Sure, Grant," Jason gave him his approval. "If you'd like to add to the blessing in your own way, that'll be great. Go for it."

As Grant also looked at me, I told him, "The Lord be with you, Grant. We're certainly blessed with your experience."

"Thank you, Keith," said Grant, placing his hand on my shoulder in a display of mutual faith. He then proceeded downstairs to the basement by himself.

When Grant emerged from the basement several minutes later, he acknowledged to Jason, Carl and myself that his own additional blessing was completed, and that everything had gone well. Since this was obviously something personal to him regarding his faith, I respected his method and experience without asking him for details.

Approaching Luis and Marjorie, Jason then told them, "Well, this pretty much wraps up our investigation here today. As you know, Keith has blessed the entire apartment, with the exception of the upstairs bedroom which Clayton keeps locked. What we'll do now is go back to TAPS Headquarters in Rhode Island, review our evidence, and then our next step will be to come back and let you know our findings. Now, do either of you have any questions at this time?"

"No," said Marjorie, "I think that pretty much covers it all. We want to thank you all very much, for all that you've done for us!"

"Yes, thank you so much!" said Luis, gratefully shaking hands with Jason.

"You're very welcome; we're glad to help in any way we can," Jason told them both.

Luis then came over to me and warmly shook my hand as well. "Thank you, so much," he told me. "Come see us again. And you make sure you bring your lovely wife with you next time!"

"That I will, Luis," I promised him.

Marjorie placed her arms around me, and said, "So good to see you again, Keith. And thank you, again, for everything you did for me today. Tell your wife we missed her, and we look forward to seeing her again."

"She'll be glad to hear that, Marjorie," I said. "And it's been so good seeing you again, too."

Marjorie then asked Jason and me, "So, when can we expect to see this episode on your new show...what's the name of it again?"

"'Ghost Hunters'," replied Jason. "And as of yet, I really have no idea exactly when this particular episode will air. But, as you know, the series itself will be premiering in mid-October."

Coming over to join us, Carl said. "And we'll certainly keep in touch, so we'll be sure to let you know."

"Yes, please do that," said Marjorie, embracing Carl. "And you make sure you come up and visit us again, like we were just telling your brother. In fact, I'll make spaghetti for you when you come up again!"

"Oh, that sounds delicious!" said Carl. "We'll be sure to be back, now."

Marjorie also gave Brian a hug, telling him, "So good to see you again, too. And I'm glad you didn't get sick this time!"

"I'm glad too, believe me!" Brian told her.

As I was packing up, Clayton (who was now considerably more at ease than he'd been earlier, when the pressure had been on him) approached me. He appeared anxious to share the details with me, about how his only sister had met with her untimely demise a few years previous. "They initially tried to rule it as a suicide," Clayton informed me. "But after examining her, the coroner declared that not only was she shot, she was also severely beaten beforehand."

"I'm so sorry to hear that, Clayton," I commiserated with him. "Where was her body found?"

"Actually, not too far from here," said Clayton. "She was found along a path right down in the woods nearby. Me an' Lisa go walking there sometimes."

"So, did they ever find out who did it?" I asked.

Shifting his weight back and forth, Clayton replied, "Well, they figure it was drug related, an' there was a lot of cover-up involved. An' the coroner was supposed to testify, and reveal his findings to the court. But, he himself died, less than a week before he was supposed to reveal his report on my sister's death."

"He died? How??" I asked.

"He himself was murdered, shot to death, although they never found out who did it," said Clayton. "In fact, I even got copies of the newspaper articles about it all. I'll give you a copy, to take home with ya."

In the kitchen just before we left, both Lisa and Marjorie insisted that Carl take a container of Chinese food along with him, for the long ride home. They also spoke with both Carl and I about their impending eviction, which was partially due to a sudden and dramatic rent increase. Carl asked, "How long are the landlords giving you, before the final decision is made?"

With a sigh, Marjorie replied, "Well, we've only got until the first of next month to get this resolved, which I know is only a couple of weeks from now. But don't worry, we'll fight this in court if we have to!"

Unfortunately, another reason the family was facing possible eviction, was the result of Clayton's stubborn refusal to allow the housing authorities into the padlocked upstairs bedroom for a full inspection. However, both Marjorie and Lisa seemed to feel confident that they had valid legal grounds, for denying the housing authorities access into the room.

Outside in front of the condo several minutes later, as Carl and I were loading equipment into the van, we discussed some basic aspects of the case. Carl asked me, "Do you personally feel that there's any validity to Clayton's claims, about there being dangerous demonic entities sealed up in that padlocked bedroom?"

"Personally, no," I replied. "At least, I doubt it. But, who knows? I could be wrong. I just didn't sense any 'pulsating evil' emanating from the bedroom door."

"Well, I tend to agree with you on that point," said Carl. "It's most likely nothing more than Clayton's own personal psychosis. The main problem is that Luis and Marjorie and Lisa are diametrically opposed to disagreeing with Clayton on this issue, or on anything else for that matter. And they're also under the disillusionment that they can somehow use this in court, to prevent a full inspection of the apartment."

I asked, "Do you think they actually believe that the court will accept Clayton's testimony, that this room is dangerously haunted?"

Carl said, "Well, from the way Marjorie was talking about it, she seems to feel they have a pretty good chance. Of course, when Marjorie told me that, I initially wanted to advise her, 'I wouldn't count on it, Ma'am.' But of course, I kept it to myself."

"Just as well," I said. "Hopefully, when the reality of the situation sets in, they'll see reason. Anyway, we've all done our part; now all that remains is for us to review and collate our evidence. I just wonder what Jason's opinion is of everything that went on today."

"Hey, guys!" said Jason, suddenly stepping over to join us, and slapping his hands on our shoulders. "Did I just hear my name mentioned?"

"Hey, Jason, speak of the devil!" I said. "Yes, we were just discussing how the entire investigation went today, and wondering what your take is on everything that went down."

Jason said, "Well, as you guys were just discussing, we'll have to go over all the footage from today. And it's unfortunate, Keith, that Marjorie's son Clayton wouldn't allow us access in that locked upstairs bedroom, so you weren't able to complete the blessing. But, I want you to know, as always, you guys both did a great job today, and I really appreciate everything."

"Thanks, Jason," said Carl. "So glad that at least we were all kept safe."

"Yes, thanks, Jason," I said. "It's always great working together with you on a case."

Just outside of Lewiston on our way back home, we stopped for refreshments at the first pizza restaurant we came to. By now, I was fortunately beginning to feel considerably less drained than before.

At the conclusion of our meal, I briefly stepped outside into the parking lot for a breath of fresh air, and to clear my mind just a little. As Jason had told us, we'd all done our best, and in that we could feel satisfied. Soon we'd all be back home with our families, with an interval to rejuvenate ourselves before our next upcoming case... whatever that may turn out to be.

Suddenly, I heard the sound of footsteps quickly approaching me from behind. Swiftly turning, I recognized the figure of soundman Frank, hurrying towards me. Frank touched my left arm and asked me, "Keith, just before we left the house, who did the family give that container of Chinese food to? Was it you, or your brother Carl??"

"Well, it was Carl," I replied.

Without another word, Frank turned and dashed off in the opposite direction while holding onto his hat, in search of Carl. Obviously, word of the Chinese food had just gotten out, and caused Frank to develop a desperate craving!

THE REVEAL

Three days later, Jason and Grant, along with the film crew, returned to Pine Hills in Lewiston. When they were seated at the kitchen table with Marjorie, Luis, Clayton and Lisa, both Jason and Grant told the family how good it was to see them again. Luis said affably, "It's so nice to see you fellas again, too."

Marjorie asked, "Where's everybody else this time?"

Jason explained, "Well, this is just the reveal, where we share our findings with you. If it were an actual investigation like the last time we were here, then we'd naturally have the rest of the team with us."

"Oh, I see," said Marjorie.

Grant then told the family, "So, we've reviewed our findings, and as Jason has just explained, we're here to go over them with you. First of all, I'd like to ask you people how things have been here, since our last investigation which took place three days ago."

Marjorie answered, "Oh, things seem to have quieted down quite a bit here. We haven't experienced anything at all for the past few days, not even at night."

Luis added, "It seems you guys really took care of the problem, and we really appreciate all that you did."

"Yes, thank you, very much," Lisa added with a smile.

"You're entirely welcome," said Grant. "That's what we're here for. And Marjorie, how have you been feeling?"

"Oh, quite well, I've gotten most of my energy back by now," she replied.

"And how are you doing with the spiritual oppression you were experiencing?" Grant asked her. "Have you experienced any more of those attacks, where you feel your personality's being taken over?"

"No, not at all," said Marjorie. "Ever since Keith prayed over me the other day, I've been feeling so much better. It seems that the demon, or whatever it was, is really gone from me now."

"Well, I'm very glad to hear that, Marjorie," said Grant. "Keith and his brother Carl have been with us a long time. Now, as far as our other findings are concerned, we did manage to pick up some rather high readings on our Electro Magnetic Field detectors, both in the basement, and in the upstairs hallway, particularly right outside the padlocked bedroom door."

Jason then said, "As I'm sure you're all aware, the main problem is that we couldn't properly complete our investigation of the entire condo, or Keith's blessing of your home, because of Clayton keeping that bedroom closed off. This being the case, I'm afraid we'll have to rule our findings as inconclusive."

Turning to Clayton, Grant said pointedly, "Alright, Clayton, I'm going to appeal to you one last time, and to the rest of your family as well, to allow us into that bedroom. As Jason, myself, Steve and Keith have already explained to you, no evil spirits are going to attack you for opening that door. In fact, I can guarantee that you and your family will not be in any personal danger whatsoever. So, what do you say?"

Nervously, Clayton replied, "I-I'm sorry, guys, but…but I just don't feel I'm ready for that yet. There's nothing in there but a bed, an' some boxes of junk, mostly old magazines. I just keep it locked, so the evil spirits that are in there won't be released. But I had an appointment with my new doctor yesterday afternoon, an' she might wanna put me on some new medication… s-so maybe next time I can do it. But not right now."

"Final answer?" asked Grant.

"Y-Yeah. Final answer," said Clayton. Apologetically, he added, "Sorry, guys."

"That's all right, it's cool," Grant told him. Glancing around at the others, he asked, "And how do the rest of you feel about this?"

Following an awkward moment of silence, Marjorie spoke for the rest of her family: "We'll, it's up to however Clayton feels about it. As you can see, it would obviously terribly upset him."

"Yes, it would," Lisa agreed.

Luis remained silent, and appeared somewhat befuddled.

With a shrug, Grant told them, "Fair enough. That's your decision, and we respect that."

Jason added, "Of course, there are few absolutes in this field of investigation, anyway."

"In the meantime," said Grant, "as both Keith and Carl explained to you, the best possible way to prevent the activity from reoccurring, is to maintain a positive atmosphere within your home. Work together as a family as much as possible, and try to lend support to each other."

"We will," Marjorie assured Jason and Grant. "And once again, I'd like to thank you and the rest of your people, for all you've done for us."

Luis added, "Yes, thank you all so much. And just remember, you're all welcome back here to visit us, anytime!"

Grant said, "And we just may take you up on that offer sometime."

Jason told them, "If you need anything at all, don't hesitate to give us a call. Okay?"

"Will do, young fella!" said Luis.

Lisa added, "Yes, and be sure to keep in touch with us."

After the cameras were turned off, Clayton asked Jason and Grant, "So, you guys said that you got some high readings while you were in the basement, right?"

"That's right," said Jason.

Sounding somewhat anxious, Clayton told them, "Y'know, that's where the psychic we had over here said that the body is buried, so there might still be something there. I-I mean, I still don't like to go down there by myself."

Grant reminded him, "Well, you know, Clayton, both Keith and I did a thorough spiritual cleansing in the basement the last time we were here. If anything, I'd be more concerned about the bedroom upstairs, which you wouldn't allow us access to. But, like I said, that's entirely your call."

During the drive out of Lewiston, with Jason behind the wheel of the new TAPS van and Grant in the passenger's seat, Jason commented, "Well, this has to fall under the category of one of the most bizarre cases we've ever been involved with. We certainly didn't find much in the way of concrete evidence, which is what it seems the family was hoping for."

"I agree, they were really looking for us to provide verification of paranormal activity," said Grant. "As Carl likes to say, the 'Holy

Grail' would be finding a full-bodied apparition. Unfortunately, that just didn't happen here."

"Also, you have to take into account that there's undoubtedly mental illness involved in this situation, which complicates matters," said Jason. "One thing I intentionally avoided mentioning to the family, was their impending eviction. And the primary reason for their eviction is their stubborn refusal to go against Clayton's wishes about that locked bedroom. Let me ask you something, Grant. Did you get the impression that the entire family is frightened of Clayton?"

"Honestly, yes, I did," said Grant. "In fact, I get the impression that they're just as terrified of opposing Clayton – and this includes his girlfriend, Lisa - as Clayton is of someone going inside that bedroom."

"Yeah. That's exactly my impression, too," said Jason. "Unfortunately, there's obviously just no way of getting through to Clayton about this. He's definitely an unstable character, and he won't see reason."

"Well anyway," said Grant, "if nothing changes in their situation, then in a few weeks it'll be out of their hands entirely. Clayton can't prevent the bedroom door from being opened, if he and his family have been evicted from the premises."

Turning off an exit ramp that led onto the main highway, Jason said, "I don't know, Grant, this whole situation gives me an uneasy feeling. Not just with Marjorie's alleged possession, which Keith seems to have helped her with. And don't get me wrong, both she and Luis seem to be very nice people. But then, there's this business about the sister being murdered, and then the medical examiner meeting with foul play as well. And in between the first investigation back in January and now, the other son violently meets his end."

"I hear ya," said Grant. "I guess we'll just have to wait and see what develops from here."

"In the meantime, as least the family seems to have been put at ease for now," said Jason. "And that's the important thing, knowing that we all did our best, to give them some measure of reassurance."

"Yep," Grant agreed. "When all's said and done, that's what it's all about."

They then tapped their knuckles together in a gesture of camaraderie.

Several days later, my brother Carl received a telephone call from Clayton's girlfriend, Lisa. Later that same day, Sandra and I also received a telephone call from her. She informed us all that the eviction of the Ray family had finally gone through, mainly due to Clayton's refusal to unlock the upstairs bedroom door and allow the health inspectors to perform a complete house inspection. Lisa also informed us that she'd had to terminate her long-term relationship with Clayton, because of his increasingly abusive behavior towards her.

The three of us sympathized with Lisa. We were also naturally curious to know more details about the eviction, and if she knew what was found in the padlocked upstairs bedroom.

Lisa explained to us that the day following the eviction of the Ray family from their condo, she had agreed to meet with two of the housing inspectors, to assist in gathering whatever remaining items the family might have left behind. The housing inspectors had indeed gained access to the locked upstairs bedroom… and basically all they'd discovered inside was a bed frame with an old, somewhat stained mattress, along with some dusty cardboard boxes strewn about the floor containing old clothes and outdated magazines. In fact, the only items they found that were even remotely objectionable were some wall posters and some subversive literature, which might have been considered socially offensive.

Lisa had also later found out during a telephone conversation with Marjorie, that a new, unused TV set, as well as an expensive bureau, all originally belonging to Lisa, had also been stored within the bedroom. Just prior to their eviction, Clayton had somehow been able to overcome his fear of the bedroom long enough to retrieve these items, and they were now at the new apartment which the Ray family had just relocated into. Of course, Clayton was still convinced that the evil spirits, which had now been released from the bedroom, would seek their retribution upon whoever next moved into that condo!

Sandra and I, along with the rest of the TAPS team, all found the final revelation of the "padlocked room" to be rather anti-climactic, to say the least. After all the fuss Clayton Ray had made, we had at least anticipated that there might be some sort of occult paraphernalia contained within the room, or perhaps a stash of some illegal substance, or maybe even human remains! Obviously, no forensic testing was ever performed within the room. Suffice it to say that we never received any reports of anyone ever being attacked by vengeful spirits, as the result of the bedroom finally having been opened and inspected.

EPILOGUE

Throughout the ensuing year following our last visit to Lewiston, Marjorie and her family kept in occasional contact with Sandra and Carl and me. Lisa also kept in communication with us, although she never resumed her relationship with Clayton. Not unexpectedly, all of them were acutely disappointed that the episode of "Ghost Hunters" in which they were featured was never aired, although they'd twice seen it advertised.

All throughout this time, Marjorie Ray remained free of any spiritual oppression or possession.

In late June of 2005, Marjorie began to complain of a general weakness, combined with abdominal discomfort. After undergoing a series of medical tests, she was diagnosed with colon cancer, which was apparently already in an advanced stage. In July, she was admitted into a local nursing home to recover from cancer treatments. After a little over a week, Marjorie had begun regaining much of her strength, as well as her appetite, and near the end of the second week, her overall condition had improved to the point where she was ready to be discharged. On August the 1st, the evening before Marjorie was to return home, her husband Luis and her son Clayton came to visit with her as usual, and found her sitting up in bed, laughing and joking with everyone about how anxious she was to return home. She even announced that she had a craving for Chinese food. Luis and Clayton promptly left for Chinese take-out, promising to be back as soon as they could, so they could all celebrate her last night in the nursing facility together.

However, when Luis and Clayton arrived back at the facility scarcely forty-five minutes later, they were regrettably informed by the staff that Marjorie had suddenly and quite unexpectedly gone into cardiac arrest, and passed away. Her death at age 74 had been very quick and tranquil, and she had not suffered.

Chapter 14

The Dover Demon

It was mild and seasonably cool on this Thursday evening of April 21, 1977, as three teenage high school students drove along Farm Street in the Boston suburb of Dover, Massachusetts. The time was approximately 10:30 PM, and Bill Bartlett was behind the driver's wheel, chatting with his two friends about the activities they all had planned for the upcoming weekend. While in mid-sentence, the 17-year-old driver began to slow, as the headlights of his car illuminated what appeared to be some sort of animal creeping along a low stone wall near the side of the road. Bill at first assumed it might perhaps be a dog, or even an exceptionally large raccoon. However, as the thing came into full view, he found it difficult to believe what he was actually seeing.

Clearly, this was totally unlike any sort of creature Bill had ever seen before. Although basically humanoid in form, it could have been no more than perhaps four feet tall. The most noticeable aspect of this creature was it's large, watermelon shaped head, with no visible facial features except for two large, reflective orange orbs for eyes. The skin that covered the creature's spindly body appeared to be peach colored, and completely hairless. Although it walked upright, it held onto the rocks tenaciously with its elongated, amphibian-like toes and fingers.

"What the-?!" Bill exclaimed to his two friends. "Guys – did you just see that?"

"See what?" asked his friend Mike.

"Yeah, what?" his friend Andy asked from the back seat.

"That, back there, whatever the hell it was!" said Bill. "Didn't either of you just see the thing?"

"No," said Mike, "we were both busy talking. What was it?"

When Bill had described the creature he'd seen to his two friends, they excitedly urged him to turn back. "No way," he told Andy and Mike. As they continued to persist, Bill was finally persuaded, albeit reluctantly, to turn around and drive back along the stretch of Farm Road. However, whatever had been there climbing along the stonewall was now gone.

Upon returning home, Bill Bartlett made detailed drawings of the bizarre creature he had witnessed earlier that evening.

It was shortly before midnight that same evening on Farm Street, a little over a mile from the spot where Bill Bartlett had sighted the creature, that 15-year-old John Baxter was walking home from visiting his girlfriend. Just up ahead in the darkness, John noticed a small figure on the same side of the road walking directly towards him. Wondering if this might be someone he knew, John called out, "Hello? Who is that?" When there was no reply, John stopped. As he did so, the figure also came to a halt. They were now perhaps about twenty feet away from each other. "Hey, who is that?" John called out once more.

But again, there was no response, only the sound of peep frogs chirping in the distance. As John watched, the shadowy figure suddenly began moving off the side of the road while still facing him. It was then that he could just barely make out two large, glowing orange eyes cautiously staring at him. With a shock, John realized that although this thing stood upright, it was definitely not human. Its large, watermelon shaped head appeared completely out of proportion with the rest of its frail looking body. Long spindly fingers and toes clutched onto nearby small rocks as it moved. For a moment, John apprehensively thought that the creature might be about to attack him. But instead, the small alien-like being merely used its elongated toes and fingers to slink off into the woods and slowly make its way down a nearby gully.

Now seized with fright, John Baxter fled the rest of the way home along Farm Street, hardly even daring to glance back at the darkened road behind him. As soon as he was safely back in his house with his family, John also drew an illustration of the otherworldly creature he'd just encountered.

    The following evening, Friday April 22, 18-year old Will Taintor was driving along Springdale Avenue near the downtown section of Dover. Seated beside him in the passengers seat was 15-year-old Abby Brabham. Although Will's friend Bill Bartlett had mentioned to him about spotting a strange creature along Farm Street the previous night, Will had not bothered mentioning the incident to Abby. It was around midnight as they neared Abby' home, when she suddenly spotted something just up ahead of them. The first thing Abby noticed were two large round eyes reflecting in the headlights. The eyes were set within a bulbous head that was set on top of a rather small, spindly peach-colored body, which appeared to be hairless. Long, spider-like fingers and toes clasped onto the mound of earth upon which it perched, watching them as they approached. Abby cried out for Will to look as his car passed by, and he too caught a quick glimpse of the misshapen creature. "Oh, my God!" gasped Will. "That's the same thing Bill Bartlett told me he saw last night." The only difference from Bill's description was that the large eyes appeared to be reflecting greenish in color, instead of orange.

    Nearly in a panic, Abby pleaded, "Please, Will, just get us out of here!!" Will stepped on the gas, and raced the rest of the way to Abby's house.

    Although an intensely thorough investigation by authorities was conducted throughout the area after these sightings were reported, no trace of this elusive and mysterious creature could be found. All who knew these four young witnesses testify that they were not prone to hoaxes or fabrications, and that they'd all seen something that truly terrified them. And although their descriptions matched, Bill Bartlett and John Baxter presumably did not even know each other at the time of the sightings.

    Soon after these reported sightings, Cryptozoologist Loren Coleman, who resides nearby to Dover and who himself investigated the case, was the first to refer to this unknown creature as the Dover Demon. And yet, if it did actually exist, what could it possibly have been? According to the illustrations made by eyewitnesses Bill Bartlett and John Baxter, the creature did somewhat resemble a classic alien in description. However, instead of being a small gray, it appeared to be more of a "small peach," for lack of a better term.

The Dover Demon has not been spotted again since those two nights in April of 1977. However, to commemorate the 30th anniversary of the event, the crew at "Spooky Southcoast," a Massachusetts radio show hosted by Tim Weisberg and Matt Costa, decided to dedicate an episode of their show to the Dover Demon. For their broadcast they chose the evening of Saturday, April 21, 2007, exactly thirty years after the original sightings had taken place. In the studio besides Matt and Tim, were Chris Balzano of Massachusetts Crossroads Paranormal, and myself. Tim introduced us by saying, "Of course, we have our old friend Chris Balzano of Massachusetts Crossroads Paranormal with us. Also here with us in the 'Spooky Studio' tonight, filling in for Science Advisor Matt Moniz, is demonologist and founder of NEAR, Keith Johnson. While he usually hunts down a different type of demon, Keith has long been fascinated with the Dover incident and will be sure to bring a fresh perspective to the table."

On the phone with us during the live broadcast were two distinguished guests: Cryptozoologist Loren Coleman, who had first coined the name Dover Demon, and paranormal researcher and author Jeff Belanger, of Ghost Village.com. Matt Moniz, the Science Advisor for Spooky Southcoast, would also be in contact with the studio by cell phone, reporting live from the actual locations where the Dover Demon was originally sighted. Accompanying Matt was paranormal researcher John Horrigan of Monster Mash and Mystery Tour.

It was just after 10:00 PM as Matt and John arrived at the beginning of Farm Street, where teenager Bill Bartlett had been the fist to glimpse the elusive cryptid, and where John Baxter had encountered it only hours later. (Farm Street in the present still appears much the same as it probably did back in 1977.) As Matt slowly drove his car through this darkened area, it was relatively easy to imagine the peach colored, hairless thing with the bulbous head and the spindly fingers, gingerly scaling along the stonewall bordering the surrounding woods.

John asked Matt if he knew exactly where the Dover Demon was sighted here on Farm Street. "No, I'm not sure of the exact spot," replied Matt. "But we're definitely in the vicinity right now. It sure must have been a startling experience, suddenly seeing that thing creeping along the side of the road in the middle of the night."

John added, "And of course, here we are driving along here, intentionally keeping an eye out for anything unusual. Back on that night in 1977, none of those teenagers had been expecting to meet up with anything out of the ordinary, which made their experience all the more shocking."

"Good point," Matt agreed. "And that's especially true of John Baxter's too-close-for-comfort encounter with the creature, since he was alone on foot instead of being in a car with his friends."

While driving along, they also speculated on exactly what the Dover Demon may or may not have been. Matt commented, "Over the years, there have been many theories ranging anywhere from a deformed child, to a rabid dog or raccoon, to a wandering baby moose."

"None of which makes any real sense," John said with a chuckle.

Matt said, "Of course, there have been other equally bizarre theories. Some people have attributed the sightings to the teenager's over-active imaginations, although everyone who knew them at the time believed them to be sincere. Others believe it may in fact have been an actual demon, or even an extra-terrestrial. Someone once even put forth the proposition that it may have been some sort of mutant primate, like a bald chimpanzee."

"A bald chimpanzee?" John asked with a laugh.

"Or the proverbial missing link," Matt further speculated. "I'd personally lean more towards the extra-terrestrial explanation. Or, perhaps it could even have been some sort of hybrid creature, as yet to be classified."

"I suppose just about anything's possible," said John. "Of course, 'Dover Demon' was just the name Loren Coleman came up for it at the time. I guess it just had kind of a catchy ring to it. Makes it stick in your mind."

Back in the studio, Tim Weisberg and Matt Costa played a recorded interview with John Baxter, pertaining to what he experienced on the morning of Friday, April 22, 1977 at 12:30 AM. Tim, Matt, Chris and I then chatted with Loren Coleman and Jeff Belanger about the history of the incident. At one point, a call came in for me from a caller who wished to know if I, personally, believed that this creature known as the Dover Demon might have been an actual demonic entity. I responded that in my opinion, this was a presumably lost, solitary creature, apparently of an unknown species, as opposed to something of a malevolent nature. Loren, Jeff, and Chris agreed with me on this point.

We then received a call-in from Matt, who gave us a brief progress report regarding his and John's on-site investigation. After having traversed the entire length of Farm Street several times in both directions, they had failed to encounter anything remotely out of the ordinary. They were now about to head across town to their next destination, which was Springdale Avenue. This was the site where both William Taintor and Abby Brabham claimed to have witnessed the creature on the evening of April 22, 1977. At least there, they hoped to locate the exact spot where the Dover Demon had last been sighted. Matt's cell phone connection then began breaking up. Tim advised him, "You and John try checking in with us again a little later, Matt."

Without too much difficulty, Matt and John managed to come to Springdale Avenue. When they'd driven about a quarter mile along Springdale, John asked, "Now what spot exactly are we looking for?"

Glancing at the sides of the darkened road, Matt replied, "As far as I know, we're supposed to come to a little overpass of sorts, where a brook runs directly underneath the road."

After finding the exact spot, Matt parked his car along the side of the road several yards away from the small overpass. He and John then got out and walked over to the area where the Dover Demon reputedly was last sighted. Within the first twenty minutes or so, the breeze from off the nearby brook began to pick up, causing the temperature to noticeable drop. Also, no less than eight cars drove by within that time period, each of them slowing down as the drivers and passengers peered out the window at John and Matt. John commented, "Looks like we're drawing a lot of curious stares from the locals. They must be wondering just what we're up to."

"It'd be great, if we could actually conclude our investigation by providing an eyewitness account," said Matt. He and John then walked up a nearby incline. Using battery powered torches, they began visually surveying the darkened, wooded area surrounding them.

Suddenly, another car approached, and began slowing to a stop. This time, it turned out to be the local police, who'd been alerted to reports of dozens of other "Demon hunters" in the area. Matt and John readily identified themselves to the two officers, and explained that they were investigating on location for the live "Spooky Southcoast" broadcast. Upon hearing this, the officers seemed quite impressed, and told both Matt and John that they'd be allowed to continue their investigation without harassment. After the two officers had left, Matt called into the studio once again to give us another update. "Yes, we've just been paid a visit by Dover's Finest," he informed us. "But after we explained to them exactly who we were and what we're doing here, they kindly allowed us to continue our investigation. In fact, from what the officers told us, there are quite a few other people out here tonight searching for the Dover Demon. But apparently no one's had any actual sightings as of yet, including us."

While Matt and John never did wind up encountering the infamous Dover Demon that night, the Spooky Southcoast broadcast turned out to be an enjoyable and enlightening experience for all involved. And what better way could there have been, to commemorate the 30th anniversary of the original sightings!

To the present, there have been no conclusive reported sightings of the creature known as the Dover Demon, since the two successive nights of April 21st and 22nd in 1977. Whether it was some lost otherworldly being, or perhaps something of subterranean or even inter-dimensional existence, the Dover Demon remains an enigma… simply leaving us with another reminder that we may not be alone in this universe. Let us hope that this solitary creature, wherever it may have come from, eventually managed to find its way back home.

Chapter 15

Spirit Well

In the southwest section of North Scituate, Rhode Island, some of the local residents may recall the legend of a supposed "spirit well," which is said to be located just off of Plainfield Pike, between Carpenter and Nipmuc Roads. According to the legend, many years ago two children fell into this well and were drowned... and it is said that on moonlit evenings, the spirit of their mother can still be heard sobbing for her lost children.

Back in the 1970's when I was an adolescent, a few of my friends and I would sometimes traverse this lonely stretch on moonlit nights. Although we never came across the legendary well or heard the ghostly sobbing, we did perceive the odd sensation of being watched and even "followed" by an unseen presence. What we perceived as fleeting shadowy figures would also frequently be seen moving about in the darkened woods of this area. Any actual evidence of this alleged haunting, however, remained ambiguous at best. In fact, over the years, I began to wonder if it had been nothing more than a local urban legend after all.

Thus it was that fairly recently, I decided to make a legitimate attempt to acquire any possible evidence which might lend validity to this story of an alleged haunted well. My search began, appropriately, at the North Scituate Public Library. Searching through the town archives, I of course found numerous references to various families who had lived in the area prior to the advent of the Scituate Reservoir, which was constructed between 1921 and 1925. But there was no specific reference that I could find, relating to two children having met their deaths by accidentally falling into a well. Not that this necessarily means the incident did not occur. It may well have been a true incident, passed down though oral tradition. Prior to the mid-19th Century, local town records were sometimes scantily kept, and many have been lost over the years. However, there was nothing I personally found during my research to support the historic fact of this particular tragic incident.

Also, some time had elapsed since I'd heard of anyone having experienced anything unusual in this particular area. Then, just recently, my wife Sandra and I gave a Halloween lecture on true vampire case histories, at the invitation of Fr. Robert Bailey at the St. Maria Goretti Church in Pawtucket, Rhode Island. The lecture was well attended and afterward two women, a mother named Karen and her adult daughter Carrie, approached us, anxious to share an unusual experience they'd had.

According to the mother and daughter, they'd been driving along the length of Plainfield Pike in Scituate during the early evening hours. Suddenly, they both caught a glimpse of what they described as young children, peering out at them from the nearby woods along the side of the road. When Karen and Carrie slowed down to get a better look at the ghostly children, they'd simply vanished. In fact, Karen and her daughter Carrie had both experienced this phenomenon on more than one occasion when driving along this exact area. The sightings so disturbed them that they decided to start avoiding this particular area altogether, especially at night. Of course, while driving along Plainfield Pike they would naturally be passing by both Carpenter and Nipmuc Roads, which is where their sightings of the children took place. I then asked them if they'd ever heard the story of the "Spirit Well," into which two children had supposedly fallen and met their deaths many years ago. Karen and Carrie replied that they'd never heard this story but that it did make sense, according to what they'd both witnessed in this location.

And so, the investigation into the children of the Spirit Well in Scituate remains ongoing. Should anyone reading this have any added insight or information, we heartily encourage you to contact us at New England Anomalies Research.

Chapter 16

The Secrets of Precious Blood Cemetery

Woonsocket Historical Cemetery #6, also known as Precious Blood Cemetery, is located on the corner of Rathburn Street and Diamond Hill Road in the City of Woonsocket, Rhode Island. With approximately 28,904 burials, it is the largest cemetery in Woonsocket and is maintained by Precious Blood Church. Although it is known as belonging to Woonsocket, a large portion of the cemetery is also in Blackstone, MA. There have been no new lots or single graves available since June 1, 1955. Known for some of its amazingly beautiful statuary, there is also a small, poorer section near the back of the cemetery that is obscure and mainly hidden from view. In this area simple, decaying wooden crosses are all that mark the graves. However, the most striking feature of this cemetery is located on top of the cemetery's summit. This is the tomb of Aram Jules Pothier, born July 26, 1854, in the Province of Quebec, and died Feb. 3, 1928, in Woonsocket. He served as the Governor of Rhode Island from 1909 to 1915 and 1925 until his death in 1928. He also served as Lieutenant Governor of Rhode Island from 1897 to 1898. Of all the exquisite monuments within the grounds of Precious Blood Cemetery, this is by far the most noticeable… not only for the fact that it is built on the highest elevation of the cemetery, but also because it seems to have been designed to resemble an ancient Greek amphitheater. In fact, it is even complete with columns. It is also said that when Governor Pothier was helping to design the particulars of his final resting place, he specified that his body (which is interred within the pedestal section of the monument) not be encased within a casket. Also, there are small openings, or windows within the pedestal which supposedly allow for viewing inside. The alleged reason for this was that Governor Pothier wished to always be close to the people of the city of Woonsocket, which he served so dutifully in life.

Precious Blood Cemetery is also the final resting-place for Marie Rose Ferron, New England's only documented stigmatist. Marie Rose Alma (Roselma) Ferron, also affectionately known as "Little Marie" was born 24 May 1902 in a stable in the Province of Quebec, Canada. She and her family became residents of Woonsocket, Rhode Island in 1925. Marie Rose Ferron died in 1936 as a claimed stigmatic, bearing the wounds of Christ's Passion, and she was buried in Precious Blood Cemetery. Her body was exhumed in 1947 to verify that she had been a stigmatist. When the body was examined, it did not appear to have decomposed and the stigmatic evidence was deemed conclusive. To this day, people often flock to pay homage at the gravesite of Maria Rose Ferron in Precious Blood Cemetery. Some of the faithful even gather there in the hope of receiving a miraculous cure.

Precious Blood Cemetery was also the victim of a devastating flood that took place in August of 1955, when Tropical Storm Diane caused the waters of the nearby Blackstone River to overflow through the cemetery grounds. Because much of the cemetery is on highly elevated ground, the flood waters caused many of the graves to be completely flooded out. This resulted in literally dozens upon dozens of caskets being washed out of the cemetery and being swiftly carried away by the overflowing waters of the Blackstone. One of the caskets even wound up being temporarily lodged in the raceway at Slater Mill in Pawtucket.

There is another story dating back to the time of the flood, shared with me by fellow paranormal researcher Thomas D'Agostino. According to the story, a Woonsocket resident was having an illicit love affair, which was suspected by his terminally ill wife. His wife forewarned him, "If you marry that woman after I die, I'll come back to haunt you!" Well, after the man's wife did eventually pass away, he wasted little time in marrying his mistress. However, during the flood of 1955, his first wife's coffin allegedly floated down from Precious Blood Cemetery and finally settled on her former husband's back lawn...with the coffin lid open. The man supposedly never recovered from the shock.

Now, with all this history, you would think that if any of our local cemeteries were to boast a reputation for being "haunted," Precious Blood Cemetery would certainly be among them. And it was partly for this reason that this became the favorite cemetery of my close friend and associate Brian Harnois, very early on in his paranormal investigating career. Another reason, of course, is the fact that Precious Blood Cemetery was located very close to Brian's original Woonsocket residence. What originally attracted Brian to Precious Blood Cemetery was of course some of the breathtaking statuary. However, it was when he'd originally organized the Rhode Island Paranormal Society that he first began some serious paranormal investigation at the cemetery

RIPS initial group investigation at Precious Blood included members Brian, Rich, Eric, Eric's girlfriend Theresa and also Heather, who had just recently joined the group. It was a pleasant, mildly cool evening with a clear night sky overhead. They split up into two teams to cover the expansive cemetery grounds, eventually meeting up with each other again at the Governor Pothier monument on the summit. So far, none of them had experienced any definite paranormal activity within the cemetery. However, once they began exploring the more secluded section at the far end of the cemetery, Brian's eyes suddenly began to water, and he felt a prickling sensation on the back of his neck. "Guys... there's something here, I can feel it," he alerted the others.

Nervously, Theresa asked, "What is it? What are you sensing?"

"I'm not sure," said Brian. "But whatever it is, I don't think it's anything good."

Heather then glanced over at the nearby Blackstone River and gasped audibly. Everyone else turned to look at her and asked what was wrong. Pointing to the Blackstone, Heather said, "I see something moving over there by the river! Do you guys see it?"

Glancing over to where Heather was pointing, they all saw what appeared to be a shadowy figure at the water's edge. From what they could see, the solitary figure appeared to be that of a female with long dark hair, moving about in an undulating fashion as if dancing. In case this was a real-life person, Brian called out to the figure, but it paid them no mind.

Since they all agreed that this was not a trick of the light on the rippling water, Rich began videotaping the figure and the others who had cameras with them took several photos. Then the "dancing lady" was suddenly no longer there. "She's gone," said Brian. "I guess whoever or whatever she was, she must've caught onto the fact that we were filming her."

Rich said, "But at least I managed to catch at least several seconds of footage of her before she vanished. I could see her through the viewer plain as anything."

"Alright!" Brian said excitedly. "At least we got proof tonight, dude!"

Unfortunately, when they later reviewed their evidence, no trace of the "dancing lady" came out on the video footage, although Rich was certain that he could plainly see her while he'd been taping. Neither did the image appear in any of the photos they'd taken. Although Brian was disappointed that he and his team members were unable to capture any photographic evidence that night, his passion for investigating at Precious Blood Cemetery was kindled.

Brian's interest in this particular cemetery of course continued long after he had stepped away from RIPS and joined with TAPS. In fact, the original logo on the TAPS website was a photo of an angel statue, its head bent in sorrow, which was taken by Brian in Precious Blood Cemetery. Because of the cemetery's close proximity to his house, Brian would quite often take a stroll through the cemetery grounds, both in the daylight and during the nighttime hours. Although he never witnessed the "dancing lady" again, he did experience the uncanny feeling that something not of human origin was sometimes nearby. He always seemed to experience this feeling at the far end of the cemetery, near the Blackstone River. Brian theorized that this was because of the running water serving as an energy source, which an inhuman spirit might be utilizing.

Because Brian and Sandra and I were such a close team during the year leading up to the advent of the Ghost Hunters TV series, he would often mention to us how anxious he was to give Sandra and I a tour of Precious Blood Cemetery in his home city of Woonsocket. He also frequently expressed a desire that the three of us together might conduct a nighttime investigation at the cemetery. Finally, the opportunity presented itself on one of those rare weekends that we did not have any prior cases to attend to.

It was early on the evening of May 1st 2004 that Brian, Sandra and I arrived at Precious Blood Cemetery. A full moon was rising as Brian pulled his white Malibu past the cemetery gates and continued along the narrow paved pathway for a hundred yards or so before turning right and parking his car. The evening air was warm and mild as we ventured forth, with Brian enthusiastically leading us. The brightness of the full moon created a sort of eerie false daylight, enabling us to view much of the statuary without the aid of a flashlight.

One of the first places Brian led us to was the grave of Marie Rose Ferron, the Rhode Island mystic who bore the wounds of the stigmata. "This is our official Rhode Island saint," said Brian, pointing to the long, flat, beautifully inscribed monument. "People still come from all over the country and even from as far away as Canada to visit her grave. There have even been miraculous cures known to take place here." I took a photo of the monument before we moved on.

As we continued along the inclined narrow pathway, Brian paused to point out a familiar looking angel statue. "Do you guys recognize this?" he asked us.

After glancing at it, I said, "Yes, this is obviously the angel you used for the original TAPS logo."

Sandra commented, "Oh, yes, I thought it looked familiar. I knew I'd seen it someplace before."

Moving on, we passed by many other beautiful examples of religious sculpture, including a life-size crucifix with a weeping Madonna and Mary Magdalene at the foot of the cross. Because of the pale glow cast by the moonlight, many of these silent stone figures seemed to take on an uncannily life-like appearance, as if they might suddenly be rendered capable of motion and speech.

Brian also pointed out the grave of several priests of Canadian French heritage, as well as a bishop, and even a monsignor. Sandra commented that there were certainly a lot of French names on the stones and monuments in this cemetery. Brian explained that this was predominantly a Canadian French cemetery and that even some of his own family was buried here.

Sandra was also anxious to see the location where Brian and his other team members had witnessed the "Dancing Lady." Brian assured her, "Don't worry, you'll see that. It's near the back of the cemetery. But first, I want you and Keith to see the Governor's burial place."

We eventually arrived at the most noticeable monument within the entire cemetery, which was the amphitheater-like monument of Governor Aram Jules Pothier. Like a professional tour guide, Brian announced, "Here we are at the Governor's monument. This is what I've been telling you about. It kind of looks like the Coliseum, doesn't it?"

I agreed, "You're right, especially with the columns. It also reminds me of an ancient Roman or Greek amphitheater."

Sandra commented, "It sure stands out here against the sky, especially in the moonlight."

Gazing at it a moment, I could almost imagine an ancient Greek tragedy being performed here, with the actors being illuminated by the light of the full moon and flaming torches.

Brian enthusiastically explained to us that the Governor had personally designed this monument and had it built while he was still alive. He went on to tell us that Precious Blood had originally been four smaller cemeteries, which the Governor had incorporated into one. Prior to that, much of the grounds we were now standing in actually used to be a wooded area.

Both Sandra and I were impressed with Brian's knowledge of the cemetery's history. Brian also reminded us of the Governor's last wish- that he be laid to rest within the base of the monument with small window openings, so he would never be completely separated from the people and the city he so loved in life. "And if you look carefully inside one of these slots, you can actually see his skeleton," said Brian.

"The head's gone, though. People who live around here say that, after the Governor's death and placement here, you could actually smell the body decaying for about a year. You couldn't even approach this place, it smelled so bad."

Personally, I began to have my doubts. It seemed to me that city and state health regulations would have prohibited a putrefying body, entombed within a sepulcher, from being exposed to any source of outside air and causing a public health risk. However, Brian insisted that the Governor's body could be seen, and since there were indeed some small apertures within the wall of the base, it seemed that we were about to find out. The first of the small apertures we inspected was covered over, with both a wooden board from the inside and metal screening on the outside. And we certainly weren't about to attempt vandalizing it, just to get a glimpse.

The next one we inspected was open and would hopefully allow for an unobstructed view. "Alright!" said Brian. "Let's shine our flashlights in there and see if we can see the Governor himself."

"Have you ever been able to see him before?" I asked Brian.

Brian replied, "Yeah, sure I have! At least, I've been able to see some of what's left of him."

Brian and I shined our flashlights though the slot (which was about eye level) and peered in. Even with the beams shining from two flashlights, the interior of the base was only partly illuminated. In fact, it hardly looked like a crypt at all but more like a darkened basement, filled with debris. Sandra also took a turn viewing but could not make out much of anything. Suddenly Brian exclaimed, "There he is! There's the skeleton, I see it!"

"Where?" I asked. "I don't see it."

"It's right over there, dude!" said Brian, maneuvering the beam of his flashlight. "See it? Right over there, I've got my light trained right on it."

Carefully peering though the slot once again, I could just barely make out what looked like some sort of a shelf… on top of which was what appeared to be a rib cage. Or, it could also have simply been a pile of debris. "Oh yes, I can see something now," I said. (In fact, if these were indeed the actual mortal remains of Governor Pothier that I was looking at, then I could only imagine the effects which the flood of 1955 must have caused, with the late governor merrily floating and bobbing about in there!)

We tried taking some photos through the small opening, but unfortunately, we could not seem to get a sufficient angle with the flash. Next, Sandra suggested that she try videotaping though the small aperture. "Good idea," said Brian. "Now at least we'll have this preserved on video."

While Sandra was standing beside Brian with her camcorder held as close to the opening as possible, I quietly stepped back several paces to get a camera shot of the two of them. Of course, I hadn't realized that Brian assumed that I was still standing right there right beside him. "Isn't that right, Keith?" he asked as he concluded a sentence. When I did not immediately answer, he glanced around. Not seeing me, he became instantly alarmed. "Keith?? Keith???"

I immediately came sprinting back over to them.

"Don't freakin' DO that!!" Brian exclaimed in frustration. "What's freakin' wrong with you?!"

"You didn't know I was over there?" I asked.

"No!" he said. Sandra burst out laughing.

Brian then escorted us up some stone steps, to the top of the base. "Watch your step," he cautioned us. He also informed us "You can actually crawl in there to where the Governor's buried."

"Oh, really?" I asked.

With a laugh, Sandra said, "I don't think I want to!"

Brian said, "There's a stone that's loose on the stairs. If you pull the stone away, you can crawl right in there." He then escorted us to the top section of the base, and demonstrated to us just how loose one of the stones comprising the steps actually was.

"Oh, yes, it's definitely loose," Sandra agreed. "I'm sure vandals have been in there."

"That's why the Governor's head's missing," said Brian.

"There's a name for people who do things like that," I said.

"What's that?" asked Brian.

"Ghoul," I replied ominously.

Sandra asked Brian, "Have you ever been in there?"

Brian replied, "Oh, hell no, I ain't goin' in there with all them damn bones sittin' in there!"

(Again, I began to wonder about the legalities of the Governor being laid to rest outside of a coffin. Then again, I figured that having money and being in a position of high authority does have its advantages. Perhaps the Governor also had a phobia about premature burial, especially if his body was not to be embalmed. And just maybe the Governor's decision was also partially influenced by the multiple bodies housed in the famed catacombs in France, which he may perhaps have visited during his lifetime.)

The three of us then stood on the upper platform of the pedestal. Looking out over the expansive cemetery grounds and the Blackstone River from the Governor's monument was quite breathtaking, especially in the moonlight! Sandra attempted to take a video shot of the view. But she found that the camera battery had now completely drained, even though it had been almost fully charged just a short while ago.

Brian then led us into the very back section of the cemetery, which was also the poorer section. What markers existed there were considerably smaller than in the front and middle sections. Some of the graves did not have stone markers at all. Instead they were adorned with simple wooden crosses... some with names inscribed, some without. Sandra remarked, "Gee, Brian, you were certainly right about this part of the cemetery being secluded. In fact, it's rather dismal."

"Yes, it is," Brian agreed. "In fact, it's right around here that I've always sensed the 'inhuman.'"

"Are you sensing the inhuman now?" I asked.

Brian said, "No, not at this moment. But I can always tell when it's around, because my eyes start to water, and I'll see shadow figures darting about." (Fortunately, I had prayed with Sandra for our protection earlier that evening.)

Brian also pointed towards the Blackstone River, and told us, "Right over there is where Heather and I and the rest of the group saw the 'Dancing Lady.' We were watching her dance right on the water there for several minutes."

I had to ask, "Are you certain that it wasn't just an optical illusion, caused by reflections and the rippling of the water at night?"

Brian explained, "Oh, we were pretty sure that this couldn't have been an illusion, because we got a close enough look to rule out that it was any sort of reflection. She was in dancing right near the edge of the river."

"On solid ground?" asked Sandra.

"That's right," said Brian. "Her shadow came all the way back over here, and there were no flags waving or anything that would've caused a reflection. We even tried to see if any reflection exactly like that could be recreated, but it couldn't. In fact, Heather can attest to the fact that she actually appeared there."

Sandra said, "It's too bad that nobody had a camcorder going."

"Oh, we actually had a camcorder going, and we took five still shots," said Brian. "They would not take a picture of her. All five of my still photos were black, and the camcorder would not record. She would not let us take a picture of her."

"Stubborn little wisp, wasn't she?" asked Sandra.

Brian said. "Yeah, I was hoping that she'd come out tonight. That was the most gorgeous thing I've ever seen in my life. I was like, 'Oh, my God.' But unfortunately, she only appeared to us that one time. I've never seen her since."

I commented, "It must have very moving experience."

"Oh, yeah," Brian agreed. "There she was, right on the Blackstone."

While we were still in the back section of the cemetery, Brian momentarily excused himself to take a call on his cell phone, and then to make another quick call. Sandra and I occupied ourselves for the next fifteen minutes or so by wandering among the simpler headstones and wooden grave markers of the poorer section, taking photos as well as video and audio recordings. Brian then rejoined us, and asked, "Get anything interesting yet, guys?"

"Well, not that we've observed so far," I said. "Of course, we still have to review our recordings. But the atmosphere does feel very dismal back here."

Sandra said, "Yes, it almost feels oppressive. And it's a lot damper than the front section, because of the water being so close by."

"You're right," said Brian. "In fact, my eyes are starting to water now, on and off. I'm feeling a certain heaviness around here right now."

Before we moved on from this part of the cemetery, I prayed an "Our Father" out loud.

While leaving the back section, we discussed the possibility, that the near proximity of this end of the cemetery to the Blackstone River might indeed be conducive to paranormal activity. We also speculated on whether or not the inhuman spirit that Brian had encountered was confined to that particular section of the cemetery, or whether it was free to roam about. Brian's opinion was that since the cemetery was originally comprised of what were four different sections, the inhuman entity might still be confined to one particular section.

Sandra asked me, "What do you make of that, Keith? Why would the inhuman spirit be confined to one particular area?"

I replied, "Well, this is consecrated ground. However, it's probably been at least partially desecrated, through vandalism and possible cult activity. Brian mentioned that the inhuman comes here to feed."

What was more, we speculated that if the 'Dancing Lady' had been an actual phenomenon, then perhaps 'she' was also restricted to the area of the banks of the Blackstone. (Of course, Sandra and I had not personally witnessed either of these manifestations for ourselves.)

Along the way back Brian pointed out a statue of a man wearing a robe, devoutly holding a child. "Keith, see if you can tell me who that's a statue of," he said.

"St. Joseph," I replied.

Brian laughed, and said, "Pretty good! Joseph's my middle name, 'Brian Joseph Harnois.' But how'd you know that was St. Joseph?"

"Well, I assumed it was, because he's depicted holding the Holy Child," I said. I paused to take a photo of the statue, with the full moon directly above it.

We continued on, and were almost at Brian's car, when something on the ground just to our left suddenly caught Sandra's attention. It seemed to be a mound of light colored fur. "What is that?" she asked, stopping short.

It now appeared to be a small, dead animal. Brian and Sandra stepped forward, and Sandra shined a flashlight on it. It turned out to a desiccated cat carcass. "Ohh!!" Sandra let out a cry of dismay. "Ohh!! That's disgusting!!"

Looking more closely, we saw that the cat was mutilated pretty badly, with an infestation of bugs crawling over it. Brian commented. "Something's gorged itself on it. It looks like something 'Chewbacca' was eating."

"It looks pretty hacked up, too," I said. "This poor cat may have even been a victim of animal sacrifice."

Brian said, I'm getting the heebie-jeebies from that now."

And then I recalled that the date was May 1st, and that it was also a full moon. I explained to Brian and Sandra, "This is actually 'Beltane' on the Pagan calendar, which is a seasonal celebration. And last night was 'Walpurgisnacht' which is also a traditional religious holiday. Unfortunately, there are certain cults that celebrate these occasions by performing ritual sacrifices... and what better time, than that of a full lunar cycle?"

Brian said, "Jeez, I hope there's none of 'em still lingering around here." Sandra agreed.

"Well, it's usually the 'amateurs' who do things like this," I said. "And that of course makes them very dangerous."

We decided not to linger there much longer.

Minutes later, as we were driving away from the cemetery and discussing what an interesting adventure we'd just had, I asked Brian if it would be okay if I popped an audio cassette into his tape player, and reviewed some of our audio. "Oh, yes, definitely, go ahead," he told me.

I rewound the tape to the section I'd been recording shortly before we'd left. There was Brian asking me about the statue of St. Joseph, and my response, followed by the clicking of my camera as I took a picture. And then we could hear Sandra gasping in shock, as we came across the desiccated cat carcass.

In the back seat of Brian's car, Sandra said, "That's still upsetting me, thinking about that poor cat."

"Yeah, I know, huh?" Brian agreed. "Sometimes you never know what you'll find in cemeteries at night."

"I really should have thought about what night this is beforehand," I said.

As we continued listening, I suddenly detected a faint whispering voice right after ours. "Did you guys just hear that?" I asked.

Brian said, "Yeah, I sure did. It sounded like someone whispering, but it didn't sound like us."

I rewound the recording a bit and played it again, this time turning up the volume. Immediately after Brian said, "I'm getting the heebie-jeebies from that now," about the mutilated cat carcass, a male voice distinctly whispered: "Good people... what's a dead cat??"

We played it back and listened to the EVP several times, to make certain that was exactly what it said. The message was plain enough to be definite.

As Brian drove along, we speculated on whether this might have been the inhuman spirit that Brian had told us about. Assuming it was, then that may have answered the question, as to whether it was bound to the back section of the cemetery or if it was free to roam about, since the voice was recorded nearer to the front of the cemetery. Or, as I speculated, perhaps it was a "rogue" spirit that had been summoned or drawn in by a ritual sacrifice, and was still hovering about, observing us. That would certainly make sense regarding the "Good people" reference it had made, since we were there merely to investigate and not sacrifice. But of course, there was really no conclusive way of knowing the origin of this whispering voice. We were simply thrilled that we'd managed to capture such a concise EVP on audio.

Unfortunately, as is sometimes the case with Electronic Voice Phenomena, the recorded spirit voice eventually lost clarity, not long after the recording was first made. Yet, our recorded voices remained just as clear, and did not diminish in clarity. While there is most likely a completely natural explanation for this (perhaps having to do with the fact that our voices were much stronger to begin with), I've also known of other examples where an EVP will noticeable fade or even completely disappear off the recording by the very next day. It's almost as if the spirit was simply lending its voice to the recording, on a temporary basis. At least a little of my EVP recording still remained, although it seemed to have rather rapidly gone from a "class A" to a "class D."

A few years after Sandra and I had first visited Precious Blood Cemetery with Brian, we returned on a chill December evening with some member of our own organization, New England Anomalies Research (NEAR). Present besides Sandra and myself were NEAR members Kim Brager and Renee Smith. Our friend Joseph Petrucci had also accompanied us to the cemetery on this particular evening, as part of his training to become a paranormal investigator.

While we were there, we suggested giving our members a view of governor Pothier's remains, since the video footage we'd taken before was inconclusive at best. However, the small openings in the monument were now all sealed, preventing anyone from viewing inward. The loose stone in the stairs had also been repaired, meaning that the interior of the Governor's crypt was no longer accessible except through the locked iron door. (Not that any of us were seriously considering entering it that night anyway.)

Because there was snow on the ground and the night air was quite frigid, Sandra soon felt her feet starting to become numb. We decided to call our investigation short, and to linger in the cemetery no more than another fifteen minutes or so. As Sandra and I walked together, she happened to have the external microphone of her small tape recorder clipped to her overcoat collar, near her neck. About twenty-five feet away, Joseph Petrucci was also attempting to capture EVPs. Speaking into his own tape recorder, he asked, "Are you walking through the graveyard?"

Later that night, after the investigation had concluded and Sandra and I were sitting in our car reviewing the recordings we'd just taken, we heard Joseph's voice in the near distance, asking, "Are you walking though the graveyard?"

A clear voice, sounding as if it were speaking directly in to microphone Sandra had clipped to her collar, answered: "Yes!"

Once again, it seemed as though we were being observed by an unseen entity within the grounds of Precious Blood Cemetery. Although Joseph had asked the question, no EVP was picked up on his tape recorder. We wondered if perhaps it spoke directly into Sandra's tape recorder, because it may have perhaps recognized her and me from before. From what Brian had previously informed us, he himself often seemed to be recognized when wandering through this particular cemetery.

Today, Precious Blood Cemetery in Woonsocket remains a place where visitors can view some breathtaking statuary, and visit the final resting place of Marie Rose Ferron, who bore the wounds of the stigmata in life. The place offers a wonderful daytime excursion, where the monuments can be seen in their full beauty. And based upon our own personal research, as well as that of others, we believe that there is a certain amount of genuine anomalous activity within the grounds of this historic cemetery. With that being said, however, we also caution anyone against venturing there at night. Because of repeated vandalism that unfortunately continues to take place at Precious Blood Cemetery, as well as cult activity, neighbors within the vicinity now routinely watch the grounds at night. They will immediately alert the local police if they notice anyone entering the cemetery after dark. We therefore recommend visiting Precious Blood Cemetery during the daylight hours.

Investigating the Governor's tomb in Precious Blood Cemetery, Woonsocket, RI.

Chapter 17

The Hauntings of Old Slater Mill

Old Slater Mill, located beside the Blackstone River in Pawtucket, Rhode Island, is truly an icon of American history. This is especially so, considering the fact that it is the birthplace of the United State Industrial Revolution. The entire Slater Mill historic site is actually comprised of three buildings: the Sylvanus Brown House, the Wilkinson Mill, and Old Slater Mill itself. Each of these buildings has its own unique history…each are seasonally open to the public for private and group tours… and all three buildings have a reputation for being haunted. Since my brother Carl and I have both been employed as tour guides at the Slater Mill site, we can personally vouch for some of the activity there.

Allow me to begin by sharing a brief history and description of each of these buildings that comprise the Slater Mill complex. This may actually shed some light as to why the buildings may in fact be haunted. I will also share what phenomenon has reportedly been experienced in each of these three buildings.

The Sylvanus Brown House

First built in 1758, the quaint Sylvanus Brown House ~ also known as Memory Cottage ~ was once occupied by two brothers, Ebenezer and Nathaniel Jenks. The brothers lived there with their separate families, sharing separate halves of the house. This meant that at one time, there were 22 people living in this two-story colonial home, eighteen children and four adults. In 1785, the house came into the possession of a skilled local artisan named Sylvanus Brown. When a 21-year-old Samuel Slater first arrived in Rhode Island in January of 1790, at the invitation of Moses Brown, he was an overnight guest of Sylvanus Brown in this house. Although Moses Brown and Sylvanus Brown were not blood related, apparently Moses considered Sylvanus a good judge of character, and personally requested that Sylvanus scout-out the character of this newly arrived young Englishman and future business partner, Samuel Slater. Sylvanus Brown later assisted in overseeing the construction of the Slater Mill dam, and eventually also became a close business partner of Samuel Slater.

Sylvanus Brown died in this house in the year 1824. Throughout the ensuing 134 years various other families lived in this house. In fact, it was fully occupied right up until the year 1960, when it had to be moved from its original location to make way for the expanding Intestate highway. Because of its local historic significance, all 40 tons of the house was transported by platform truck to the Slater Mill site. When a new foundation for the house was finally completed in 1972, the Sylvanus Brown House became a permanent fixture at the Slater complex.

Within the first floor of the Sylvanus Brown House, there is a small room off to one corner of a main bedroom, which at first appears to be a closet. In reality, this small room – now used for storage – originally served as the "birthing room" where mothers-to-be, having gone into labor, would go to deliver their children. It goes without saying that this was most often an agonizing ordeal, considering that these births took place in an era prior to any modern anesthetics and in unsanitary conditions. In fact, the two most common causes of death for women in early America, were fire (due to cooking over large hearths) and childbirth.

It must also be remembered that throughout early American history, even when death occurred from natural causes for both men and women, it often took place at home. The Sylvanus Brown House was no exception. After all, this was an era when hospitals and nursing facilities as we know them today simply did not exist. Up until at least the early part of the 20th Century, occupants of this and other early American homes usually lived most of their entire lives there, caring for their infirm loved ones, and eventually dying at home.

Although both the birthing room and the master bedroom (presumably the room in which Sylvanus Brown expired) are both located on the first floor, it is actually the upper section of the house that is reportedly the most haunted. Because the second floor section is in a state of general disrepair, visitors are not usually brought up there. It is made up of three fairly spacious bedrooms, which are now primarily used to house storage. When the Slater Mill staff have ventured up there, they often report an uncomfortable feeling of not being alone and of being watched, even if no one is up there with them. Sometimes the feeling of a presence is so strong, some staff members have felt reluctant to remain up there for any length of time.

One morning, one of our tour guides named Jennifer decided to briefly explore the upstairs area by herself, out of curiosity. While up there, she too began to experience the uncanny feeling of being watched. She then felt what she described as a pressure enveloping about her waist, making it difficult for her to breathe. Needless to say, Jennifer quickly left the upper area, and returned back downstairs.

On another occasion, a staff member named Michelle was leading a group of visitors on a tour through the first floor section, when she heard the unmistakable sound of footsteps walking about in an upstairs room directly above her. Michelle had just unlocked the house herself, and no one would have been able to gain access to the upstairs. Quickly checking the upstairs area, she found it to be completely vacated. Although somewhat unnerved, Michelle simply continued with the tour in an upbeat, professional manner. However, she never forgot her experience.

One Friday afternoon in September of 2008, as the last of the tourists were leaving for the day, a woman approached my brother Carl and informed him, "I want you to know, that I'm not given to hallucinations. But I just plainly saw a young girl, wearing what looked like an old fashioned dress, looking out from one of the top floor windows of the Brown House. I looked away for a second, to make certain I was really seeing her... and when I looked back again, she was still there."

Carl had just locked and secured the Sylvanus Brown House, having first checked the entire house to ascertain that no one was still in there. He of course checked again, but found it to be completely empty.

However, there is some recent indication that the first floor may also be haunted. On an evening in March of 2009, Carl and several members of The Paranormal Investigators, who were visiting from

Long Island to conduct a paranormal investigation of the buildings, overheard a distinct peal of girlish giggling while they were on the first floor inside the Sylvanus Brown House. The giggling seemed to emanate directly from a room in which a large antique loom is set up, although certainly no one else was in their at the time.

Two distinct names have also been detected on EVP (Electronic Voice Phenomena) within the Sylvanus Brown House, one of them saying, "Becca" and the other saying, "Sally." The name "Becca" was also picked up intuitively by Carl's companion Dina just prior to the EVP being recorded, and may be short for "Rebecca." The name "Sally" was captured on an audio recording by a tour guide named Jan, in response to her having asked, "Do you have a name?"

The Wilkinson Mill

Construction on this impressive three-story structure was begun in 1810 and completed in 1811. It is named after its designer and chief builder, Oziel Wilkinson, and is constructed primarily out of original New England rubblestone. Oziel Wilkinson and his eldest son David were originally blacksmiths in the town of Smithfield, Rhode Island, who eventually became business partners with the team of Almy & Brown some time after relocating to Pawtucket. With the addition of young Samuel Slater to Almy & Brown's mill, the business rapidly expanded, and soon required a separate service facility to repair the mill machines and to manufacture new parts… hence the addition of the Wilkinson Mill. Family ties between Samuel Slater and the Wilkinson family also developed. Soon after his arrival in Pawtucket, 21-year-old Samuel Slater met 17-year-old Hannah Wilkinson, daughter of Oziel. They were married less than a year later, creating family ties along with business connections.

Unlike over at the Slater Mill, no women or very young children were ever employed at the Wilkinson Mill…only skilled machinists, carpenters and blacksmiths, or apprenticed boys learning their trade. The pay rate was generally much higher than at Slater Mill as well. An experienced laborer at the Wilkinson Mill could certainly support a fair-sized family on his weekly wage. In fact, he could perhaps expect to earn more money in only a month or two, than a typical New

England farmer might earn over the course of an entire year! But make no mistake; conditions in the Wilkinson Mill were often harsh and brutal. Industrial accidents resulting in workers being maimed were not uncommon. The noise from the machinery was deafening, and would cause significant hearing loss over a period of several years. The mill air normally smelled rancid, owing to the putrefying tallow (animal fat) used to grease the gears, in an era before petroleum products were in use. Over the course of the day, the fluid from the greasy tallow would steadily drip down onto the wooden floor, causing the floor to be too slippery for the men to wear their leather soled shoes or boots. To prevent serious slips and falls, the men were required to work barefoot year round. The mill's interior was often stifling hot in the summertime, and freezing cold in the winter months. Workdays were long, often up to 14 hours or more when daylight permitted.

Added to this was the constant, horrendous vibration from the 10-ton water wheel located in the pit below the building. In fact, the rubblestone walls of the Wilkinson Mill had to be constructed three feet thick, to prevent the entire three-story structure from tumbling down like the walls of Jerico! Yet the wheel had to be constantly run at full force, powered by the rushing waters of the Blackstone River, to keep the machines running at max efficiency on all three floors.

Maintaining the huge wheel itself within the dank water wheel pit was an arduous task, requiring long hours of incredibly strenuous and often hazardous toil. It is said that Samuel's Slater's 13-year-old son William once met with a terrible accident when servicing a similar rotating wheel of approximately the same size. The unfortunate lad slipped off, causing one of his legs to be crushed. Although he was lucky to have survived, his leg could not be saved, and was later amputated from the knee down by an attending physician.

It is not uncommon for visitors and staff alike to report experiencing an eerie feeling within the interior of the Wilkinson Mill. As my brother Carl explains, "The building is very old, and contains a lot of memories. The three-foot-thick rubblestone walls of the mill have high quartz content as well as limestone, and even minute traces of gold sediment. Combined with the heavy amount of flowing water necessary to power the 20,000-pound wheel, this could be very conducive to residual, or 'playback' activity."

(The effect of energy being generated from within the wheel pit, possibly causing residual phenomena to occur, would be known as the "Pizer effect.")

On one occasion our former Site Director, Janice Kissenger, experienced a possible encounter with two otherworldly beings. It was a late afternoon just before closing, and Janice was walking through the first floor workshop of the Wilkinson Mill, past the array of antique machinery located on either side of her. When she was about halfway through, she suddenly felt a strong sensation of pressure pushing against her chest area, causing her to come to a halt. It was then Janice began somehow perceiving what she described as a heated altercation taking place between two men, who were perhaps former workers at the mill. In fact, according to her perception, the two men even seemed to be trading blows, and were evenly matched. Finally, Janice managed to move forward, and actually "pushed" her way through them. The experience left her very shaken. Janice later learned that others (including her office assistant Chandler) have also felt a very eerie sensation in this exact spot, and she would thereafter no longer walk through this section of the Wilkinson Mill unaccompanied.

When the TV series Ghost Hunters was filming an episode on the hauntings of Slater Mill, the TAPS investigators seemed to find some activity in the wheel pit of Wilkinson Mill. Using a K-2 Meter placed upon a fold-out wooden chair, Jason Hawes and Grant Wilson began asking that if there was a spirit presence with the pit, could it communicate with them through a series of blinks? With the K-2 blinking on and off, Jason and Grant allegedly established communication with the spirit of a nine-year-old boy named "Edouard" who had once worked in the mill, and who had apparently died there.

Old Slater Mill

What is now known as Old Slater Mill was opened in 1793 as Almy, Brown & Slater, with a staff of two adults and nine children. It was the money and vision of Moses Brown, a successful Quaker merchant, which allowed the mill to be built on the site of the Blackstone River in Pawtucket. Then the remarkable Samuel Slater arrived from Belper, England, and helped them get started. Having apprenticed in the mill of Jedediah Strutt for seven years, young Samuel Slater was able to successfully replicate the Arkwright water-powered machines, which he'd become thoroughly familiar with in England.

Because Samuel Slater had replicated and implemented the advanced water-powered spinning technologies he'd mastered in England, the business rapidly prospered. When Samuel Slater died at the age of sixty-six in 1835, he was worth, by one biographer's account, over ten million dollars, and owned thirteen separate mills. For a time, Samuel Slater was one of the wealthiest men in the country, making him truly one of America's original success stories. During his lifetime, two United States Presidents, President James Monroe and President Andrew Jackson visited Samuel Slater and toured his mill. Such was his reputation in later life, that it was said that once someone had been employed by Samuel Slater, and had left the mill in good graces, he or she could find work just about anywhere else in the entire country.

Old Slater Mill in Pawtucket, RI.

Moses Brown, who'd originally invited Samuel Slater to join him as a business partner, was also an early abolitionist. Being a Quaker, he disapproved of slave labor. But apparently, he had no objection to child labor within the mills. In a correspondence to one of his pro-slavery brothers in the shipping business, Moses Brown boasted, "In my mill, we do not use slaves. We employ children." And that was obviously considered acceptable. Children had small and dexterous fingers to operate the machines. They were plentiful and could easily be replaced, if one of the children became sick or injured. They trained and learned rapidly. Most importantly, you did not have to pay a child as much as you would an experienced adult worker. The children working in the mill usually ranged in age from six to twelve years of age. For well over a century-and-a-half, the primary workforces at most of the textile mills throughout New England were young children, and Slater Mill was no exception. (To Samuel Slater's credit, he did voluntarily offer the children who worked in his mill a rudimentary education for four hours on Sunday afternoons, teaching them religious instructions and basic academics. He began by teaching them himself on his one day off, and later hired student teachers from Brown University.)

Just as at other mills at the time, Slater Mill undoubtedly also saw its share of horrendous mill accidents. For example, there is the oft-told true story of a young woman named Mary Kenyon, who lost a finger while she was weaving on a. power loom. While there is no record that Mary Kenyon actually worked at Slater Mill itself (most probably it was a similar textile mill within the vicinity), her story is just one example of accidents that were not uncommon at Slater Mill. And, just like at Wilkinson Mill, the work hours were long and tedious, typically extending to twelve or more hours per shift, with only one half hour allotted for lunch and a quick visit to the "toilet tower" (which conveniently emptied straight down into the Blackstone River).

Both staff and visitors at the 1793 Old Slater Mill itself have reported experiencing what seems to be a mischievous spirit presence. Of course, just like Wilkinson Mill and the Sylvanus Brown House, the Slater Mill building now functions as an active museum, which displays a restored working textile mill.

Richard Danforth, who presently holds the position of Educational Coordinator at Slater Mill, is a studious man of a practical nature who had taught in the Pawtucket school systems for 30 years. Early one evening in 2005, Richard was attempting to "arm" the 1793 Slater Mill building, with the motion sensor system. As he entered his personal code, the green LED screen repeatedly read SYSTEM NOT READY, which indicated that the security system had somehow been breached. Mr. Danforth checked both the up and downstairs areas, including the weave room and attic, to see if any doors or windows were ajar which might breech the circuit. Everything in the Mill seemed secure. Upon phoning the security system headquarters and explaining the problem, Richard was informed by an agent monitoring the system that their sensors indicated what seemed to be "a sizeable group of women and children" moving back and forth through the upstairs section. Richard and another of the staff again climbed the stairwell and searched around, only to reconfirm that nothing was amiss. The agent then advised Richard to leave the building unarmed that night, and assured him that the next day their technician would check out the system at Slater Mill.

Next morning, the technician arrived at the site, and proceeded to thoroughly examine the wiring, circuitry and connections for any possible cause of the disruption. Everything was clear and functional. To this day, neither Richard Danforth nor anyone at the security system headquarters can explain why the system for a span indicated much moving to-and-fro in the upstairs of Slater Mill.

Such an incident occurred again early one evening in July of 2008, when the curator at Slater Mill, Andrian Paquette, received a call from the Pawtucket Police Department requesting that he return to the site. They had been alerted by Sonitrol, who reported that their sensors indicated a gathering of people "milling about" in the upstairs section of Slater Mill. Upon inspection, the area was once again found to be vacant.

Also in the Old Slater Mill building, there was the occasion when members of the Slater staff were hosting a catered social function, which was being held in the upstairs area. My brother Carl happened to be keeping duty in the gift shop downstairs. At one point, a young woman who was a member of the catering staff ventured downstairs and pointedly asked Carl, "Excuse me, but is this place haunted or something?" Carl wanted to know why she asked. The flustered young woman replied, "Well, while I was upstairs just now, something pushed the serving tray I was carrying from behind, and nearly caused it to topple. When I turned around, there was absolutely no one behind me!"

In April of 2007, Carl happened to be leading a group of 4th grade school children through Slater Mill. They were about halfway though the mill, when Carl heard what sounded like the somewhat muffled voice of a little boy crying out. The sound seemed to have emanated from over in the bell tower, which was just around the corner out of sight. One of the young girls in the school group asked Carl, "Did you just hear that?"

"Yes, I did," he said. After excusing himself, Carl immediately rushed over to investigate, but found no traces of anyone in the area of the bell tower. All of the school children were also present and accounted for.

With all the reported hunting phenomena being reported at the Old Slater Mill historic site, my brother Carl eventually came up with the concept of organizing a series of public ghost tours through the mill buildings. The initial tours were held for several weekends during the Halloween season of 2008. According to plan, they consisted of a half-mile stroll along the Blackstone River, and concluded with a mini-tour of both the Wilkinson and the Slater mill buildings. Also in both buildings, a brief paranormal investigation would be held, in which those attending would be invited to participate.

From the very start of the Slater Mill ghost tours, paranormal activity at the site seemed to noticeably pick up. Perhaps this was partly the result of the added recognition it was being given. Even before the initial ghost tour officially began, the activity seemed to accelerate. Early on Friday evening, September 19th, 2008, just as the initial ghost tour was commencing, there was another reported sighting from a tourist, of a little girl in antiquate clothes peering out from an upstairs window of Slater Mill itself.

Throughout the first season of the ghost tours, participants repeatedly reported being touched by an unseen hand while moving though the darkened recesses of Slater Mill in particular. One such person was Rosemary Danforth, who is the wife of Educational Director Richard Danforth. Rosemary was touched on her elbow during one of the nighttime tours she attended inside of Slater Mill. At the time, there was no person close enough to her to have made physical contact.

On yet another occasion, on a Friday morning during the ghost tour season, staff member Alan McGillivray – himself a veteran schoolteacher of more than thirty years – was in the attic of Slater Mill waiting for the curator, Andrian. Suddenly, Alan was roughly shoved from behind. He instantly turned around, but saw no one nearby in the large attic that could have shoved him. Needless to say, the experience left him more than a little mystified. The fact that Alan is a down-to-earth individual with no previous interest in the paranormal lends credence to his personal testimony.

During the 2009 and 2010 ghost tour seasons, there have also been continuing attempts at spirit communication, in all three building comprising the Slater Mill site. Since I am usually taking audio recordings during the tours, some of these attempts at spirit communication have produced some rather clear examples of EVP.

One evening as a tour group was being led through the darkened Slater building, Carl momentarily switched on an antiquated throstle spinning machine, to replicate one of the sounds which 19th Century factory workers would have been familiar with. After shutting it off, Carl asked, "Did you work in this mill… in Slater Mill?"

When I played back my audio recording, it was at this point that sounded like a young girl's voice could clearly be heard saying, "Yes."

On a subsequent ghost tour, while Carl and I were leading a tour group through the darkened interior of Slater Mill, Carl asked, "Did you work here with children?" This time, it was high-pitched voice that whispered a very definite "Ah, yes!" on the recording.

There is also some indication that at least one spirit entity within the Slater Mill is adverse to flash photography. On more than one occasion in the mill, when investigators have called out "Flash" to warn others that they are about to take a flash photo in the dark, I've received a very definite "No!" in response on EVP. For some unknown reason, this seems to happen most frequently in the vicinity of a large, life-like framed portrait of Samuel Slater.

And the reports continue to come in. Due to the fact that the activity seems to be escalating within all three buildings on the site, we find that we must now also proceed with added caution. Tourists at night have even occasionally been reduced to tears, as the result of hearing phantom voices, or being poked and prodded by unseen fingers.

Reviewing these accounts, can it be stated conclusively that the site of Old Slater Mill in Pawtucket is in fact haunted? Is it perhaps populated by a work force of ghostly laborers, persistently showing up for their tedious shifts? Or could it be some unseen force of a more deceptive nature? Or perhaps even a thought form, generated by the recognition which the "ghosts" regularly receives? Considering the rich history of these historic buildings, one could at least suggest that those weathered structures have absorbed plenty of memories. For the present, our investigations into the haunting activity of the Slater Mill historic site remain ongoing.

Chapter 18

The Phantom Dogs of Hell's Gate

In the town of West Greenwich, Rhode Island, there is a local urban legend of a woman named Mary Brown, who supposedly relocated to Rhode Island from Salem, Massachusetts many years ago to escape the witchcraft persecution. With her came the only two friends she possessed in the world, which were her two mongrel dogs, a large one and a smaller one. Although she is said to have originally lived for a while in the town of Exeter, she apparently found herself unwelcome there, her reputation having followed her, and she eventually settled in a relatively obscure area of West Greenwich. There, Mary Brown lived a reclusive existence, with her two loyal canines providing her with the only source of companionship and protection she knew. Exactly when or how Mary Brown departed this life, as well as what became of her two dogs is lost to time and legend. The area where her modest hovel once stood is located off of what is now known as Plain Meeting House Road, down a long and winding driveway which used to be marked by a small wooden gate. Because of Mary's double reputation for being not only a local recluse but also a witch, this particular area is rumored to be quite haunted, and the gateway has been given the connotation of "Hell's Gate."

Over the years this particular stretch of property has gone through a variety of owners, who have for the most part left it in rural condition. In the 1950's a brief shoot-out took place here, involving a small group of local racketeers who were staked out by Federal agents. To my knowledge no one was killed in this skirmish, and the racketeers were successfully taken into custody. The small, dilapidated shack in which the hoodlums temporarily took shelter still stands, visibly ridden with bullet holes.

Some say that the ghost of Mary Brown still haunts Hell's Gate and the surrounding area. She has even supposedly been glimpsed walking nearby along Plain Meeting House Road during the nighttime hours.

But the most often reported sighting is that of Mary Brown's two dogs – or rather, the apparitions of her two dogs – still faithfully keeping watch around the area of Hell's Gate, as if anxiously waiting for their mistress to return. They are always described as two mongrel dogs traveling together, one appearing to be a large shepherd-collie mix and the other one a smaller mutt with grayish fur. In my personal opinion, there may actually be some truth to this reported phenomenon, be they phantom dogs or otherwise. Although the area of Hell's Gate is now private property, this does not deter some individuals from exploring the place for themselves.

One evening, a personal friend of mine named Ray, who is a local rock singer, decided to do just that one evening. Accompanied by a friend of his, who was also familiar with the area, Ray set out on a moonlit night to explore Hell's Gate. After concealing their car along Plain Meeting House Road, Ray and his friend began making their way on foot past the entrance where the wooden gates once stood. The two of them had not been exploring for very long before two dogs suddenly dashed out from somewhere along the overgrown path they were on. The larger of the two dogs appeared to be part shepherd, while the smaller was of an indistinguishable breed. Wherever the dogs had come from, they did not seem malicious. Instead, they simply kept close by to Ray and his friend the entire time they were there, following them and sometimes even flanking them. Ray was not quite certain whether the dogs were guarding the property, or acting protectively towards them personally; it could have been either way. And then, when Ray and his friend were leaving the area, they turned to see that the two dogs were not longer with them. "In fact, we didn't even hear or see the two dogs leave," Ray said when relating this incident to me. "We just looked around and suddenly noticed that they were gone, as if they'd just simply vanished." Although Ray and his friend had both heard the legend of the two phantom dogs of Hell's Gate, it wasn't until the dogs had vanished that they began to wonder if they had, if fact, just experienced a supernatural encounter. (Incidentally, Ray's professional singing name happens to be "Ray Dog.")

Another part of the legend says that Mary Brown and her two phantom K-9's also occasionally choose to haunt the West Greenwich

Cemetery, which is located about a mile further down along Plain Meeting House Road. It is for this reason that there has been some confusion regarding the spirit that allegedly haunts this particular cemetery, as to whether she is the spirit of a witch, as opposed to being a vampire.

Nellie L. Vaughn, who died in 1889 at age 19 and who is actually buried here, has been confused with both Mary Brown, and with Mercy Brown of Exeter. Mercy L. Brown, who also died at age 19 and who is buried in Chestnut Hill Cemetery in Exeter, was posthumously suspected of having become a vampire. Apparently some teenagers in the late 1960's had decided to go vampire hunting one Halloween night, and had wound up in the wrong cemetery, eventually also finding the wrong grave. This is the reason that Nellie Vaughn has so often been confused with Mercy Brown. Now, add to this the similarities between the names Mercy Brown (a suspected vampire) and Mary Brown (a suspected witch), and you get a triple confusion!

Those who have encountered the phantom dogs at the West Greenwich Cemetery claim that the two dogs refuse to enter the cemetery itself. Instead, they will remain outside the cemetery entrance, bark, and anxiously pace back and forth. It remains unclear whether the two dogs are guarding the cemetery grounds in a territorial manner, or are trying to warn anyone who is about to enter the cemetery – or anyone who has already entered it – of impending danger.

Personally, I have had one possible encounter with the two phantom dogs of Hell's Gate. It was a shared experience, with noted researcher and author Rosemary Ellen Guiley. Rosemary, having researched and written extensively on the subject of vampire lore, happened to be in New England during Halloween week in 2006, and asked me if I would mind giving her a tour of the Nelly Vaughn cemetery. Naturally, I told her I'd love to. Thus it was that on the late morning/early afternoon of Thursday, November 2, Rosemary and I met at Historical Cemetery #2 along Plain Meeting House Road. It was a typical damp, overcast, New England Fall day, with intermittent drizzle. During a break in the rain, I gave Rosemary a brief tour of the cemetery, and pointed out to her the burial spot of Nellie L. Vaughn. After we'd taken several photographs, Rosemary suggested that we attempt an EVP session.

Standing beside a large concrete tomb that is in the center of the cemetery, Rosemary switched on her small pocket tape recorder, only to find that the fresh batteries she'd just loaded into the recorder had completely died. (Battery failure, of course, it not unusual when investigating locations where paranormal phenomena reputedly occur.)

Rosemary excused herself to go and get some fresh batteries from her car, which was parked next to mine just outside of the cemetery. No sooner had she turned to leave, however, then she froze in her tracks, for at the entrance of the cemetery were two mongrel dogs – one large and one small. The larger of the two dogs, which looked like a tan and white shepherd/collie mix, barked twice at her. It then quickly turned and moved away followed closely behind by the second dog. Rosemary explained to me, "Oh…I have a slight fear of dogs, because I was once almost attacked by one as a young teenager when I was riding a bicycle."

Author and paranormal researcher Rosemary Ellen Guiley explores a cemetery nearby to Hell's Gate in West Greenwich, RI.

Out of curiosity, I dashed to the cemetery entrance and glanced around the stonewall that surrounds the cemetery, only to see that the two dogs were no longer anywhere in sight. I then quickly ran out to the street nearest the cemetery, which was the direction the dogs had seemed to be heading for…but again, there was no trace of them. Somehow, it just did not seem likely that they could have gotten completely out of sight that quickly, without making a sound as they left. Possible, of course, but unlikely.

When I returned to Rosemary inside the cemetery, and informed her that the two dogs were no longer anywhere in sight, she breathed a sigh of relief. Naturally, since Rosemary was not from the area, she'd never heard of this very local legend of the two phantom dogs. I then quickly filled her in on the legend. "That was strange," she agreed. "Now that you mention it, I didn't hear any sound at all when those two dogs moved away." Rosemary and I both lamented the fact that had the dogs had appeared and vanished before we'd had the opportunity to snap a photo of them.

From my own perspective, after the larger of the two dogs had barked twice, there was something slightly unnatural about the way he'd turned and moved out of sight behind the stonewall by the cemetery entrance. It's difficult to describe. But somehow, I almost had the impression that I was watching a movie with the sound turned off; that's how silent they were.

And so, Rosemary and I were left to ponder if we had indeed shared a genuine paranormal encounter, with the two phantom dogs of Hell's Gate. And if it was genuine, why did they appear to us then and there, at that particular day and time? Was it perhaps because I knew of the legend, and was therefore able to relate it to Rosemary, after she'd been briefly startled by the appearance of the two dogs? Or, was the explanation for what we'd experienced a more mundane one, simply meaning that two wandering mongrels matching the description of the "phantom dogs" had momentarily crossed our path, and then eclipsed themselves with uncanny stealth and speed?

The remainder of our investigation that dreary November afternoon resulted in nothing unusual. For now, the legend of Mary Brown and her two ethereal companions remains just that...a legend. Personally, I did not feel at all threatened by the appearance of the two dogs. Then again, catching a brief glimpse of them in the middle of the day, even if it was damp and overcast, is obviously a different scenario than meeting up with them in the darkness of night. Occasional sightings still continue to be reported to this day. And in retrospect, there may also be some measure of comfort, in that the phantom dogs of Hell's Gate may still represent the love and loyalty once shared, between a lonely recluse and her two cherished companions in life.

Chapter 19

Brian's Uninvited Guest

It was shortly before filming began on the first season of Ghost Hunters that Sandra and I, along with Brian Harnois, were on a TAPS investigation involving a family that lived upstairs in a second floor apartment in Massachusetts. A certain amount of paranormal activity was taking place within the upstairs apartment that night, which included anomalies captured on video and examples of EVP. At least one family member present had also been physically assaulted. The only problem was, for some unknown reason Brian seemed to be the only one among us not experiencing much of anything that evening. This proved to be very frustrating for him. As he later recalled, "I was upset. I was there, and everyone else was experiencing things. I wasn't experiencing a damn thing. I'd go into a room. I'd leave, and all hell would break loose. I'd walk back in, and it would die down. I was like, 'Hell, I can't do nothing here tonight!' I literary spent that last four hours just sitting on a couch."

The clients had previously gone to a local haunted asylum to investigate and take photos, and what seemed to be a little girl spirit had followed them home. They'd subsequently contacted TAPS, asking us for help. Our investigation that evening concluded with Sandra and myself performing a religious cleansing, which seemed to have a positive effect. However, if Brian was feeling somewhat disappointed at not having experienced any significant activity that night, he wouldn't be disappointed for long. It seemed that the little girl spirit had decided to follow him home, too.

Indications of this first occurred about two nights later, when Brian started hearing light disembodied footsteps walking about in the living room of his apartment. At the time he lived on the third floor of an old Victorian era house, located in Woonsocket, RI. Although it was originally one big Victorian house, the present owners put a division in the middle to make it a duplex, and converted the two sections into separate apartments. The only way to get to his apartment was to enter though the first floor kitchen, and then go up two flights of stairs. Because Brian enjoyed his privacy, this seemed to be the ideal living arrangement for him.

One evening, shortly after the night he'd first heard the footsteps, Brian was in the living room by himself reading a book, when he suddenly heard what sounded like a little girl giggling. Realizing he'd left the TV on, he got up and shut it off. But he could still hear the muffled sound of a little girl giggling from somewhere nearby. Brian began walking around, searching though each room of his apartment, but there was nobody else there. After waiting awhile in silence, he heard the giggle again. "Heh-heh-heh-heh!"

"You gotta be kidding me," he said to himself out loud.

Brian then recalled that the landlord and his family had a little five-year-old niece who sometimes came over to visit with them. Maybe it was her he was hearing downstairs. He waited, and heard it once more, a distinctive little girl's giggle. Brian then figured he'd better go downstairs and see for himself, whether or not the niece was making the noise. "If she's down there, I will be so grateful," he thought on his way down to the first floor.

The landlord's wife greeted him when he knocked on the door. Trying to sound casual, Brian said, "Hi, I just thought I heard a little girl running around and giggling in the building, and was just wondering if it was your niece visiting."

The landlord's wife answered, "Oh, it couldn't possibly be her, because she hasn't been here in a week."

With a shrug, Brian said, "Oh, I guess I must've been hearing things from outside, then. Sorry to have bothered you."

"No bother at all, Brian," the landlord's wife said pleasantly.

So Brian simply went back upstairs, saying to himself with a sigh, "Alright, here we go." He knew that he'd unmistakably heard the distinct sound of a little girl, running around and laughing from somewhere close by, definitely from within the building. In fact, he had to admit that it had even sounded as though it could have been coming from right inside his own upstairs rooms!

    That night, Brian woke up somewhere around two o'clock in the morning. For some reason, he had the uncanny feeling that he was not alone in the room. Wondering if something had just happened to wake him up, he groggily glanced around his darkened bedroom. Looking out from where his bedroom was, he caught a sudden flash of movement over in the living room. In the dim illumination cast from a nearby streetlight outside, Brian could just barely make out something moving along the floor, past his bedroom doorway. He rubbed his eyes to make certain he was really seeing this. "Aw, I must've just been dreaming," he thought to himself. But when he looked again, it was still there, crawling past his bedroom door, along the hallway. At first he hoped it might be a mouse, trapped underneath a towel. Brian slowly got out of bed, thinking, "If it comes around that corner, I'm pouncing on it." He stood there for about two full minutes, waiting in silence for it to come around the corner. But it never showed up. Finally he stepped out around the corner, only to find nothing in sight. When he turned on the lights and inspected each room, there were no discarded towels left anywhere, and certainly no sign of a mouse moving one along the floor!

    Very shortly before the TV show Ghost Hunters premiered, Brian had just returned after an exhausting day and night from filming the Race Rock episode for Season 1. It was about 5:00 AM when Brian returned home. He discovered that while he was gone, workmen had been there tending to some much needed repairs on the roof. In fact, they had apparently put tar paper down, and it had just rained outside. As a result, some parts of the ceiling had leaked though, leaving a sticky, powdery residue in various spots on the floors of his rooms. This sticky residue was all over the stairway as well. What was more, Brian noticed that there were little bare footprints all over, as from a small child scampering around. "Who's gone in my rooms? What the hell??" Brian said in exasperation. His first thought was that the landlord's little five-year-old niece had somehow gained access in there while he'd been away.

He immediately went back downstairs, and knocked on their door again.

The landlord and his wife were just getting ready to go to work. They both greeted Brian, and apologized for any inconvenience that the roof repairs might be causing him. Remaining calm, Brian asked, "By the way, has your little niece been here?"

The landlord's wife replied, "Well, yes, but she didn't go up in your room. She was down on the first floor the whole time. We don't let her go upstairs by herself, because we don't want her to slip and fall."

Befuddled, Brian simply returned upstairs. Before going to bed, however, he took photos of the footprints, as proof that someone with very small feet must have been up there.

Another strange turn of events came after Brian borrowed an antiquated, tattered little girl's dress from the Stone's Public House in Ashland, Massachusetts after a night of filming there, because he wanted to "study it" at home. (It was rumored that this dress had once belonged to a young girl who'd been tragically killed in a train accident, on the train tracks right outside of the building.) Brian basically wanted to see if anything was connected to it. He kept the tattered little girl's dress in his possession for a period of two weeks. To Brian's surprise, all paranormal activity in his apartment ceased throughout those two weeks. There were no unusual noises in the building, no sounds of the little girl running around, or any repeated ghostly appearances. Brian once again became accustomed to getting a good night of uninterrupted sleep.

However, the tattered little girl's dress which he'd borrowed from Stone's Public House eventually had to be returned, on the day that "the reveal" was filmed on location for the conclusion of the Ghost Hunters episode. And according to Brian, almost immediately after the dress was returned, all hell seemed to break loose in Brian's apartment. That very night after he'd returned the dress and come back home, items were found scattered about in each room. Rapidly moving footsteps, sounding as if they belonged to a small child, could now be heard prancing about the apartment at all hours of the night. Once again, Brian went downstairs and questioned the landlord and his wife, only to again be informed that their niece had not been visiting with them. Brian soon reasoned that the spirit of another little girl might have been attached to the dress he'd taken with him from Stone's Public House. And now that the original little girl spirit had been suddenly deprived of her new playmate, she was expressing her displeasure by throwing a typical childish temper tantrum.

The next night, after spending the whole day home in his apartment, Brian retired for the evening shortly before midnight. At about two forty-five in the morning, he awoke, once again keenly sensing a presence in his room. After glancing at the digital clock, he turned over...and was greeted by the dim yet solid figure of a little girl, kneeling at the side of his bed, and gazing intently at him. She had wet-looking straight black hair, similar to the little girl in the movie "The Ring." (Brian had just seen the movie, and so was even more freaked out by what he was now seeing.) Because the only light switch was above her head, Brian realized that he'd have to go even nearer to her if he wanted to turn on the light. "Wonderful!" he silently thought to himself. "I've got no one around, and I'm going to die!"

After taking a deep breath, Brain leapt out of bed out of bed, and dashed across the room. Somehow without pausing, he'd also managed to switch on the overhead light. He glanced back in the now illuminated bedroom, and saw that the little girl was still there in the room with him, sitting on the floor, and watching him. She was sitting with her head lowered and her arms wrapped tightly around her knees. All Brian could see of her face was her two dark eyes, still silently watching him with an unsettling stare, with her long dark wet-looking hair cascading down past her shoulders. And then she was suddenly no longer there. Thinking back on it, he'd only seen her with the light on for perhaps two or three seconds, although it certainly made quite a lasting impression on him. Brian later described it as the weirdest thing he'd ever seen in his entire life.

Finally, out of sheer exhaustion and exasperation, Brian spoke out loud to his uninvited guest, saying, "Alright, that's it. You can't show yourself anymore. Really, you've just been creeping me out. If this doesn't stop, I'm gonna have to go sleep on the couch downstairs, for God's sake! Please don't do this any more. Don't do this. You can be here. You can live here. You can chill out. You can do whatever you want. I just don't want to see you anymore. No offense. I'm just not prepared for that at two o'clock in the morning."

Thankfully, Brian's attempt at reasoning with the little girl's spirit seemed to have worked. She never again appeared to him in that apartment. Oh, she was obviously still there, as he could still overhear her giggling every once in awhile. But the major activity ceased, after Brian verbally expressed that the little girl spirit was not welcome to fully materialize herself to him, in the form of an apparition.

Brian goes cemetery tripping.

Brian eventually moved out from the Victorian house in Woonsocket. Whether or not the next tenants that moved into his former third floor rooms ever experienced any activity there, he never knew.

To end this story with a somewhat ironic twist, Brian was once relating the tale of his uninvited guest to an audience at Penn State University. This was in September of 2008, and Sandra and I, being a part of the paranormal conference that weekend, were of course in the audience. In fact, I also happened to be making an audio recording of Brian's lecture.

A short time later, when Sandra and I listened to the recording, we heard Brian concluding his story of the little girl ghost by saying, "And she never did. She never followed me." Immediately after he said this, an EVP of what sounded like a little girl's voice could be heard faintly whispering, "No... no." It seems that Brian may still have her company after all.

Chapter 20

A Skeptic's Encounter

The following true story was related in person to my brother Carl on Thanksgiving Day, 2008. On Monday evening of the previous week, our brother-in-law Joseph Bailey (husband to our sister Cynthia) had an uncanny experience that in Carl's opinion cannot be dismissed by anything apart from an irrefutable paranormal occurrence. In Carl's words, "Joe is what we'd term a hard-line skeptic, not especially religious, unconcerned with anything of a seeming other-worldly nature." In fact, Joe has on occasion good-naturedly ribbed Carl and Sandra and me, for our avid interest in exploring the paranormal. It was therefore astonishing to hear our skeptical brother-in-law actually relating a paranormal account of his own. In fact, the experience apparently had a profound impact on him. At any rate, here are the details of the story:

Joe is employed as a security officer at Twin Rivers dinner hall and casino in Lincoln, Rhode Island, formerly Lincoln Downs. During Joe's extended shift that day and evening, a coworker (aged early sixties) who had been Joe's friend stretching back to their years together as Providence Police officers, complained of what he took to be persistent "indigestion." As it turned out, those vague symptoms indicated a problem of a far more serious nature. Sometime later, this man collapsed as he suffered fatal cardiac arrest. The director of the paramedic team that arrived on the scene--unavoidably too late this time--stated he believes the deceased likely succumbed either while or immediately prior to being transported to the rescue squad.

Upon reviewing the security camera's taping of transference to the rescue, Joe observed a shadowy yet distinct figure imprinted on the tape. Unbelievably, Joe clearly recognized the face and the figure as belonging to his stricken friend, walking behind a uniformed Lincoln policeman towards the back of the emergency vehicle. Another security person saw this on the tape, thereby corroborating what Joe was seeing. Of course, upon hearing this account from our sister, then from Joe, Carl requested a copy of the security tape showing the phantom image. Unfortunately, Joe couldn't comply with his request. Not that viewing of the tape was restricted. Rather, upon replaying the tape, Joseph and his fellow security staff found that the spectral form was no longer discernible. In fact, it had entirely vanished from the tape!

These events which were related to Carl and which I've documented here, seem all the more credible because Joseph is a practical, rational individual working in a position of high responsibility and trust. He is accustomed to maintaining his composure under stressful conditions, trained to rely on his observational abilities and not at all given to flights of fancy.

For you reading this retelling of a "skeptic's" encounter within the paranormal realm, your comments and personal experiences are always welcome.

Chapter 21

Paranormal Realities

Recently we were once again in the Ghosts R N.E.A.R. studio with a return visit from our good friend David Manch, who is author of "There Are Ghosts In Our World, But Are They All Real?" We also welcomed a first-time visit from New England Paranormal's Pat Rabideau.

Dave is also the case manager for New England Paranormal, the case manager for The Atlantic Paranormal Society's home team, and the founder/director of Southern New Hampshire Paranormal. Pat is an investigator and tech specialist with New England Paranormal. Our interview with Dave and Pat was certainly an enjoyable event, and some very pertinent information on updated equipment and investigation techniques was discussed.

As Dave explained to us in his own words, "I've recently been utilizing an invention of mine known as the 'FaraDave Cage', which is an upgraded version of a Faraday enclosure. This is based on the principles of renowned scientist Michael Faraday. Such enclosures are typically made of a fine mesh of either copper or silver surrounding a more rigid enclosure that holds a recording device. The mesh is then grounded by a wire that's attached to the enclosure by an 'alligator clip' and plugged into the ground fault connector of a household electrical outlet. The practical application of this design prevents most RF (radio frequencies) or other electromagnetic fields from entering the enclosure, thereby keeping stray cell phone signals, radio waves, WI-FI, or household electrical contamination from affecting the recording of any analog or digital recorder inside the enclosure. The person who helped conceive this device is our tech specialist here, Pat Rabideau. The name 'FaraDave' was actually Pat's idea; I'm not that bold."

Pat elaborated, "It's a nylon mesh, but it's coated with silver, and the silver acts as a conductor. The one we've brought with us here is about one foot long and about four inches wide. It's built for most equipment that you can carry, like a digital voice recorder or an EMF detector. The inside is lined with plastic mesh, which creates a dome effect. And the bottom is lined with foam, which acts as a cushion. The lining also has to be durable enough to create some rigidity, to protect the equipment inside. And once you've placed the equipment inside, you pull the drawstring taut, so what you have is a closed system. If the mesh is not is not secured all the way around, then electromagnetic waves can move through and cross-contaminate your evidence."

On the topic of cell phone interference, Pat also mentioned, "Cell phones are actually getting lower in frequency, so that they can have a longer range. The lower the frequency, the longer the range you can get from electromagnetic fields. That's why most radio communications are microwaves, and very low frequency, which is why an insulating device like the FaraDave cage is very important."

Dave added, "That's especially true, since you're bombarded by those waves wherever you go. One of the things that we now look for whenever we go on investigations, is are there any cell phone towers within viewing distance of the house? And if there are any, then there's a good chance that we may experience some cross-contamination, because of the way it's transmitting the radio frequencies, or microwaves. And we have had that happen."

Pat said, "And especially if you're using a K-2 Meter and a cell phone within the same room, the K-2 is going to light right up. Because your K-2 measures radio frequencies, along with a wide range of things. But you take that same K-2 and put it in the enclosure, and then put your cell phone right on top of the cage and make a phone call, and the K-2 will not light up."

Sandra commented, "The K-2 Meter does seem to be very sensitive to a lot of what's going on in the environment. Would you recommend that a K-2 really only be used in conjunction with an enclosure like this?"

Pat replied, "I would say, that I would be leery of any measurements you take with the K-2, without a FaraDave cage. The K-2 can measure RF and microwave frequencies. So because the K-2 measures RF, you can be anywhere in a house and all of a sudden get a spike because a signal came through a window, or it was conducted even through your equipment. The IR beams on your equipment can actually carry a signal."

Sandra asked, "And what about the HD video camera? How does that add to the efficiency of investigations?"

Dave replied, "The HD video camera has almost obvious benefits, in that it has much greater clarity and reduced subtlety of objects or other phenomena that would otherwise tend to blend into the image, and make it difficult to determine what it is. In a recent case that New England Paranormal investigated, it wasn't the video quality of the camera that yielded exciting evidence, but the audio that it captured. This is an often overlooked source of evidence on investigations, and the high-quality audio of video recorders is often capable of recording some significant EVP evidence."

I then asked, "Now, for some of our viewers who may not be totally familiar with the term Electronic Voice Phenomena, would you mind briefly defining that for us?"

Dave explained, "Electronic Voice Phenomena is actually something that's been around for quite a long time. Thomas Edison was the first one to attempt recording what he called 'voices of the dead.' Although no one understands exactly how it works, there are several theories as to how we are able to record these voices from people who obviously aren't present in the room when the recording is made. If spirits are comprised of an electric mass, then it would make sense that they would attempt to communicate via an electronic sound wave, rather than an acoustic sound wave, which you make when you talk by causing vibrations throughout the air. So, an electronic device is actually going to be able to record that electrical sound wave, even though you can't hear it audibly because your ears are designed for picking up acoustical sound. And when you play it back, you have a voice that wasn't audible when it was recorded. So, in a nutshell, an EVP is simply a disembodied voice that you didn't hear at the time the recording was made, but upon playback it's there."

After the taping of Ghosts R N.E.A.R. took place, and we were all relaxing at our favorite local coffee shop, Dave and Pat were kind enough to personally share with Sandra and myself some details of an interesting case, which they were both recently involved with. What makes this story of particular interest is that Dave and his team members had been implementing some new "cutting edge" technologies during paranormal investigations, and had recently upgraded some of their equipment. Two examples of this upgraded equipment of course included a FaraDave enclosure, and an HD (or high definition) video camera. Their goal was to hopefully be able to obtain convincing pieces of evidence, which would give credence to the continued use of these devices during investigations.

This particular investigation took place at a residence located in eastern Massachusetts. When the homeowners contacted New England Paranormal, they were reportedly being kept awake at night by the sounds of a young female voice laughing and speaking. This usually occurred while they were in bed, on an almost nightly basis. Other disturbing activity was taking place in the home as well, such as cold spots, intermittent knockings on the walls, and household items being mysteriously misplaced, only to be later discovered in unusual places.

The house that the clients occupied was a split-level design. During NEP's investigation of the main level, the team members placed a digital recorder within a FaraDave enclosure, making certain that it was securely inside. They left this set to record in the master bedroom. They also left the HD video camera recording in the living room, facing the hallway and toward the doorway of the master bedroom. (The digital recorder possessed a recording capacity in excess of 50 hours with a flash memory, or "memory card." The HD camera was capable of recording up to 8.5 hours on a memory stick.)

When the NEP team reviewed their evidence from the Massachusetts home, they found impressive results. The digital recording captured an EVP of what sounded like a young girl's voice saying, "I'm sorry," which was picked up several minutes into the recording. As mentioned, the FaraDave enclosure had been extensively tested beforehand to ensure it was not capable of allowing any type of EMF or cell phone interference to enter and possibly contaminate the recording.

The audio clip captured on the HD video camera was even more astounding in its volume and clarity. At one point, a young girl's voice very clearly stated, "Mommy." In lining up the time frames, the "Mommy" EVP was recorded only a few minutes before the "I'm sorry" EVP that was picked up in another room on the FaraDave enclosure-protected recorder. To rule out noise contamination, there were no children in the home at the time, and the windows were shut securely as it was quite cold outside.

Dave also theorized, "In the time-lapsed world of paranormal communication, several minutes apart may as well be several seconds, so the two clips may well be the same spirit communicating a single message."

Dave certainly considered this to be quite a successful debut for both pieces of equipment. As of this writing, New England Paranormal is working on the development of other ways in which to analyze the surrounding environment during investigations. Some of these methods may be in conventional use by other investigative groups, while other methods may not be. Certainly each and every group is unique in some ways, and many investigators have their own individual approach to investigating paranormal phenomena.

Shortly before concluding our conversation with Dave and Pat within the comfortably warm coffee shop, and venturing back outside into the chilly December evening to begin warming up our cars, I asked Dave what he'd like to see accomplished in his quest for exploring "paranormal realities." In his affable way, Dave replied, "Well, the more ways in which we look at what is happening at locations where paranormal activity is suspected, I think, the more ways we're brought closer to a better understanding of what the paranormal world truly is."

Sandra and I readily agreed.

From the Demonologist's Assistant:

Sandra behind the scenes of Ghosts R N.E.A.R.

I sincerely hope you have enjoyed reading Keith's second installment of the Paranormal Realities book series and look forward to reading Book III as much as I do.

Though in the past few years I have become Keith's ever-present sidekick in 'The Work' (as those in this particular branch of the field call it), I have not always been part of the adventure due to one reason or another. Some of these stories are as new to me as they are to you- particularly investigations which took place prior to my membership in The Atlantic Paranormal Society (TAPS).

Keith and Sandra at 'Work".

Anyway, I would just like to say what an honor it has been to be able to work by Keith's side. His gentle manner, his faith, his genuine desire to help those who seek him out, not to mention his endless patience and devotion to our son (who suffers with severe autism), make it quite a privilege to be the 'Demonologist's Assistant'.

May God bless,

Sandra Johnson

About the Author

Keith and Sandra Johnson are regularly called upon to assist individuals in dealing with alleged malevolent paranormal phenomena or potential inhuman infestation in their homes and together have over 40 years of experience as paranormal investigators.

Keith has had an interest in the paranormal since he was a teenager when he had phenomena occur in his own home. In the seventies, he was a member of the paranormal research group Parapsychology Investigation & Research Organization, out of RI College.

Keith has been featured on the SyFy Channel's Ghost Hunters, as a consulting demonologist, and both he and Sandra are former core members of The Atlantic Paranormal Society (TAPS).

They have been featured as demonology consultants in two first season episodes of the A&E series Paranormal State as well as assisting with documentaries dealing with the paranormal including New Gravity Media's '14 Degrees'.

The pair are co-founders of New England Anomalies Research and host a local TV talk show dealing with paranormal topics called Ghosts R N.E.A.R. which airs locally in Rhode Island and can also be seen online.

Keith is the author of the 'Paranormal Realities' book series that chronicle his experiences as a paranormal investigator.

You can learn more about them by visiting www.nearparanormal.com.

CPSIA information can be obtained at www.ICGtesting.com
Printed in the USA
BVOW030922190911

271406BV00002B/10/P